ROMANTIC FRIENDSHIP IN VICTORIAN LITERATURE

Romantic Friendship in Victorian Literature

CAROLYN W. DE LA L. OULTON
Canterbury Christ Church University, UK

ASHGATE

Published by
Ashgate Publishing Limited
Gower House
Croft Road
Aldershot
Hampshire GU11 3HR
England

Ashgate Publishing Company
Suite 420
101 Cherry Street
Burlington, VT 05401-4405
USA

Ashgate website: http://www.ashgate.com

British Library Cataloguing in Publication Data
Oulton, Carolyn, 1972–
    Romantic Friendship in Victorian Literature. – (The Nineteenth Century Series)
    1. Friendship in literature. 2. English literature – 19th century - History and criticism.
    I. Title.
    820.9'353'09034

Library of Congress Cataloging-in-Publication Data
Oulton, Carolyn, 1972-
    Romantic Friendship in Victorian Literature / Carolyn W. de la L Oulton.
        p . cm. – (The Nineteenth Century Series)
    Includes bibliographical references.
    1. English literature – 19th century – History and criticism. 2. Friendship in literature.
    3. Male friendship in literature. 4. Female friendship in literature. 5. Love in literature.
    6. Gender identity in literature. 7. Homosexuality in literature. 8. Lesbianism in literture.
    I. Title.
    PR468.F75O86 2007
    820'9'353–dc22   2006032274

ISBN 978-0-7546-5869-6

This book has been printed on acid-free paper

Printed and bound in Great Britain by MPG Books Ltd, Bodmin, Cornwall.

Contents

The Nineteenth Century Series
General Editors' Preface

The aim of this series is to reflect, develop and extend the great burgeoning of interest in the nineteenth century that has been an inevitable feature of recent years, as that former epoch has come more sharply into focus as a locus for our understanding not only of the past, but of the countours of our modernity. It centres primarily upon major authors and subjects within Romantic and Victorian literature. It also includes studies of other British writers and issues, where these are matters of current debate: for example, biography and autobiography, journalism, periodical literature, travel writing, book production, gender and non-canonical writing. We are dedicated principally to publishing original monographs and symposia; our policy is to embrace a broad scope in chronology, approach and range of concern, and both to recognize and cut innovatively across such parameters as those suggested by the designations 'Romantic' and 'Victorian'. We welcome new ideas and theories, while valuing traditional scholarship. It is hoped that the world which pre-dates yet so forcibly predicts and engages our own will emerge in parts, in the wider sweep, and in the lively streams of disputation and change that are so manifest an aspect of its intellectual, artistic and social landscape.

Vincent Newey
Joanne Shattock
University of Leicester

Acknowledgements

Jacket cover: *The Favourite Poet*, Alma Tadema, by permission of National Museums, Liverpool (Walker Art Gallery).

Part of Chapter Two first appeared in *Dickens Quarterly*, vol. XXI (September 2004) as '"My undisciplined heart": Romantic Friendship in *David Copperfield*'.

Part of Chapter Four first appeared in *Wilkie Collins Society Journal*, vol. 7 (2005) as '"Never be divided again": *Armadale* and the threat to romantic friendship'.

Introduction

A Kind of Enchantment

The Victorian debate about marriage and the changing place of women in a male-dominated society has been well documented. Feminist critics have gone on to analyse the importance of female friendship in terms of the 'woman question' and the ambivalent status of unmarried women; accepted behaviour in the context of friendship has informed work on masculinity, for instance by Richard Dellamora and Matt Cook; further studies of both male and female relations in the period have discussed the significance of 'romantic friendship' as a euphemism or perhaps displacement for what we would now term homosexual or lesbian feeling. In *Between Men: English Literature and Male Homosocial Desire*, Eve Sedgwick insightfully qualifies such a view, commenting: 'What *counts* as the sexual is … variable and itself political' (15). But long before the upsurge of gay and lesbian studies, the nineteenth century itself had hosted a long-running debate about the nature and role of friendship in its own right.

Given the segregation of male and female youth in particular, it is hardly surprising that friendship between members of the same sex should have assumed a high degree of importance. Much of the discussion put forward by writers and journalists concerned with the subject takes friendship between the young as its focus. Equally predictably, the question of moral influence at such an impressionable time is the basis of ongoing concern. Significantly, writers on the subject return again and again to the passionate impulsiveness of youth and the dangers inherent in such undirected passion. But equally, not all friendships are assumed to arise from youthful ardour, nor does writing on the subject confine itself entirely to the young. It is helpful to consider the range of expression permitted – and considered appropriate – to various types of friendship, often associated with different life stages.

Within this context, I am specifically concerned with the phenomenon of romantic friendship and its perceived relationship to friendship in general, as an ideal that enjoyed a high, although sometimes ambivalent, cultural status for most of the nineteenth century. This form of friendship depended on both strong feeling and what may now seem startlingly rhetorical expression. Friends could describe their response to each other in terms of love and mutual dependence, in language that initially appears, at least by later standards, to have been uncircumscribed in the extreme. Elizabeth Mavor, author of the biography of the Ladies of Llangollen, has described romantic friendships as 'Edenic', at least:

> before they were biologically and thus prejudicially defined. Depending as they did upon time and leisure, they were aristocratic, they were idealistic, blissfully free, allowing for a dimension of sympathy between women that would not now be possible outside an avowedly lesbian connection. Indeed, much that we would now associate solely with a

sexual attachment was contained in romantic friendship: tenderness, loyalty, sensibility, shared beds, shared tastes, coquetry, even passion. (Mavor, xvii)

But as John Rosenberg warns: 'we would be naïve to assume that there were no worms in the pre-Freudian sexual garden, or that the Victorians failed to spot them' (Rosenberg, 305). Social approbation was granted only on certain terms, a proviso which could initially have acted as a strength. We are accustomed to locating greater personal freedom within the more liberal social value systems of the twentieth and twenty-first centuries. But it is plausible to suppose in this context that a less permissive society, such as Victorian England, could actually contain greater freedom, in its very strictures and the rules governing expression. Where the limits of expression are carefully considered and generally acknowledged, the threat of ambiguity or misinterpretation is correspondingly less. A widespread knowledge of what is acceptable and what is not informs nineteenth-century writing on romantic friendship, and allows it a range of expression within the limits established (the interest shown by essayists and writers of conduct manuals belies the supposition that proponents of intense friendship were guided solely by their own emotional dictates). It is ironic, then, that by the end of the century, the image of 'unconscious innocence' that romantic friendship had successfully promoted emerged as the very ground on which its claims could be attacked.

By the 1890s the theories of sexologists had come, irreversibly, to locate a specifically sexual tendency in the intensity and self-sufficiency of romantic friendship. As Havelock Ellis was to put it in 1897 in his famous study *Sexual Inversion*:

> … conventional propriety recognises a considerable degree of physical intimacy between girls, thus at once encouraging and cloaking the manifestations of homosexuality.
>   These passionate friendships, of a more or less unconsciously sexual character, are certainly common. (Ellis and Symonds, 85)

In the same work, Ellis warns that 'A woman may feel a high degree of sexual attraction for another woman without realising that her affection is sexual …' (80). This assumption that intense emotional responsiveness necessarily implied a sexual force, whether or not it was fully recognised by the subject herself, has been a persistent one. But this reading of romantic friendship as sexual actually reinforces an already present fear of the intrusive elements that it claims to be responsible for locating. Insisting that women had not hitherto questioned the appropriateness of their own responses, Ellis claims authority to interpret those responses, supposedly for the first time, within the framework of socio-medical discourse.

In a recent study, *Intimate Friends: Women Who Loved Women 1778–1928*, Martha Vicinus usefully analyses the ways in which a range of late nineteenth-century discourses sought to impose constraints on female self-definition:

> By the late nineteenth century some number of social commentators, political and sexual activists, and sexologists were struggling to define both heterosexuality (and its essential corollary, marriage), and homosexuality (and its presumed loneliness). Their unattainable

goal was a stable sexual identity for everyone. Their psychomedical discourse gave lesbians a wider choice of vocabulary but a narrower choice of roles. (Vicinus, 173)

But again, this account foregrounds the sexual in its contention that a 'stable sexual identity' is unattainable. Certainly, the sexologists' interpretations were characterised by a rigidity that could hardly fail to create feelings of anxiety, not only in women who would later term themselves 'lesbian', but also in those who had never before seen reason to view their own responses in this light. The vulnerability of intense feeling to just such appropriation becomes clear in the light of Gesa Stedman's study of emotion in the nineteenth century:

> Individuals (physically) experience emotions but they can never access them without first acquiring knowledge of the social relevance, and appropriateness of certain feelings; thus, the social can never be absent from any kind of emotional experience and its representation. (Stedman, 9)

In the course of this book, I will show how writers were already engaged in just such a process of interpretation and representation; romantic friendship had always been dependent for its survival on its capacity for self-regulation, and this is how it was initially able to combat the 'findings' of sexologists at the end of the century.

In common with all subsequent scholars in this area, I am indebted both to the work of Carroll Smith-Rosenberg and to Lilian Faderman's classic *Surpassing the Love of Men: Romantic Friendship and Love Between Women from the Renaissance to the Present*, although my own research into romantic friendship as a primarily heterosexual ideal accessible to both genders necessarily influences my reading of the phenomenon. Faderman's central premise, as I read it, is that women's romantic friendship would now almost certainly be constituted as lesbianism, but that this was either not available as an identity or would have been indignantly rejected by those involved. Such a rejection, according to Faderman's line of argument, would depend on an appeal to a cultural ideal that was itself necessarily and by definition unselfconscious. As a result romantic friendship could not withstand the scrutiny of sexology because the fostering of anxieties about the nature of such feelings made them inexpressible in the previously ratified terms. In other words, it depended almost by definition on the absence of anxiety. According to this view, the separation between romantic friendship and what we would now term homosexuality becomes largely irrecoverable (even in retrospect by participants in romantic friendship themselves), but an acknowledgement of changes in what is considered appropriate can help to explain what now appears contradictory in nineteenth-century friendship ideals.

As I understand Faderman's position, however, our post-Freudian collective consciousness means that interpretations of romantic friendship will inevitably be filtered through, or at least seen in relation to, current definitions of homosexuality; particularly if this is not seen as depending on a recognisably sexual responsiveness, the lines become very difficult to draw. My main divergence is in the establishment of a perceived pattern within which romantic friendship defines itself. Crucially, I see its status as depending on a deliberate rejection of erotic elements, not an ignorance or even unthinking denial of erotic potential – in my account, therefore, not only can a level of anxiety be accommodated, but as the century progresses it becomes something like a necessary condition of romantic friendship. The claim that the subject is ignorant of her (or indeed his) own desire is in theory the most effective weapon that could have been brought to bear on romantic friendship at the end of the century. In her later book *Odd Girls and Twilight Lovers: A History of Lesbian Life in Twentieth-century America*, Faderman notes a seeming paradox, in that romantic friendship gained ground (particularly in America) even as sexology attempted to pathologise it. She attributes this anomaly to the increase in economic opportunities for women at the *fin de siècle* – a career could provide reasonable justification for refusing marriage and provide the wherewithal for an independent life. Moreover, the creation of a lesbian subculture acted to counteract social pressure on women to seek heterosexual marriage. Faderman notes that:

> For most women, who were of course socialized not to challenge their culture's ideology about acceptable behavior, with the turn of the century began the death knell of romantic friendship … but it was also the beginning of a lengthy period of general closing off of most affectional possibilities between women. The precious intimacies that adult females had been allowed to enjoy with each other earlier – sleeping in the same bed, holding hands, exchanging vows of eternal love, writing letters in the language of romance – became increasingly self-conscious and then rare. (*Odd Girls and Twilight Lovers*, 4)

But a further paradox, in English fiction at least, is that *fin de siècle* novels are persistent in representing female romantic friendship as a wholly orthodox form of expression. Some writers are careful to reinstate the heterosexual love plot with a marriage at the end of the text, or even the death of the heroine's friend. But others suggestively privilege the friendship of women over the prescribed marriage, which though it does take place, appears in a secondary or subordinate position in the text. Reviews of these novels as they appeared suggest an absence of anxiety that is surprising in the light of Faderman's discoveries. It is plausible to suggest that if sexology insistently conflated behaviour, gender identity and sexual object choice, then passionate women were less susceptible to attack if they displayed features and behaviour that had been designated as feminine (see *Odd Girls and Twilight Lovers*). But it is likewise a viable supposition that if female friendship in particular was resistant to the attacks of sexologists, then the ideal itself must have been predicated on a fairly sophisticated understanding of what could safely be accommodated and what could not.

Since Faderman's landmark study *Surpassing the Love of Men*, the continuing development of queer theory on the one hand and feminist criticism on the other has involved a corresponding interest in the nature of romantic friendship between members of the same sex. In these contexts, Faderman's assertion that same-sex romantic friendship was not necessarily sexual in nature has been contested by various critics, including Martha Vicinus, Lisa L. Moore and Emma Donoghue. Moore sees Faderman as 'dismissing sexuality from her account of romantic friendship' (Moore, 9) – in fact, Faderman's account allows for a high level of ambiguity and uncertainty in the experience and understanding of this type of relationship. Where these critics implicitly agree with Faderman is in their very blurring of the lines between what would now be constituted and expressed as sexuality and what at the time of writing was formulated as an expression of friendship. In presenting romantic friendship as one aspect of the history of sexuality, such accounts necessarily suggest a kind of uniform progression towards self-identified lesbianism.

The difference is predominantly one of emphasis – where Faderman suggests that many women who experienced intense but possibly chaste friendships with members of their own sex would have readily defined themselves as lesbian in a later age, later critics have often insisted on a higher level of self-awareness on the part of the women themselves, suggesting that they deployed the rhetoric of female chaste attachments as a necessary survival strategy, successfully fooling a proportion of the social commentators who then wrote about them in terms of approbation. But both approaches allow for an unproblematic convergence between expressions of emotion and same-sex desire. For instance, in her analysis of predominantly pre-nineteenth-century passion between women, Donoghue conflates romantic friendship with women's elopements and their marriage to each other where one of the parties was disguised as a man:

> Many writers do not seem to have understood what they were writing about; they offered the facts of a case in isolation, having no conceptual framework about passion between women to help them interpret the story. And finally, many women and some men wrote about love between women in the lofty terms of romantic friendship, admitting no connection between this and sexual passion. (Donoghue, 9)

As Donoghue's work suggests, Victorian narratives include a surprising number of instances where women appropriate traditionally male roles. Notably in Elizabeth Gaskell's story 'The Grey Woman', the luridly named Amante ('beloved') rescues Anna from her villainous husband and disguises herself as a man, and the two women escape to a life in hiding as supposed man and wife – once a suitable male replacement has been found, Amante is conveniently murdered and the traditional order is more or less restored (Anna's remarriage is not exactly legal, although it is justified on the grounds that she could have obtained a divorce, but needed to sustain the illusion that she was dead). But the transgression of gender rôles may be detailed, even necessarily punished, as is arguably the case here, irrespective of any obvious erotic response. Female-authored texts such as George Eliot's *Romola* support the substitution of woman-centred relationships for the marriage tie where that has failed, and this often takes the form of a pseudo-marriage. In Eliot's novel, Romola redeems her husband's sin in persuading the naïve Tessa that they are married, giving her a lock of her own hair as he has already done, and ultimately taking her to live with her, and even educating her children when Tito is murdered.

While I would acknowledge the potentially erotic nature of many female-centred (or male-centred) relationships, I would contend that such a focus on awareness or ignorance tends to preclude the more difficult question of how feeling might be safely regulated. The complexities of romantic friendship in fact offer a framework within which the question of sexuality can be treated in some depth. In this context, homo-eroticism is not an anomaly that may or may not be recognised by the subject – in a range of literary texts it is presented as a threat to social stability that must be shown to be rejected by an initially too trusting victim, or where the friendship is upheld, outlawed by the loving friends themselves.

In her study of homosocial desire among men, Eve Sedgwick notes the importance of intense male friendships in Victorian fiction, observing that they are similar in:

> the lack of remark surrounding their union and in the shadowy presence of a mysterious imperative (physical debility, hereditary curse, secret unhappy prior marriage, or simply extreme disinclination) that bars at least one of the partners in each union forever from marriage. (*Between Men*, 174)

She interprets these homosocial pairings as subtly indicating, although not necessarily acknowledging, an erotic element in male friendship models of the time; such friendships are not fully differentiated from the accepted sexual experiments of the educated male middle class, who she claims 'operated sexually in what seems to have been startlingly close to a cognitive vacuum' (173). But a distinction needs to be drawn between the confused rhetoric of the middle-class gentleman who attempts, however unsuccessfully, to rationalise or reject his youthful sexual aberrations, and the carefully structured outlines of same-sex friendship. The very point she makes about the inability of one character in a text to marry suggests the way in which romantic friendship needs to justify celibacy as an alternative to marriage – this justification does not preclude the presence of an erotic undertone, but it does show writers' awareness of the issue, and their efforts to pre-empt suspicion. I would apply Lisa Moore's analysis of female relations to friendships between either sex, in her identification of the 'tension between "romantic friendship" and female homosexuality ... as a basic, if sometimes unstated, cultural assumption'.

In the introduction to her study *Intimate Friends*, Martha Vicinus makes a conscientious attempt to historicise female relationships and identities; taking up Faderman's point, she reminds us that 'The various *representations* of same-sex love exhibit significant continuities throughout the period under discussion, but their *significance*, as well as *attitudes* towards them, show considerable variation' (xxiv). She is careful to acknowledge at the outset that:

> identity history can be limiting: more interesting and difficult questions can be asked about friendship, intimacy, sexuality, and spirituality than who had what kind of identity when. ... [she is convinced that] all categories and definitions must remain provisional. (xxviii)

But despite this creditable attempt to remain objective, Vicinus's work is largely concerned with identifying an erotic element in women's responses to each other, and in tracing the means by which this experience is encoded through an appeal to established ideals (such as mother–daughter love). The 'who had what identity when' itself tends to suggest an inevitable progress towards some form of lesbian identity.

Chapter One

Ennobling Genius: Writing Victorian Romantic Friendship

Of all the threads, where'er my glances ran,
Like that of Friendship I could none discern;
Such goss'mer lightness all the rest surpassed,
And oft I looked if I perchance might learn
Howe'er intact such fragile length could last.
('Friendship', 1886)

In an 1896 article, the then Bishop of Winchester, Anthony Thorold, offered eight purposes of friendship: counsel, defence, appreciation, correction, society, intercession, aid, sympathy. Elsewhere in the same pamphlet he referred to Christ's love for his apostles as combining 'the two essentials of friendship everywhere – the intimacy of companionship, and the readiness for sacrifice' (Thorold, 12). Similarly, in 1893 Sir Maxwell Herbert commented that 'In friendship, as in love, the test of reality is the readiness to sacrifice – sacrifice of time, of money, of exertion, or whatever else. Sacrifice lies at the root of the primitive idea of devotion' (Herbert, 406).

But despite the endorsement of such reputable figures, the status of friendship was complex throughout the Victorian era. Routinely celebrated in novels and poems, its centrality was usually displaced only by the inevitable love plot. Certainly, it was understood that this triumph of marriage towards the end of the third volume would signal a diminution or disruption of the friendship through which the plot itself might well have been mediated – in parodic vein, Dora Spenlow's romance with David Copperfield is largely orchestrated and supervised by the romantic Julia Mills, who promptly disappears to India once the successful outcome is seen to be attainable. Pre-dating the Victorian tradition, Jane Austen's Emma realises her own love for Mr Knightley when she believes that she may have lost him to her friend Harriet (her intimacy with whom does not survive the happy realisation of her mistake). But this assumption did not preclude debate on the nature and function of friendship among members of the same sex both before and after marriage.

Throughout the century, novelists, poets and essayists had debated the status and worth of friendship in its various forms, both in relation to marriage and gender norms, and as a manifestation of moral and social character. The popularity of the theme is manifest in the prolific sales of tracts on the subject – Sarah Ellis is well known as an exponent of female duties, but less remembered works were likewise popular in their own time: Sarah Tytler's (Henrietta Keddie's) *Papers for Thoughtful Girls*, for instance, went through nine editions between 1862 and 1875. That friendship was enormously important as an ideal is further suggested in the rhetorical terms in which it was often expressed, a rhetoric that has since often been taken uncritically as pointing to erotic undertones in same-sex relationships of the time.

The various accounts of friendship offered by journalists, authors and writers of conduct manuals testify both to its importance and to its ambiguity. The often ambivalent discussions of the topic that surged from the press at this time are largely united in claiming that friendship is essential to the development of social and spiritual faculties. Again, the ultimate end of friendship is foreseen in its displacement by the more intimate relation of marriage, although most writers allow that it should continue in a secondary position even after this event (in an age that vigorously promoted the male-only clubs of the West End of London for bachelors and married men alike, it would be extraordinary to find male friendship at any rate consigned altogether after a certain age).

Again, there is disagreement about what constitutes genuine friendship. The more conservative appraisals will allow it to exist only in a sedate and restrained form, even where marriage has not intervened to render it redundant. According to this formulation, the excesses of 'romantic friendship' belong in another category altogether, as being not friendship at all, but a precursor of love indulged in by high-minded, although innocent, youth – spectacular in its display of emotion, this type of relationship is held to be sincere, but not enduring. Making an explicit comparison with the uncertainties of flirtation even as he invokes the sanctities of religion, Herbert comments that:

> even friendship – the more sober and rational kind of human intercourse – is not the simple matter it might be supposed to be. It is a holy thing, yet most capricious, and is no more under command of the will than faith.' (Herbert, 400)

The accompanying social proscription of homosexual relationships has caused later commentators to identify English romantic friendship with what America termed 'Boston marriages', in many cases a convenient euphemism for homosexual attachment. Such seeming inconsistencies are in fact compatible with the nineteenth-century ideal of romantic same-sex friendship, in which even physical admiration may play a part without necessarily incurring opprobrium or suspicions of a homo-erotic dimension. Writing from a slightly different angle, Faderman warns that the licence of expression accorded to women in the middle years of the century was based on a refusal to acknowledge anything they might wish to do to each other, and that male expression was correspondingly more constricted. (*Surpassing the Love of Men*, 152) But in youth at least, the worship of peers based on physical admiration was an accepted phenomenon. In Dickens's *Our Mutual Friend*, to give but one example, Bella Wilfer and Lizzie Hexham are instantly attracted by each other's physical appearance. The narrator's approbation of this response is mediated through John Rokesmith, who says to Bella that, 'Just as you are attracted by her beaut- by her appearance and manner, she is attracted by yours.' (*Our Mutual Friend*, 519). Significantly, the correction here is to avoid an admission that Rokesmith himself is conscious of Bella's beauty, which he was about to give away in describing the permissible effect of each women's attractiveness on the other. Bella subsequently approaches Lizzie in the familiar language of romantic friendship, 'I wish you would tell me whether you ever had any friend of your own sex and age', following up her question with: 'I wish you could make a friend of me, Lizzie' (524).

Romantic friendship, then, was regarded as separable from its more orthodox counterparts even at the time of its highest appeal, and a reading of nineteenth-century essays and tracts (whether they fully support it or not) helps to explain the knowing scepticism with which the phenomenon has so often been reviewed since. In the case of writers commenting on the ideal and its manifestations, as in the intense exchanges between friends in literature, the language is often all but indistinguishable from the erotic language of lovers, and it is crucial for this reason to contextualise such exchanges.

Striking elisions, as same-sex relationships are described in terms of 'love' or 'intimacy', suggest the way in which friendship could be presented, before the closing years of the century, in terms that make it appear, to a modern reader at least, startlingly variable and fluid. As both Victorian observers and later critics have pointed out, the very lack of unrestrained contact between the sexes would in itself help to account for the mode of passionate expression available to friends of the same sex. Intense friendship stood to offer not only a permissible outlet for female sensibility in particular, but even a useful means of displaying a susceptible and responsive nature to potential suitors, without the danger of compromising restrictive feminine codes of behaviour.

That nineteenth-century writers were aware of the potential eroticism in female bonds can hardly be in doubt. Martha Vicinus has recently shown that the legal profession, for instance, was caught in a Catch-22 in its treatment of lesbian evidence; obliged to take a stand, lawyers and judges were trapped in a position of compromise – they would not know what they could not help knowing, and so made strategic appeals to the cult of romantic friendship. This stance is borne out by the transparent enough hints of an American writer, William Alger. In his preface to *The Friendships of Women*, published in 1868, he declares firmly that: 'In treating such a theme as friendship, the worst dangers are hardness and levity on the one extreme, exaggeration and mawkishness on the other, and cowardice and squeamishness between' (Alger, xii). Having set out his stall for a non-squeamish treatment of women's friendships, Alger manages to avoid any further reference to their erotic possibilities. But as I will show, literary treatments tacitly acknowledge what is seen as a threat, and patrol the boundaries accordingly.

In some accounts, romantic friendship is indeed conscientiously distinguished from friendship proper, occupying its own allocated space somewhere between the sedate and sober friendships of later life and the first passion associated with courtship and love. The physiologist Alexander Walker, in a much-reprinted essay on intermarriage (it is shown on the British Library catalogue with a date of 1838, and makes a final appearance there in an 1897 edition), identifies romantic friendship as a largely pubescent phenomenon, connected, in the case of girls at least, to the reproductive organs:

> Now, may be observed, not merely the preference which draws one sex towards the other and is restrained by fear and reserve, but extravagant friendships and secret confidences

between individuals of the same sex. And in this way seemed [*sic*] to be first formed the greater number even of sympathetic and benevolent dispositions, as well as romantic ideas and illusions of every description. (Walker, 27)

William Alger similarly presents youthful friendship as a necessary stage of development, elevating the capacity for feeling. He urges his readers not to mock what he sees as the excessive feeling expressed by young women, on the grounds that:

> sentimentality, frozen under the cutting breath of derision, resembles that loathsome ice-lake of poison in the Scandinavian hell. Sentimentality, fired by the glorious contagion of self-forgetful admiration and loyalty, is raised into sentiment, or even divinized into enthusiasm. (Alger, 8)

In her series of essays published in 1857 as *A Woman's Thoughts About Women*, the popular novelist Dinah Mulock (later Craik) clearly explicates the difference between youthful romantic friendship and the more staid relations which she saw as destined to succeed it, in terms of a natural progression. The following passage is worth quoting at length, if only for its detailed description of a socially sanctioned rite of passage, whereby romantic friendship emulates and ideally prepares for the state of marriage that will finally supersede it:

> Probably there are few women who have not had some first friendship, as delicious and almost as passionate as first love. It may not last – it seldom does; but at the same time it is one of the purest, most self-forgetful and self-denying attachments that the human heart can experience: with many, the nearest approximation to that feeling called love – I mean love in its highest form, apart from all selfishness and sensuousness – which in all their after-life they will ever know. This girlish friendship, however fleeting in its character, and romantic, even silly, in its manifestations, let us take heed how we make light of, lest we be mocking at things more sacred than we are aware.
>
> And yet, it is not the real thing – not *friendship*, but rather a kind of foreshadowing of love; as jealous, as exacting, as unreasoning – as wildly happy and supremely miserable; ridiculously so to a looker-on, but to the parties concerned, as vivid and sincere as any after-passion into which the girl may fall; for the time being, perhaps long after, colouring all her world. Yet it is but a dream, to melt away like a dream when love appears ... (137–8)

This analysis of the function of female friendship stresses its importance as not simply a precursor of, but in a very real sense a preparation, or rehearsal, for marriage. In this account, the parties enact approved feminine traits of self-forgetfulness and purity. But such passionate friendship is simultaneously approved and undermined in other writing of the time, as more than one essayist holds up friendship as an ideal, only to suggest that it is unlikely to last for life.

Sarah Ellis, for instance, devotes a chapter of her much-reprinted *The Daughters of England* to 'Friendship and Flirtation'. While commending the uplifting tendency of friendship among like-minded individuals, she insists that true intimacy between two people can only exist within marriage. A suspicion of the apparent boundlessness inherent in female romantic friendship and doubts as to its viability are expressed by both male and female writers of the period. Ellis, for instance, points out that the uncertainty of youth often seeks the influence of a more knowing friend (and this becomes an important theme in the fiction of the time). Arguing for faithfulness in friendship, she warns that none the less, there is:

> a rashness and impetuosity in the formation of early friendships which of themselves are sufficient to render such intimacies uncertain and of short duration. (*The Daughters of England*, 330)

In an unlikely parallel with this writer of conduct guides for young ladies, the sensation novelist Charles Reade was later to make the point that the 'enthusiasm' of first friendships is ultimately fated to make way for marriage at some stage. The knowing mother of the heroine in *Hard Cash* (1863) is coolly dismissive of the fanaticism of her daughter's young friend:

> She had seen so many young ladies healed of so many young enthusiasms, by a wedding ring. (*Hard Cash*, 8)

Jane Hardy, the object of this satirical comment, will later be overtly dismayed at her friend Julia's forthcoming marriage to her brother, and confides to her diary that:

> so in one afternoon's correspondence ends one more of my Christian friendships with persons of my own sex. This is the eighth to which a carnal attachment has been speedily fatal. (305)

Other writers' treatment of this type of friendship among men similarly suggests a pattern in which passion for friends of the same sex gives way to a marriage plot. Novelists' and poets' treatment of the theme – the main focus of this study – is reflected in various essays of the time, for instance by Percival Pickering, whose essay on friendship claims a high place for understanding between members of the same sex, but warns that ultimately:

> Marriage must, and in some degree should, interfere with friendship, and can generally supply to the affections, and even understanding, far more than friendship can offer. (Pickering, 48)

Even this brief survey reveals a contradictoriness in the most 'mainstream' or popular writing on the subject. The most fundamental clash may be between the intended spouse and the ousted friend, but even without this development, the problem remains of how romantic friendship should conduct and define itself. Inconsistencies in the Victorian response to emotional display render the manifestations of feeling within friendship a serious problem for those who wish both to appear sincere and to act within appropriate boundaries. To complicate matters further, romantic friendship does not always employ this term as a means of self-description, and careful reading is required to distinguish it from alternative versions. Most confusingly for later readers, it is not unusual for a writer to deprecate romantic friendship and then to praise spontaneous and intense bonding between friends, at different points in the same essay.

An unsigned article in *The Cornhill* on 'The Ethics of Friendship' (vol. 10, 1864) provides a classic example of this tendency. The writer imperatively dismisses as irrelevant from his or her account the type of romantic friendship formed at school,

> since it resembles love rather than friendship, and is distinguished by a fervid enthusiasm, a tormenting jealousy, great sensitiveness, and an utter absence of all calculation, distrust, or even prudence.

but cannot refrain from an invitation to the reader to recall such friendships: 'Yet in memory how fragrant the incense burned at that shrine, how genuine the idolatry, how complete the sacrifice!' (299–300). The writer goes on to describe the admission, as an adult, into a select group of friends as 'one form of Paradise' (300), and later enthuses: 'It is probable, however, that the most perfect form of friendship must always be that which arises between two human beings only' (302). In yet another shift, the essay deprecates the excesses of Continental romantic friendship, as opposed to the restraint of the English:

> Though the causes which go to establish friendship, and endow it with permanence and vitality, are everywhere the same, yet the mode in which it is manifested, and the fashions which govern the display of it, are in a large measure regulated by other things, as race, education, birth, social position, and constitutional temperament. In this country no one looks for the volubility, the effervescence, the ardent chivalry and enthusiastic devotion to an idea, which are natural to the French and Irish – and the passionate effusion, the audacious absence of self-restraint, the sentimentalism, sometimes maudlin, sometimes heroic, which characterize the German, are, according to our insular notions, not only strange, but ludicrous. (302)

The essayist cites a particularly overworked passage in which a pair of German friends 'fell silently into each other's arms, and with bowed heads poured forth all the tears that burned within them' (302) to demonstrate the point, maintaining that:

> Among very young people and women there is, of course, a greater licence permitted in such matters, but, in general, the more highly civilized and polished the society, the greater the tendency to avoid demonstrative feeling in public; and this is true of all countries, but more especially true of England. (303)

The attempt to associate intense friendship with women and the very young is characteristic of nineteenth-century writing on the subject, and will surface repeatedly in the course of this study. More perplexing is the manner in which the essayist openly celebrates intense friendship in words (one form of Paradise) and simultaneously deprecates its outward expression.

More recognisably in keeping with the ideals of the twenty-first century, a number of writers depict strong feeling held in check by social custom and supposedly natural reticence – the association of this particular ideal with English manliness has been a persistent one.

But one reason for this seeming contradiction in some accounts of friendship ideals – again, it is one that is apparent in a range of commentaries – is the changing cultural perception of what constitutes 'intensity' in the first place. Taking youthful romantic friendship as a benchmark, writers were able to disavow its excesses while upholding forms of expression that were by comparison fairly restrained. In *Lady Audley's Secret*, for instance, this distinction enables Braddon's narrator to ridicule schoolgirl friendship that expresses itself in book dedications, while praising one adult friend's obsessive search for the other's putative murderer. At this distance in time, it is only possible to speculate on the reciprocal influence within Victorian culture of *soi-disant* romantic friendship and the less extreme forms purveyed by realist literature and conduct manuals. But as the comments of contemporary essayists attest, even the more conservative forms of friendship could accommodate expression that would now be regarded as intense in its bearing. This is how conservative writers were able to contain emotional elements in their account of friendship while relegating 'romantic friendship' *per se* to women, and more particularly to the very young.

A case in point is Ouida's *Under Two Flags*, first published in 1867. Focusing on the voluntary exile and dispossession of the Honourable Bertie Cecil, the novel is ostensibly upper-class in its values – the narrator repeatedly attests to the restraint and reticence inherent in the hero's personality, characteristics which are attributed with similar narrative insistence (amounting almost to anxiety) to his better-born counterparts. Cecil is nicknamed 'Beauty' for his pleasing appearance, while his almost equally good-looking friend goes under the sobriquet of 'the Seraph'. But here again a focus on physical good looks need not imply an unusual level of intimacy. Despite this blatant appeal to the mutual admiration of attractive men, the relationship between the two does not allow one to confess private anxieties to the other while both are leading a privileged existence in England. Only when Cecil is believed dead under the imputation of crime is his friend allowed to mourn him 'with passionate loving force, refusing to the last to accredit his guilt' (*Under Two Flags*, 231). Cecil's faithful servant is permitted to show devotion in following him into service in the French Foreign Legion, but even this altruistic love is not fully acknowledged by the narrator until the moment of his death, when Rake's loyalty to his former master is significantly described, in an echo of the David and Jonathan story, as 'a fidelity passing the fidelity of woman' (409). Again, the Seraph is permitted a passionate outburst on being reunited with Cecil after twelve years, but this is justified by the presence of a firing squad who are on the point of shooting his old friend for an assault on a senior officer.

It is not perhaps wholly coincidental that this final expression of a passionate love is offered in the Arabian desert, far from the constraints of English culture, and that the witnesses to it are all French (a nation characterised in the text as far more impulsive in their emotion than the English).

The story ends with Cecil's rescue by a woman whose love he does not requite and who dies in his place, and his marriage to the more eligible Venetia, sister to the Seraph. What is notable about this sensational story is its inconsistent treatment of passion between friends – Cecil has to descend the social scale and face exile abroad before he can experience strong feeling in all its immediacy, and only when he is believed to be dead, or later, when he is about to be killed in an alien country, can the Seraph express love for him. The narrator repeatedly praises the aristocratic reserve of the two characters, obviating the need to discuss their customary behaviour towards each other by parting them for much of the novel. None the less, the most moving moments in the story are those where characters – including the male protagonists – express strong feeling for one another, and Cecil's character develops through contact with a more effusive culture as much as through the physical hardships that render him 'manly' after an 'effeminate' life of privilege amongst the English nobility.

Ouida's ambivalent treatment of male emotion and the conventions governing its expression is characteristic even of sensation fiction (the genre to which her novel most fully adheres). Throughout the novel, she deprecates passionate emotion even as she prepares the ground for the highly emotional reunion between her pair of devoted male friends (characteristic also is the final marriage between the protagonist and his friend's sister, glibly resolving the question of relative status between marriage and friendship). The dilemma is apparent throughout the novel, as the supposedly upper-class virtue of self-restraint conflicts both with the exigencies of the plot and with the narrator's increasingly open attraction to passionate expression. In common with other writers, the narrator finds one solution in simply denying or ignoring the intensity of the relationship portrayed.

At some level, romantic friendship could even be deployed as a repository for passion from which writers or self-appointed social critics might wish to distance themselves – as I will suggest, Thackeray questions the sincerity and worth of fashionably romantic effusions as a means of validating the more restrained version of friendship offered by his heroes. As I have noted above in my discussion of the *Cornhill* article, in drawing attention to the excesses of romantic friendship, writers could paradoxically outline an adjacent 'space' in which to explore quite elevated expressions of attachment without sacrificing the imperatives of 'English restraint'. Furthermore, within romantic friendship itself a similar deflection technique can be used to great effect by an able narrator. I will be paying considerable attention in subsequent chapters to the way in which one character's innocence is highlighted by another's comparative knowingness – by drawing attention to the potential for erotic passion through the corruption of a would-be seducer, writers are able to stress by contrast the purity and idealism of their heroes and heroines.

At one level, then, romantic friendship was doubly necessary to those writers who were least drawn to its impassioned forms of expression, but who wanted to portray their characters in the act of forming close attachments to members of their own sex. As I will show in Chapter Four, in satirising excessive demonstrations of regard, a writer such as Thackeray could disclaim an effusiveness of which he had himself a stock of fond memories, while pre-empting possible criticism of the sentimental friendship he wished to convey.

But the failure to draw clear distinctions could have serious implications even at the time, as one anonymous essayist points out (ironically, without himself offering a clear definition):

> We are too careless in our use of terms; we apply the same words to the false as to the true, to the selfish as to the pure, to the passing as to the permanent. And thus it is that the name of friendship has been profaned, and the reality of friendship has come to be doubted. (*Sayings About Friendship*, 55)

Given the immense importance attached to close friendship at the time, carelessness of definition could – and perhaps did – give ammunition to satirists who impugned the female capacity for loyalty in particular. As this writer complains, the indiscriminate or purely fashionable use of a term such as 'friendship' is ultimately likely to debase the idea it describes, as when Thackeray's Becky Sharp shamelessly employs the language of romantic friendship to manipulate the despised Amelia, whom she parodically vows to love 'for ever and ever and ever'.

In attempting to redress the balance, essayists offered some highly complex (sometimes bewildering) disquisitions on the nature of 'real' friendship – which may or may not be romantic, and may or may not incorporate elements of intense expression. A conscientious attempt to define friendship in all its manifestations comes from Thackeray's daughter Anne, who offers a particularly useful set of distinctions in lamenting what she sees as a tendency to neglect friendship in a world concerned with what she terms 'meaningless repetition'. In an 1873 essay in *The Cornhill* (collected the following year as part of *Toilers and Spinsters and Other Essays*) she recalls her own friendships and invites the reader to do the same, suggesting:

> One means perhaps passionate emotion, unreasonable reproach, tender reconciliation; another may mean injustice, forgiveness, remorse; while another speaks to us of all that we have ever suffered, all that we hold most sacred in life, and gratitude and trust unfailing. (Anne Thackeray, 'In Friendship', *Toilers and Spinsters*, 291)

A scholarly treatise on friendship by the Sunday School missionary Henry Trumbull, published in America in 1892, but making copious use of English literary sources, is of considerable interest in its attempt to analyse the nature of close friendship. In the defiantly titled *Friendship the Master-passion*, Trumbull discusses the etymology of the word itself and offers a lengthy appraisal of friendship rituals in various parts of the world. Insisting on its importance and sacredness (by no means a given in England by1892, as we will see), he argues:

> The common thought is, that 'love' and 'friendship' merely differentiate *degrees* of affection; and that intensity and devotedness are the distinguishing characteristics of 'love' in comparison with 'friendship'. But the place given in both classic and sacred story to the illustrations of self-sacrificing friendship proves that no lack of depth and fervor limits the force and sway of this expression of personal attachment. Greater love hath no man than that love which is shown in friendship, at its best and truest manifestation. Not in its measure, but in its very nature, is an unselfish friendship distinguishable from a love which pivots on a reciprocal relation, secured or desired. (Trumbull, 17)

Trumbull makes some big claims for friendship as 'the pre-eminent and surpassing affection of the human heart' (57), largely on the basis of its altruism – '"Love" is supposed to involve some possessory relation with the object of attachment, while "friendship" does not necessarily imply any such relation' (16); indeed, he goes so far as to assert that:

> Friendship is love, with the selfish element eliminated. It is an out-going and an on-going affection, wholly and inherently disinterested, and in no sense contingent upon any

reciprocal relation between its giver and its object, nor yet upon its return or recognition. Friendship, in short, is love apart from love's claim or love's craving. (118)

Incidentally, this analysis seemingly precludes any conflict of interests between friendship and marriage. But as I will argue, such a case for friendship as being less possessive than romantic love is not necessarily supported by relationships in the texts I will be considering.

As is becoming apparent, the distinction between sexualised responsiveness and romantic friendship is such a difficult one to establish, partly because of the terms in which it was framed in the nineteenth century, the term 'passion' being applied seemingly indiscriminately to both intense friendship and sexual attraction. Significantly, in discussions of the nature of friendship, commentators (sometimes quite unselfconsciously) use the rhetoric of love and marriage, as well as religion and fraternity, to pinpoint the ideal they wish to inspire or analyse. Indeed it is even possible as late as the 1880s to equate the two, a comparison that writers seem not to have found particularly problematic:

> ... that mysterious link of mutual understanding and sympathy ... which cannot be accounted for, which eludes analysis, which yet makes, when the sex happens to be identical, the indissoluble friendship of a David and a Jonathan, a Karlos and a Posa; and, where there is a difference of sex, brings about that rarest wonder of the world, a happy marriage. (Cholmondeley, *Sir Charles Danvers*, 219)

The connotations of 'passion', less fully exploited in the early twenty-first century, can of course include any strong feeling in addition to the most immediately obvious meaning of sexual arousal. Nineteenth-century usages include the still familiar noun, for instance, in which a person can be described as being 'in a passion', suggesting rage. Well into the twentieth century, the word was still being used to describe the hero worship encouraged in single-sex boarding schools – having a 'pash' or passion for (later, a crush on) an older pupil enjoys a long tradition in this carefully regulated context.

Notably in mid-century literature, while intense friendship can be ambiguous – and this is a theme variously explored by the writers to be considered – it can also act as a safety valve, providing an appropriate outlet for passionate feeling that would otherwise be inexpressible. The expression of love and the sacrifice of self that romantic friendship appears to offer its proponents are similarly celebrated in literary portrayals of sibling loyalty. Famously, the family circle in Victorian writing serves as a locus of strong feeling that can only be appropriately expressed – by women at least – in a domestic setting.

Dickens's Christmas story *The Battle of Life*, Wilkie Collins's novel *The Woman in White* and Christina Rossetti's poem *Goblin Market* all present intense responsiveness, physical and emotional, between female characters. However, despite critical attempts to equate this feeling with sexual attraction, it should be remembered that in each case the protagonists are sisters (or half-sisters in the case of Marian and Laura); unless we are to accept that these writers are depicting incestuous behaviour in terms of unqualified approval, such portrayals surely point towards a key function of romantic friendship – it does not simply sublimate, but rather displaces socially proscribed passion. The feeling between sisters in the texts cited above is enabled in each case by their family relationship – romantic friendship is not socially sanctioned in quite the same way, but in one sense it mimics the values attributed to loving brothers or sisters.

The social value of romantic friendship is problematic, partly because of its defining qualities of exclusivity and intense focus – Trumbull notes that 'He who is capable of friendship at its best, cannot be a true friend alike to all. The very intensity of the sentiment demands a positive limit to the extension of its scope' (Trumbull, 93). But provided it adhered to certain rules, one of which was that it should ultimately be superseded by marriage, this kind of relationship could have a very real practical value in training the sensibilities of young men, and in particular young women. Contrary to the stereotype that has since become so influential, the approved model for women in the nineteenth century did not necessarily centre on insularity or conscious repression, but largely on social, or at least symbolic, functionality and responsibilities. Denigrating superficial education as much as assertive independence, Sarah Ellis's immensely popular conduct manual *The Women of England: Their Social Duties and Domestic Habits* makes this social aspect of women's role abundantly clear. First published in 1839, *The Women of England* sets out what might be taken as a manifesto for female responsiveness and responsibility:

> Woman, with all her accumulations of minute disquietudes, her weakness, and sensibility, is but a meagre item in the catalogue of humanity; but, roused by a sufficient motive to forget all these, or rather, continually forgetting them because she has other and nobler thoughts to occupy her mind, woman is truly and majestically great.
>
> Never yet, however, was woman great, because she had great acquirements; nor can she ever be great in herself – personally, and without instrumentality – as an object, not an agent. (64)

One way in which women could display their 'natural' qualities of sympathy as a powerful agency was through friendship shown to each other. It is, according to Maria Edgeworth, writing in 1896, 'a charming accomplishment in a friend; the only obligation a proud person is never too proud to receive' (*Helen*, 30). Romantic friendship between women was actively encouraged until the end of the century, when fears about the 'New Woman' (according to Lillian Faderman) precipitated its identification with lesbianism by sexologists. Of course, the identification of romantic friendship with a constrained form of lesbianism is impossible to prove conclusively either way – but Ellis's argument that such relationships were erotic in their very nature rests on the assumption that women whose behaviour was conventional in other respects were unaware of the real tendency of their feelings. In fact, as I will show, literary portrayals reveal a high awareness of the issues at stake, and an initial confidence in withstanding misinterpretation. While the ultimate shift in female social codes appears inevitable in the face of such scrutiny, the gradual erosion of intense language is not yet visible in the last years of the nineteenth century. The picture is further complicated by a stray remark from the influential journalist and activist Frances Power Cobbe. In an article published in 1902 she claims that:

> The tone of the highest society has become, not so much elaborately and formally polite, as in the eighteenth century, as affectionate and sympathetic almost to excess. Among very well-bred women, in particular, it is the habit to use endearing expressions and exhibit a cordiality towards acquaintances far removed from the distant courtesy of our grandparents. ('Schadenfreude', reprinted in *Prose by Victorian Women: An Anthology*, 345–6)

This comment is difficult to fathom given the age of the writer, who was 80 at the time and who describes herself as old in the same article – presumably, then, she is not adopting a persona in line with the assumed age of her general readership, but in her own youth extreme expressions would have been highly fashionable. It would be interesting to know how old her readers' grandparents are assumed to be. In the light of sexology and its suspicion of intense friendship at this period, the observation that 'excessive' sympathy has once again become fashionable, is itself unexpected. It is possible that the use of the terms 'society' and 'acquaintances' points to less intimate relations than would be implied in the term 'friendship' – what is being discussed is perhaps a passing fashion of the upper class alone rather than a perceived social trend.

Commentary by mid-Victorian writers more usually takes as read the cultural endorsement of female responsiveness as representing the norm, and this assumption is reflected in the work of the writers to be considered. Their work bears out the view that, on the surface at least:

> Victorian women in general enjoyed considerable freedom to feel and display love for each other, even allowing for literary heightening and idealization. And the freedom was at least partially a response to the constraints placed on the association between respectable men and women. (Barickman, MacDonald and Stark, 81)

That there were inevitably tensions in this ideal is a point to which I will return throughout the following chapters, but the sense in which passion is directed into particular outlets is a crucial one. Gesa Stedman has shown how certain discourses, such as patriotism and religion, were offered as 'safe pockets' of emotion, through which intense feeling could be expressed. I would argue, with Barickman, MacDonald and Stark, that these categories of allowable feeling could also include the expression of romantic friendship in a society that mistrusted the open avowal of feeling between the sexes.

Indeed, such relationships might be promoted to contain and direct passion that might otherwise have found inappropriate outlets. As Alger argued:

> the most healthful and effective antidote for the evils of an extravagant passion is to call into action neutralizing or supplementary passions; to balance the excess of one power by stimulating weaker powers, and fixing attention on them; to assuage disappointments in one direction by securing gratifications in another. Accordingly, the offices of friendship in the lives of women, – lives often so secluded, impoverished, and self-devouring, – is a

subject of emphatic timeliness; promising, if properly treated, to yield lessons of no slight practical value. (Alger, 3–4)

George Eliot's novel *The Mill on the Floss* is a study in the danger of female passion that is allowed no socially sanctioned outlet, and is first constrained in masochistic repression before coming to focus on a forbidden object. Maggie Tulliver's defining characteristic, as identified by the narrator, is her intense craving for love and affection, although it could equally be said that lack of education lies behind her depressive dependence on the feeling of others. Denied the satisfaction of intellectual attainment and with no female friend other than her cousin, the more staid and conventional Lucy, Maggie constantly strives to find an outlet for her passionate responsiveness, focusing first on her brother and later on Lucy's own accepted suitor, Stephen Guest. While ungoverned passion is shown to be ultimately catastrophic, her dangerous repression of her instincts through ascetic religion is likewise damaging to Maggie, as the rejected Philip Wakem points out to her.

Eliot was not the only writer to show concern about the restricted options for expressing female passion. A series of articles and conduct manuals of the time posit friendship as a healthy focus for female energy and passion, without which an unnatural restraint may lead to depressive illness. It is largely the suggestion later in the century that here too, sex becomes an intrusive factor that ultimately undermines the nineteenth century's apparent confidence in its own ideal of same-sex friendship. The vulnerability of romantic friendship to this type of (mis)interpretation is suggested by its contradictoriness – in a culture that promulgated male/female balance as the norm, such friendship is justified by its very exclusion of the opposite sex. Intense friendship might be seen to achieve its balance, an issue associated in the wider social context with the perceived terms of gender difference, through a certain disparity, and not through the oft-prescribed similarity of temperament. While resisting any direct reference to lesbianism, Dinah Mulock Craik warns the readers of *A Woman's Thoughts About Women* that:

> The wonderful law of sex – which exists spiritually as well as materially, and often independent of matter altogether; since we see many a man who is much more of a woman, and many a woman who would certainly be the 'better-half' of any man who cared for her – this law can rarely be withstood with impunity. In most friends whose attachment is specially deep and lasting, we can usually trace a difference – of strong or weak, gay or grave, brilliant or solid – answering in some measure to the difference of sex. Otherwise, a close, all-engrossing friendship between two women would seldom last long; or if it did, by their mutual feminine weaknesses acting and reacting upon one another, would most likely narrow the sympathies and deteriorate the character of both. (141)

Inherent in this warning about the 'dangers' of same-sex attachments persisting after youth is the suspicion that female character may deteriorate in isolation from male social influence. Craik's concerns about exclusive intimacy between members of the same sex, and the disruption of gender norms, surface as a theme in more than one fictional account of romantic friendship, and this can suggest tension in the model.

Growing concerns about social change and the New Woman, as Faderman suggests, may have influenced the shift in attitudes foreshadowed in such asides even at mid-century. That female behaviour was placed under particular scrutiny should in one sense come as no surprise in the light of the traditions of writing on this subject. Of the eight essayists considered in this chapter, three (Sarah Ellis, Sarah Tytler and Dinah Mulock Craik) write almost entirely from the specific perspective of women commenting on women; the other five (Percival Pickering, Hugh Black, Anne Thackeray and the two anonymous writers of *Thoughts on Friendship* and *Sayings About Friendship* respectively) all tend to universalise their treatment of friendship, even where they imply a male subject in their use of both examples and pronouns. It is interesting though, given the greater freedom supposedly encouraged within female friendships, that they should be subjected to more incisive commentary than their more carefully regulated male counterparts.

Several of the essays comment on the lack of celebrity accorded to significant female friendships, an omission which they attribute to the obscurity of women's lives – this assertion that women's relations with each other are somehow unknowable and unrecorded does not prevent a general preoccupation with this very area long before Havelock Ellis's intervention. What is astonishing is the sheer resistance achieved by female friendship to the (often medically sanctioned) interpretation of such commentators.

But the new sexology, and such *fin de siècle* scandals as the Oscar Wilde trial, had more immediate implications for the conventions of male friendship. For various reasons, male behaviour also underwent a change as the century progressed, and emotionalism came to be associated by the 1890s with the excesses of the aesthetic movement. In *Marius the Epicurean*, written in 1885 and set in ancient Rome, Pater suggests that the intense friendship between the aging Emperor Aurelius and his subject Fronto might require some explanation (although, perhaps unsurprisingly, the equally intense friendships between young men seemingly do not). The narrator notes:

> reiterations of affection ... which are continued in these letters, on both sides, and which may strike a modern reader perhaps as fulsome; or, again, as having something in common with the old Judaic unction of friendship. They were certainly sincere. (*Marius the Epicurean*, 226)

This slightly defensive note itself suggests an awareness of a changing attitude towards male friendship, as conservative investments in 'English reserve' increasingly conflicted with the contradictory ideal of passionate expression. This conflict is apparent in the autobiography written by Anthony Trollope for posthumous publication. Writing in later middle age, Anthony Trollope would describe his love for a friend as expressible only after death:

> These words, should he ever see them, will come to him from the grave, and will tell him of my regard, – as one living man never tells another. (*An Autobiography*, 150)

Again, Trollope adheres to the compromise whereby love was expressible without constraint within a context of mourning or protracted separation. In the last years of the century, Sir Maxwell Herbert would claim that the 'extraordinary reserve of

Englishmen' was a major factor contributing to 'make the duration of friendship precarious' (Herbert, 402).

However, this perception of social reticence is at odds with an ideal expressed by various writers earlier in the century. Extant letters between men sometimes reveal a surprisingly high level of emotionalism, and poetry in particular could be effusive in the extreme, as Walter Miller's 'To a Friend at Parting', written only a year earlier, shows:

> this then my pledge at friendship's altar sworn – I write adieu – but feel we're ever one.
> (*Offerings to Friendship and Truth*, 128)

Coventry Patmore's notorious mid-century poem *The Angel in the House* (in which the narrator's reluctance to marry at all may come as some surprise to the reader who has known it only by repute) contains a telling passage on friendship between men. Having neglected his friend for love, the narrator is joyously reunited with him when the two men learn that they are both in love with worthy objects; they walk together, 'Friendship from passion stealing fire' (*The Angel in the House*, 171).

In the earlier years of the century the young Thackeray, among others, expressed his feeling for absent friends in highly rhetorical terms, and Percival Pickering ends *An Essay on Friendship* with the famous lines from Tennyson, so often quoted out of context in our own time:

> Tis better to have loved and lost
> Than never to have loved at all.
> (from *In Memoriam*, xxvii)

Dickens's expressed feeling for his friends is itself highly, and it would seem unselfconsciously, emotional. Writing to William Macready in 1847, he declared of a new production:

> The multitudes of new tokens by which I know you for a great man, the swelling within me of my love for you, the pride I have in you, the majestic reflection I see in you of the passions and affections that make up our mystery, throw me into a strange kind of transport that has no expression but in a mute sense of an attachment which in truth and fervency is worthy of its subject. What is this to say! Nothing, God knows, –and yet I cannot leave it unsaid. (letter to William Macready, 23 November 1847, *The Letters of Charles Dickens*, vol. V, 200–201)

In a later letter to Forster he describes another man's love for the explorer John Franklin (one of Dickens's own heroes) as:

> one of the noblest things I ever knew in my life. It makes one's heart beat high, with a sort of sacred joy. (letter to John Forster, 2? March 1856, *The Letters of Charles Dickens*, vol. viii, 165)

This emphasis on the 'noble' quality of empathy, particularly in close friendships, is stressed by the famous proponent of manliness and male bonding Thomas Hughes, who asserted:

> Blessed is the man who has the gift of making friends; for it is one of God's best gifts. It involves many things, but above all, the power of going out of one's self, and seeing and appreciating whatever is noble and living in another man. (*Tom Brown at Oxford*, 72)

The claim of friendship as an index to moral status is suggested by other writers, who stress that 'It is not all who are capable of it; it is not all, it may be, who, being capable, are permitted to meet with it. A rarity of friendship demands a rarity of nature' (*Sayings About Friendship*, 51), or similarly, 'It may be that not many natures are capable of real and lasting friendship, though everyone may feel the want of it ...' (Pickering, 37).

Neither of these writers uses the word 'romantic' to describe the type of intimacy they are endorsing, but the terms in which their (remarkably similar discussions) are expressed bear all the hallmarks of romantic friendship. Intensity is offered as a notable feature of such close friendships, and the use of the word 'intimacy' in various discussions of friendship throughout the century suggests the way in which romantic friendship could be carelessly conflated with its more ordinary counterpart or even with heterosexual love.

In fiction, expressions of emotion between male characters can be extremely explicit. Tellingly, though, the scenario often focuses on a friendship forged in unusual circumstances, usually a journey, and this allows customary etiquette to be bypassed. This freedom could however suggest grounds for anxiety. In a monitory novel by J.H. Wilton, one friend at least is true to the other, but the very title suggests the rashness of such sudden intimacy. *The First Crime: or, True Friendship* details the impulsive attraction between two characters, and the journey they take together, where the narrator of the story is robbed by his friend in a place where he knows no one, and later falls suspicion to having fabricated the whole story for purposes of blackmail. The story ends with the narrator generously destroying the evidence of the whole affair, an action which is shortly followed by the death of his friend. The precipitate nature of this friendship and its emotionalism are based on an initial encounter at the theatre, where the narrator has been taken by another new friend. The next morning:

> [he] hoped I should not think him bold for confessing that he felt more deep regard and fraternal esteem for me than he had ever felt before for anyone.
> I need not say that my heart leaped with joy to learn this and to feel its echo in my breast with sympathetic emotions. (*The First Crime*, 53)

In that 'I need not say', the narrator makes a confident appeal to the shared experience of his male readers, to whom he implies further explanation will not be necessary.

It is a fact that for much of the century same-sex friendship was predicated on enthusiasm and passionate expression in words. Walter Houghton charts the rise of enthusiasm in England from the 1820s, noting that it defined itself in positive and regenerative terms, 'To admire – which is to say, *not* to criticize, still less to ridicule – was the first requirement which enthusiasm brought into English taste' (Houghton, 299). But associated as it is with intense feeling, enthusiasm can suggest both the pursuit of an ideal and a questionable lack of restraint. For instance, Charlotte Brontë alludes, in a letter to her friend's brother Henry Nussey, of 'my besetting sin of enthusiasm' (*The Brontës: A Life in Letters*, 28 October 1839, p. 69).

In *The Mill on the Floss*, Eliot reflects on the perceived human need for an inspiring higher principle of some kind, as enthusiasm replaces the striving for happiness itself as Maggie's guiding motive. In this dual focus on active choice and the deliberate surrender of personal will, enthusiasm paradoxically locates active choice in the very act of surrender itself, although in Maggie's case this renunciation is narrowly fanatical and is clearly associated – most directly in the comments of the clear-eyed Philip Wakem – with intellectual torpidity. The further contemporary meaning of enthusiasm as a general term for extremist religious fervour serves to reinforce this connotation of fanaticism. Enthusiasm, then, is itself an ambiguous term, bearing a range of possible meanings; in this context it can be taken to mean simultaneously a deliberate celebration of overpowering, idealised feeling, and the threat of such dangerous irrationality as may be produced by passion or fanatical adherence to abstract principles.

The place of enthusiasm in literature was debated by nineteenth-century writers such as Wilkie Collins, who claimed, perhaps surprisingly, in 1872 that the novelist's province was 'strictly social' (in Nadel, *Victorian Fiction: A Collection of Essays From the Period*, 384) and should cater to the man of the world for whom 'The bright world of the enthusiast is an unknown land' (389). But as late as 1890, Hall Caine was to argue in *The Contemporary Review* that, on the contrary:

> The true consort of imagination is enthusiasm, the man of imagination has never lived who was not also an enthusiast, and enthusiasm is the only force that has ever done any good in the world since the world began. ... And this enthusiasm, which cannot live at peace with realism, lives and flourishes with idealism. (481)

The dilemma faced by Victorian romantic friendship was to balance the apparent unconsciousness offered by enthusiastic idealism with a careful regulation of feeling. Feeling between friends might be mediated through the carefully chosen terms of letters or diaries, but it was also expressed through physical gesture and verbal communication. The value of such expression depended on its ability to confine itself within accepted channels while appearing to be unconstrained and spontaneous. The repression of emotion, as Sally Shuttleworth has shown, was associated with illness in women in particular – conversely, its free expression could be suggestive of insanity. Hence, 'The ever-present threat of insanity constituted the subtext of the culture of self-control' (Shuttleworth, 43). Prescriptions for self-control compete with the threat of dangerous influence exerted by friends, as I will argue in subsequent chapters. The tension between expressing passionate regard and regulating one's own emotion surfaces in a wide range of texts, from *In Memoriam* to *A Drama in Muslin*.

Gesa Stedman has shown how Victorian discourse on emotion attempts to maintain just such a balance between expression and control, a dilemma that results in manifold tensions and contradictions within writing of the period:

> The need to control the topic extends from the use of recurrent key emotion words and central metaphors to explicit rules recommended to keep the 'storms of passion' and their

effects at bay. But in equal measure the need to express the feelings is given room. The attempt at balancing both these claims results in the manifold tensions and contradictions of the Victorian discourses on emotions. (Stedman, 230)

One way in which a level of control could in theory be achieved, in the context of romantic friendship, was through a careful setting out of boundaries for the containment of emotion. The expectation that romantic friendship should be confined to extreme youth is one example of this careful ordering – while young girls may find an ideal of friendship in mutual passion, such enthusiasm is not seen as appropriate to older women. A related strategy in fiction is the splitting of characteristics between protagonists – the allocation of less conventional or socially accepted characteristics to a secondary but compelling figure is a common tactic in Victorian fiction (to cite a famous example, readers of Wilkie Collin's *The Woman in White* were less interested in the fate of the ostensible heroine than in making proposals of marriage to the 'original' of the unconventional Marion Halcomb). This classic strategy is highly effective in defusing the potential tension inherent in romantic friendship, where one character is presented as naïve to the point of obtuseness, thus ironically being rendered safe from the advances of the lascivious friend. Such dichotomies preserve the purity of one character involved at the expense of the other, and so provide a means of acknowledging the sexual threat raised by intensity and close intimacy without having to sacrifice the value of the ideal itself.

Such strategies implicitly pre-empt the arguments of Havelock Ellis and the sexologists – I will argue that Dickens, for instance, responded to the dangers of sexuality within his ideal of friendship by creating a symbolic division between enthusiasm and the erotic, nearly fifty years before *Sexual Inversion*. Stedman's analysis of the emotion/control dichotomy likewise reveals an awareness on the part of Victorian writers of tensions in their depictions of strong feeling, and the attempts of various commentators to find a resolution. Symbolic representation is one means of resolving, or at least concealing, such fractures, as Stedman points out:

> Popular metaphors serve as a kind of shorthand which makes the complexity of emotionality manageable and in a fictional text it allows readers easier access to a character's psychological make-up. But most importantly such a metaphorical continuity indicates stability in a society which was anything but stable. (Stedman, 77)

Questions of control arise in same-sex friendships, much as they do in the conventional portrayal of heterosexual love, and similarly, one party tends to be presented as self-sacrificing and dependent on the other for affection. Repeatedly, it is the supposedly dependent character with whose viewpoint the reader is encouraged to sympathise – Ozias Midwinter, Esther Summerson and David Copperfield all emerge as central characters, and Esther and David themselves control the telling of their stories. Contrary to the traditional view of feminised sacrificial figures as self-effacing or symbolically blank, these characters feel intensely, and their passionate response overpowers the stories they tell. Such intense perspective governs the narrative except, crucially, where it becomes imbued with erotic potential – in a similar strategy to the first-person narrative of *David Copperfield*, the vampire Carmilla speaks only through Laura's retrospective narration, and is in this sense denied an autonomous voice.

Such friendships may, but do not then necessarily, contain an erotic potential. In the texts under discussion, a subversive eroticism may be represented by one party but not both, and the narrative is always the province of the ingenue, who fails to see the danger represented by his or her friend. Disruptively erotic figures are firmly expelled by the end – Le Fanu's Carmilla and Dickens's Steerforth both die – and the story thus remains in the hands of the intended victim.

Carmilla's passion for young girls is seen as suspect in itself, and Laura simply finds it embarrassing. But passion for friends is not synonymous with erotic charge – indeed, these predatory and even vampiristic urges can elevate their object to a state of intense but innocent romantic enthusiasm. Steerforth's feeling for David is hardly romantic, but David himself displays a selfless ardour in this relationship, based on admiration of his captivating friend. Most clearly in *David Copperfield*, enthusiasm is deployed to neutralise the potential for erotic threat; elsewhere in Dickens, this threat is made more explicit (when *Little Dorrit*'s Miss Wade makes off with the rebellious Tattycoram, the object of this passion gives no sign of awareness, but Meagles tells Miss Wade darkly that he has heard of women such as she, who bring other women down to their own perverted level); elsewhere again, the obligatory love plot is mediated through a passionate but sexless romantic friendship, as in *Bleak House*.

Bleak House, *Armadale* and *Shirley* all posit intense friendships where a heterosexual love interest provides the ostensible focus of the plot and provides an argument against any putative erotic attachment between the friends themselves. In support of this view of the texts as confidently orthodox in their representations, it is the more intense character in each with whose point of view the reader is invited to sympathise – this is far from being the case in *Carmilla*, for the reasons I have suggested. Where highly charged language is sanctioned, it is also carefully delimited, or at least contextualised.

Parodies of romantic friendship are offered by both Wilkie Collins and Thackeray, as well as Charles Reade. In *Vanity Fair*, Becky Sharp plays on expectations of female attachment to gain her dubious ends, while the minor figure Miss Swarz is excessively devoted to Amelia but has little time in which to visit the unfashionable area to which the Sedleys are reduced after the failure of Mr Sedley's business ventures. Lydia Gwilt deliberately undermines popular stereotypes of female friendship, mocking Mother Oldershaw's assumptions of affection in her letters and flippantly questioning women's capacity for genuine feeling. But such parodies do not extend to homo-erotic expression, which is treated with much greater seriousness. The implied lesbianism of Miss Wade may well be a factor separating her characterisation from that of another man-hater, Miss Wisk in *Bleak House*. Wilkie Collins treats the friendship between Limping Lucy and Rosanna Spearman in *The Moonstone* with a seriousness that is in keeping with its tragic end. None the less the passionate feeling Lucy entertains for her friend, mediated through the narrative of Franklin Blake after Rosanna's death, is presented as disturbing in its vehemence; in *Armadale*, Lydia Gwilt had treated intense friendship as simply a subject for cynical jokes.

Certainly, an awareness of the erotic permeates Victorian writing on romantic friendship, and explains the complexity with which it is treated. Each writer under consideration apprehends such friendships differently, but in studying a wide range of texts in the following chapters, I hope to reveal a consistent pattern: intense feeling is celebrated, provided it is kept within safe limits; subversive sexuality is not contained or sublimated within the narrative, but where it appears, it is summarily expelled and the dissident figure destroyed.

The potential for erotic charge in these cases is symbolically split between two figures, the innocent enthusiast and the predatory agent of forbidden passion, whose destructive energies are ultimately turned inwards (Steerforth) or frustrated (Carmilla), leading to death or expulsion that allows the plot to be resolved. In a more ambiguous – and daring – rendering of the theme, Wilde gives Dorian Gray the option of inspiring Basil Hallward's aesthetic but possessive worship, or of submitting to the temptations figured by the dissolute Lord Henry Wotton. In this study of sensuous excess, it is Dorian's rapacity and refusal of responsibility, rather than his putative homosexuality, that brings about his destruction. Such a bold treatment is not available to mid-century writers, which is arguably why the subversive figures in the earlier texts are marginalised before being summarily expelled from the narratives in which they figure. The rules governing romantic friendship were tacitly acknowledged in literary portrayals throughout the century, and not the least important was the enduring innocence of the young and passionate hero or heroine in the face of any attempted seduction. The readiness of nineteenth-century writers to express intense feeling between friends is largely dependent on this implicit, but important, laying down of boundaries. In detailing the corruption of his central protagonist by a refined Mephistopheles, Wilde was breaking an important rule of the game.

Within accepted models of romantic friendship there are, then, conventions and symbolic registers of status recognised and mediated by Victorian writers.

The parameters and possible dangers of romantic friendship once established, it is important that a writer should be able to convey this status, for instance in the basic terms of sincerity and durability. In literature of the period, characteristically, the nature of friendship is often tested or intensified during periods of illness, as one character succeeds or fails in nursing another. In Walter Pater's *Marius the Epicurean*, the central protagonist displays loyalty to his first friend in remaining with him throughout an infectious – and fatal – disease. Such scenes are intense in focus, as Miriam Bailin has shown in *The Sickroom in Victorian Fiction: The Art of Being Ill*. As she explains:

> Nursing the sick was, for both men and women, as sanctified an act as suffering itself. As long as it was not for hire, nursing was repeatedly invoked to verify in a way no other activity apparently could the genuineness of one's affections, the essential goodness of one's character. (Bailin, 11)

In keeping with this ideal, Marius at one point 'almost longed to take his share in the suffering, that he might understand so the better how to relieve it' (*Marius the Epicurean*, 118). This empathy with the ill friend indicates the sincerity of the ministering figure's attachment, and features as a test in various friendships, whether or not they are designated as romantic.

Specifically, according to Bailin, these sickroom scenes privilege intimacy between members of the same sex:

> The Victorian sickroom is frequently portrayed as the site of a special rapport and tenderness between members of the same sex in direct or implicit distinction from the confusions and betrayals of male-female relations. (Bailin, 64)

The sickroom as site of same-sex intimacy is a recurring feature in the literature of the period. But for this very reason it can also be a threatening feature in the texts under consideration, as outsiders gain access to the family group and vampiristic urges sap the energy of the vulnerable. This threat will be clearly demonstrated in relation to Sheridan Le Fanu's 'Carmilla'.

A further anomaly is thrown up by even a brief survey of some of the major novels of the period. While male friends tend each other loyally through the most infectious illnesses and female characters nurse male lovers or daughters in particular, there is less evidence of such care between female friends. To take four Dickens novels in which the plot involves serious illness: Smike in *Nicholas Nickleby* is nursed by both Nicholas and his sister Kate; Martin Chuzzlewit is watched over by the faithful Mark Tapley; Pip Pirrip is nursed back to health by Jo Gargery despite his earlier desertion of his friend and former mentor; Eugene Wrayburn is nursed by his future wife and her friend, but also by his close friend Mortimer Lightburn. This pattern is discernible in other writers of the period: Thackeray's Pendennis is nursed through a serious illness by George Warrington as well as his own mother and future wife, while Wilkie Collins's Midwinter bases his love of Armadale on his altruism in the sickroom when they first meet.

Female friendships are not often accorded this heroic status (*Jane Eyre* is a rare example of women caring for the ill and apparently dying of their own sex). Dickens shows Ada Clare being denied entrance to Esther's sickroom in *Bleak House*; similarly, Collins's half-sisters Marian and Laura are kept from each other at times of illness or breakdown in *The Woman in White*; Magalen Vanstone in *No Name* is ministered to by her future husband when she falls ill; Rachel Verinder is guarded assiduously by *The Moonstone*'s Miss Clack purely because she wishes to convert her to vital religion and find out at the same time what has happened to the Indian diamond. Even in female-authored texts, the same anomaly is apparent. Cathy Earnshaw in *Wuthering Heights* has to make do with the dour Nelly Deane, a paid retainer; Caroline Helstone (and I will return to this) is nurtured by her mother in the crisis of her life while the eponymous Shirley is on holiday.

Same-sex intimacy is commended in the female sickroom, but it is rarely achieved outside the (surrogate) mother–daughter dynamic. Caroline Helstone, and Rosamond Trevelyan in *The Dead Secret*, are both reunited with long-absent or unrecognised mothers who see to their recovery from threatening illnesses. But this ideal is surprisingly absent from portrayals of female friendship, and where it is pursued, the would-be nurse is most often debarred, either by male medical authority or at the request of the ill character herself.

This picture is further complicated, as I have suggested, by anxieties about the very intimacy afforded by the sickroom. Alison Bashford has argued, in *Purity and Pollution: Gender, Embodiment and Victorian Medicine*, that medical practitioners and those caring for the sick themselves came under scrutiny as possible agents of 'dirtiness' or corruption. According to this account, those entering the sickroom were the focus of anxiety about both personal hygiene, and by extension, moral purity. The constant level of physical contact involved in caring for the ill person could be seen as potentially transgressive, and the liberties enjoyed in this context are a source of concern in *Armadale*, where Midwinter forms an intense bond with Armadale during his illness. Midwinter's ambiguous status as a stranger, coupled with his dangerous illness, directly inspire Armadale's care while simultaneously provoking Mrs Armadale's apparently irrational anxiety on her son's behalf. Carmilla gains access to Laura's household in just this way, despite being a stranger to the family. By assuming illness, she automatically lays claim to their protection – if caring for sufferers is an index to moral character, Laura's father can hardly refuse to take in a young girl who appears too unwell to travel further.

But this tension between the claims of illness and the suspicion attached to strangers becomes particularly interesting in the light of Bashford's study, as a level of anxiety is seen to permeate the privileged arena of the sickroom. Bashford suggests that the passage of corruption, associated with both disease and moral attrition, could be seen as functioning in either direction. In the case of *Armadale* and 'Carmilla' respectively, the family either fears (or more damagingly, fails to notice) the patient's capacity to act as conduit of moral infection. Carmilla is quite literally the source of Laura's decline – her apparent concern becomes increasingly disturbing as enervating illness is conflated with the 'cure' of impending death.

Writers such as Le Fanu are able to disturb their readers by stressing the vulnerability of the young to ungoverned passion, both their own and that of their closest friends. None the less, essays tend to stress the value of romantic friendship as a youthful ideal, showing considerably more uneasiness about emotion in later life. This ambiguity is reflected in poetry and fiction of the period, as it attempts to resolve such inconsistencies through delineation of age and the splitting of associated characteristics. The remainder of this study will assess the strategies used by a number of authors in their exploration of tensions in the basic model.

While a study of nineteenth-century poetry and prose reveals some common ground in depictions of romantic friendship, it also throws up various contradictions and inconsistencies between and within particular portrayals. In particular, the tone of discussion in essays devoted to the subject seems to bear a strong relation to contemporary gender codes. Notably, the female subject of romantic friendship is carefully gendered *as* female, and accounts of her 'nature' are defined in terms of perceived feminine qualities and social habits. Where the topic under discussion is male friendship ideals, the subject tends to be universalised – a male subject and reader are assumed but not clearly particularised at the outset, as in accounts of female relations. Chapter Three will confirm this tendency in its study of *Shirley* o female-authored text, and arguably the most conservative of those under discussion in its treatment of female friendship.

At one level it is not surprising that commentaries should tend to universalise the male subject while scrutinising the female participant in romantic friendship as being *specifically* female. Much writing on social themes follows the same pattern. What makes it odd in this case is simply that female friendship supposedly enjoyed greater freedom of expression, and might therefore anticipate a less minute observation from outside than this habit implies. A range of essays confirms that Victorians themselves were particularly aware of the freedoms permitted within female friendship. While intense male friendship is likewise celebrated, fictional accounts often posit sudden intimacies within a context of journeys, delivering their protagonists over to adventure and sometimes danger, outside the context of their everyday lives. But notwithstanding this supposedly greater freedom permitted between women, fuller provision was also made for the continuance of male friendship in later life through the cultural investment in male-only, semi-domestic spaces. Opportunities for men to maintain close bonds with each other were built into the social structure of London in particular. As Matt Cook for one points out, club culture could provide a useful space for same-sex relations of all sorts:

> For many upper and upper-middle class men the opportunities offered by the cosmopolitan West End were supplemented by a tradition of homosociality which often protected them in their exploits. The clubs and bachelor chambers in Pall Mall and St James' developed from the 1830s and formed a continuation of the homosocial worlds of public school and university. (Cook, 30)

Male friendship could to a certain extent then hold itself aloof from the allocated territory occupied by wife and family, by the simple expedient of recreating a quasi-domestic space. But the insistence on some kind of renunciation of friendship after marriage that is so prevalent a theme in essays and advice manuals of the time itself suggests the potential for conflict if friends were not prepared to give each other up.

Some level of conflict is almost inevitable, as intense feeling for a friend is no longer authorised after marriage. The metaphor of friendship as a substitute for marriage itself highlights the potential for rivalry between (intended) spouse and romantic friend. In fiction, this dilemma can be more or less convincingly resolved through the marriage of one friend to the other's relative – in *Shirley*, Caroline and Shirley marry two brothers, who are cousins to Caroline herself. Even the notoriously radical sensation fiction of the 1860s may attempt to diffuse tensions between friendship and marriage in this way. *Lady Audley's Secret*, for instance, presents an archetypal romantic friendship in which Robert Audley is galvanised by his desire to avenge his supposedly murdered friend; however, this friendship attains its status only after George Talboys has confided to Robert that his marriage has failed; furthermore, while the motivating friend is missing and presumed dead for much of the novel, his sister Clara becomes an equally powerful influence in his absence. The precise moment at which friendship is supposed to lose its force and marriage take over is blurred in this substitution of one sibling for another, as Robert ultimately marries Clara, and the errant Lady Audley is despatched to a *maison de santé* in Belgium. Of the texts under consideration in the following chapters, it is only another sensation novel, *Armadale*, in which romantic friendship is openly privileged above marriage, necessitating the death of the female interloper. As is clear from the range of texts examined here, friendship at any level in the nineteenth century is not necessarily expected to last for life, however close its bonds initially appear to be. Essayists and novelists alike ruefully acknowledge the rarity of lifelong friendships even as they celebrate their power to elevate character in youth.

Intense friendships were then associated almost automatically with the young, whose passionate energy was directed towards love of friends either in place of, or in preparation for, expected marriage. If women in particular failed to marry, their friendships were to stand in place of a conjugal tie, but the emphasis was on the stability and companionship that such supportive relationships could offer (it is no coincidence that the romantic friendships of the young are perceived in relation to 'first love' or passionate feeling for the opposite sex, while the more serious business of marriage is taken as a model for single-sex friendship between the middle-aged unmarried). Prevailing assumptions about the decline of passion in later life enforced this expectation – 'old maids' in Victorian literature may form mutually dependent relationships but they do not, or at least should not, express passionate feeling for each other. As Dinah Mulock Craik rather severely expresses it:

> It is the unmarried, the solitary, who are most prone to that sort of 'sentimental' friendship with their own or the opposite sex, which, though often most noble, unselfish, and true, is in some forms ludicrous, in others dangerous. For two women, past earliest girlhood, to be completely absorbed in one another, and make public demonstration of the fact, by caresses or quarrels, is so repugnant to common sense, that where it ceases to be silly it becomes actually wrong. But to see two women, whom Providence has denied nearer ties, by a wise substitution making the best of fate, loving, sustaining, and comforting one another, with a tenderness often closer than that of sisters, because it has all the novelty of election which belongs to the conjugal tie itself – this, I say, is an honourable and lovely sight. (139)

This passage evinces some anxiety about the appropriateness of romantic friendship that survives the youth of its professors, but the exhortation to moderate expression in later life paradoxically gives way to an implied parallel with the 'honourable estate' of marriage and might serve as an index to similar accounts of friendship as foreshadowing, or in some cases necessarily replacing, marriage itself. The ultimate example of this substitution in literature is to be found in Elizabeth Gaskell's *Cranford*, where initially at least the female residents of the town are vehemently opposed to male incursions, on the grounds that men interfere with their social regime. Notably, though, the only female character to have rejected a marriage proposal is shown in a tragic light, and several characters do make happy marriages given the chance. Charlotte Yonge was one writer among several to associate longstanding friendships with lack, writing in 1876: 'life-long friendships! Yes, they are a precious gift – often the dearest tie of single women. Happily they are many' (Yonge, 151). Even in this qualified context, the 'dearest tie' is suggestive of a substitute marriage.

Even where it involved only single men or women, this relationship between the ideals of friendship and marriage could at times be an uneasy one; the common terms in which each is described can serve to conceal an intrinsic tension in emotional discourse, as much as it suggests an insouciant naïveté on the part of some writers. Notably ambiguous is the tone of an anonymous essayist who contrives to use military imagery that is reminiscent both of religious exhortation and, more familiarly yet, the language of romantic love:

> These gentle first approaches, this ripening intercourse, this growing attraction that may end in strongest love, – we have influence over these. We cannot be too careful as to the nature of our closer companionships. Herein lies the power and the responsibility of choice: we may choose with whom we will dwell on terms of intimacy, and so choosing, we are answerable for the result. We may guard the approaches to the heart, but the heart itself once given, time only and trial can prove its trust well placed. If we would secure the citadel, it would be well to protect the outposts. (*Sayings About Friendship*, 64–5)

The thoughtless way in which this extract is able to elide the difference between friendship and romantic love, using the same image of the conquered citadel for both, again highlights both the perceived close relationship between the two, and an apparent lack of anxiety about this relatedness. But again, it stresses the need for caution, and even protection against the power of an unsuitable friend – the underlying sense of threat can be minimised only by the exercise of responsible choice.

This particular essay contains separate chapters on friendship between men, between women and on the viability of close friendships between the sexes (argued to be exceptional but not impossible). Interestingly, having emphasised that a friendship between the sexes is only eligible to be described as such if there is no suspicion of a sexual feeling on either side, the author fully approves a quotation used by Dinah Mulock Craik in *A Life for a Life*, in which the unidentified writer compares friendship directly to marriage as being 'for better or for worse'.

Where the tie between single women can almost be seen as a substitute for marriage itself, still even those who have failed to marry are encouraged to moderate their expressions of emotion, as we have seen; for those who have married, early passionate friendship should naturally give way to something more restrained:

> if it then wishes to keep up its vitality at all, it must change its character, temper its exactions, resign its rights: in short, be buried and come to life again in a totally different form. Afterwards, should Laura and Matilda, with a house to mind and a husband to fuss over, find themselves actually kissing the babies instead of one another – and managing to exist for a year without meeting, or a month without letter-writing, yet feel life no blank, and affection a reality still – then their attachment has taken its true shape as friendship, shown itself capable of friendship's distinguishing feature – namely, tenderness without appropriation; and the women, young or old, will love one another faithfully to the end of their lives. (137)

Such comparisons to marriage should not be seen as necessarily sexualising intense same-sex friendship. Rather, the comparisons reflect nineteenth-century ideals of conjugal love as moderate and tranquil, a model which as we have seen is suggested for friendship in middle age.

In isolating discussions of male and female friendship respectively in the next two chapters, I hope to point up the similarity in idealistic treatments of the subject, as well as the difference in perception between the two. This disparity is suggestive of a tradition of satirical commentary, itself satirised in *Armadale* by a witty female protagonist. This satirical interchange, involving both *Armadale* on the one hand and *Vanity Fair* and *Pendennis* on the other, will form the subject of the fourth chapter.

Romantic friendship may be conducted in terms that are no longer widely recognised, but for most of the nineteenth century it is legitimated, even as it exposes itself to satire, by its very confinement to members of the same sex. It is ironic that this emphasis on same-sex intimacy formed the very ground on which sexologists were to base their arguments at the end of the century.

Chapter Two

Extraordinary Reserve: The Problem of Male Friendship

Come then, Friendship, hover near me,
Give me strength and give me hope,
Hope that toils will not be useless,
Strength with obstacles to cope,
And when all I yearn and strive for
As my own I gladly claim,
I will ever tend thine altar
With a pure and quenchless flame.
('Youthful Friendship', L.R.R., *Cambridge Review*, 4)

Romantic friendship among young men in the nineteenth century is associated largely with the institutions of which it was a tradition, namely the major public schools and Oxford and Cambridge universities. This deliberate cultivation of feeling emphasises the sense in which romantic friendship was a product of class and education, even to some extent an artificial construct as I have already noted (the fashion in both boys' and girls' public schools for having a 'crush' on older pupils persisted well into the twentieth century). In 1893, Sir Maxwell Herbert recalled that:

> The most familiar friendships in a man's life are those sown in the natural seed-time – boyhood and youth – but though his schoolfellows may have been numbered by the hundred, those of them that became his fast friends may be counted on his fingers – most often on the fingers of one hand. (Herbert, 404)

The idealisation of such schoolboy friendships is nowhere more pronounced than in Disraeli's *Coningsby*. Written in 1844 as a defence of Conservative politics, the novel is largely concerned with the Eton friendships that the eponymous hero finds so improving and which he will sustain in adult life. The initial emphasis is notably aristocratic – Coningsby is put off his contemporary Millbank because his father is in business, and an awareness of rank and social status dominates the text. However the narrator endorses the accessibility of romantic friendship to the middle classes, quickly confiding to the reader that 'The secret of Millbank's life was a passionate admiration and affection for Coningsby' (*Coningsby*, 44). Millbank, however, is too proud to manufacture a friendship with his hero, whose awareness of social difference initially precludes any interest on his own part; the narrator's depiction of Millbank's feelings aligns him with the passionate woman, whose self-respect will none the less not allow her to make the first move:

In what fanciful schemes to obtain the friendship of Coningsby had Millbank in his reveries often indulged! What combinations that were to extend over years and influence their lives! But the moment that he entered the world of action, his pride recoiled from the plans and hopes which his sympathy had inspired. His sensibility and inordinate self-respect were always at variance. And he seldom exchanged a word with the being whose idea engrossed his affection. (52)

The two are only brought into close contact during a disastrous boating expedition. Millbank decides to swim in the river, and is only rescued from drowning by the prompt and decisive action of Coningsby. Furnished with a reason for offering homage, he takes the opportunity to write to Coningsby and thank him for saving his life:

> Now, I will say at once, that I have always liked you better than any fellow in the school, and always thought you the cleverest; indeed, I always thought that there was no one like you; but I would never say this or show this, because you never seemed to care for me … (55)

Significantly, Coningsby himself is now able to admit Millbank to terms of intimacy, because this incident has assured his own superior status – the narrator repeatedly stresses at this stage of the novel that it is Coningsby who influences those around him, for their good. His own moral improvement, as he forms a friendship with a member of the increasingly powerful manufacturing class, is only made possible by his own noble action in risking his life to save one he regarded as inferior, and 'he ended by loving the being on whom he had conferred a great obligation' (104). The centrality of these school friendships is repeatedly stressed by the narrator, particularly in the absence of a mother on whom the young Coningsby could lavish his sentiment. Isolated as he is, 'All that he knew of the power of the softer passions might be found in the fanciful and romantic annals of schoolboy friendship' (111).

The narrator enthuses over the positive influence Coningsby exerts over Millbank and his other friends at school, but his own further development requires a new romantic friendship with a character of more advanced mind. Shortly after leaving Eton he encounters the mysterious and slightly older Sidonia, whose habits of mind stimulate Coningsby's own interest in philosophical and political enquiry. This friendship will become second in importance only to his love for Millbank's sister Edith, whom he fears at one point may marry his new friend. That this transference of emotion from male friend to female lover is complete at first seems evident from the jealousy Coningsby feels, and the readiness with which he parts from his friend as a result. But this disruption of one friendship is, of course, less disastrous given the continuing relationship with Millbank, whose friendship will ultimately be assured through the familiar marriage to the daughter of the house. In a plot convention common to many treatments of romantic friendship, the central friendship with Millbank is thus renewed and made of more importance through an adult projection of love for a male friend onto his beloved sister.

As the novel works towards its conclusion and the lovers declare their feelings to each other, Coningsby infuses his feeling for both Edith and Sidonia with a romantic intensity that hardly seems to differentiate one from the other:

Entrancing love and dazzling friendship, a high ambition and the pride of knowledge, the consciousness of a great prosperity, the vague, daring energies of twenty-one, all combined to stimulate his sense of existence, which, as he looked around him at the beautiful objects and listened to the delicious sounds, seemed to him a dispensation of almost supernatural ecstasy. (341–2)

This conflation is likewise made possible, even as it seems most unlikely, by the establishment of a heterosexual love plot. In committing himself to Edith, Coningsby is momentarily able to express an admiring passion for his mentor, embedded within a complex syntax that deftly evades the question of the lover's and friend's relative status in his mind (where a choice had apparently to be made, he seemed prepared to reject his friend rather than the woman he loved, and this again acts to safeguard his later effusions). At this point in the century, adult friendship was clearly a more fraught question than the 'ardent regard' of public schoolboys. But this was to change over the next few decades.

Thomas Hughes famously celebrates schoolboy friendships among the outstandingly average in *Tom Brown's Schooldays* (1857), but such friendships operate both within an overtly Christian context and against the supposedly effete 'homosexual' subculture that the narrator darkly maintains will be familiar to some of his readers. Tom's father decides against discussing 'temptations' with him, but the narrator offers up for inspection:

one of the miserable little pretty white-handed curly-headed boys, petted and pampered by some of the big fellows, who wrote their verses for them, taught them to drink and use bad language, and did all they could to spoil them for everything in this world and the next. (*Tom Brown's Schooldays*, 182)

Positing schoolboy friendship in a context of his own vigorous 'manly Christianity', Hughes permits the delicate and intelligent Arthur to exert a redeeming influence over the older Tom, ensuring that in return he acquires a more energetic constitution through plenty of healthy exercise in the fresh air. Arthur's subsequent illness and near death permit him a religious insight and a justifying context for telling his friend that he has 'made the school a paradise to me' (240). But shortly after this conversation, Tom meets Arthur's mother, who, as the first attractive woman he has encountered, briefly but crucially deflects his own emotional reaction even as she reinforces his love for his friend. Arthur then disappears for six months, allowing Tom to benefit from his advice without the narrative having to contain any emotional charge in their relationship. The final pages specifically endorse hero worship, as Tom comes to realise his own veneration for the doctor in full just as he is leaving the school – only after the doctor's death is this feeling permitted to expand in the narrative comment that all 'young and brave souls' must 'win their way through hero-worship, to the worship of Him who is the King and Lord of heroes' (288)

Hughes steers a transparently careful course in his novel, but the moral worth of romantic friendship in boys' schools was called into question in the second half of the nineteenth century, as it was increasingly imbued with anxieties about aberrant sexual practice. John Chandos dates a shift in conventions of male friendship to school reform movements in the 1870s and 1880s. Tackling the notoriously difficult question of actual practice, he asks:

> What then *did* go on in the schools, which so agitated the moral sensibilities of the Victorians? The broad answer is that, as in the outside world, there was no uniformity in depth, only a spurious superficial uniformity. There was innocence and depravity, and all the intervening gradations of distinction. ... Romantic, sacrificial friendships and rabid sensual lusts all went on in the same community together. (Chandos, 301)

This analysis is plausible, but more important than what may or may not have gone on after lights out is the perception of reformers, with its concomitant impact on social behaviour. As Chandos notes:

> It did not seem to have occurred to any of the best-intentioned moderns of moral reform that their prescription for a cure of supposed vice might, without achieving its intended effect, do injury to existing virtues. The drying up of the springs of spontaneity and openness was a high price to pay for good intentions of dubious efficacy. (293)

It is interesting to note that emotional expression in girls' boarding schools remained the norm throughout the next century, despite such concerns.

Published in 1861, the sequel to *Tom Brown's Schooldays* details the life of an Oxford undergraduate, but reveals very similar concerns. *Tom Brown at Oxford* reinforces the ennobling quality of romantic friendship through the rather awkward expedient of dismissing the influence that Arthur has already had on Tom's development into a manly Christian. (The promise of the two friends that they will maintain a steady correspondence is seemingly forgotten by the narrator at an early stage, and there is only one allusion to its resumption towards the end. Indeed Arthur never appears, although East receives considerable attention in the final chapters.) This backsliding allows a new friend, the temperamental but essentially admirable Hardy, to offer renewal at Oxford, through a combination of intense friendship, rowing and moral admonition. The characteristic language of romantic friendship immediately comes into play, with Tom 'rapidly falling into friendship with Hardy. He was not bound hand and foot and carried away captive yet, but he was already getting deep in the toils' (*Tom Brown at Oxford*, 73). As at school, hero worship is an accepted part of this friendship, although a critical Tom reflects on the ways in which he would like to change Hardy to make him a more fitting object of such worship.

Notwithstanding the focus on individual friendship, which will gradually expand outwards as Tom becomes increasingly committed to social reform, the narrator is careful to control the expressions of regard between the two friends. Hardy cautiously tells Tom that he *likes* him and hopes the feeling is returned. The perceptive Drysdale will later point out that Hardy has told his father nothing of his invidious position as a servitor looked down on by fee-paying undergraduates, and yet Captain Hardy significantly brings about a reconciliation between Tom and his son after their most serious falling out, with the words, 'He can't keep anything from his old father; and so I drew it out of him that he loves you as David loved Jonathan' (237). In confiding in his father, Hardy reveals quite specifically that his love for his friend is not problematic (he has discreetly concealed the difficulties of his social position for several years), and this sense of transparency is underlined for the reader by the action of Captain Hardy in serving as mediator. At the same time, the disjunction between what Hardy says directly to Tom ('I like you') and the resonance of his father's comment – elsewhere the narrator has described Hardy as a 'loving soul' – points to an awkwardness in expression between the two young men. This feeling is confirmed when Tom enters Hardy's room and sees his hand trembling. Again, it is the narrator who gives an account of Tom's state of mind, with the character himself saying very little:

> Tom rushed across to his friend, dearer than ever to him now, and threw his arm round his neck; and, if the un-English truth must out, had three parts of a mind to kiss the rough face which was now working with strong emotion. (238)

Of course, Tom does not kiss his friend, and the prescriptions of English reserve are tenuously upheld, although the emotionalism in this scene is unmistakeable. In a familiar resolution, Hardy will eventually marry Tom's cousin Katie.

In the slightly later sensation novel, Henry Jackson's *A First Friendship*, published in 1863, the narrator recalls his first meeting with a charismatic stranger, when both were 18 and travelling away from home. Although William Hamilton has never yet had a friend, he has early formed an ideal of what friendship should be. Looking back, he recalls that while at school he had:

> formed my own idea of a friend. That I should, in actual life, ever meet this problematical personage was a matter of doubt with me; nevertheless, I clung to the hope that our paths in life would one day cross, or the ideal be realized. If I did not know now, when I look back to that vanished time, how true and real was the feeling I allude to, and how kindly and tenderly it is regarded in after life, I should feel inclined to stigmatize my state of mind at that period as romantic. (*A First Friendship*, 1)

Hamilton's first meeting with Robert Rutter is not dissimilar to Coningsby's romantic encounter with Sidonia in its suspension of social norms (each has taken the other for a roadside brigand and is obliged to apologise):

> Whether it was the darkness that favoured my natural shyness, or the novelty of our introduction that at once removed conventional restraint, I do not know, but there we were, talking away as though we had known each other for months. (3)

Rutter's behaviour is suspicious, in that he first appears without resources and subsequently gives his money to a sinister acquaintance without proffering an explanation (in fact, his family is being blackmailed over his father's having supposedly married his mother while his first wife was alive in a lunatic asylum, the evidence for which eventually turns out to be a fabrication on the blackmailer's part). But the narrative quickly moves to reintegrate this friendship into accepted social channels, as each friend is invited to meet the other's parent. Soon Rutter is writing to Hamilton that if he fails to visit him and his mother and sister, 'I'll erase your name from my memory, regard David and Jonathan ever afterwards as a pair of impostors, and consider the word friendship as aggravated humbug' (67).

Hamilton's trust in his friend is sustained throughout the blackmail plot, for most of which time he has no idea on what grounds the family is threatened with exposure. Tellingly, the friendship breaks down not over Rutter's failure to confide in his friend, but over his involvement with the duplicitous Victorine de Longueville, who attempts to marry him for his money. Rutter will not listen to what he terms the 'calumnies' of his friend, and turns against him altogether. It is at this point that Hamilton comments sadly, 'Alas, the close union, the brotherly intimacy of the past, were at an end! The old freedom of our intercourse had gone, never to return' (233). But Hamilton's own love for his friend is undiminished, and like Robert Audley, he will ultimately marry Rutter's sister. Again like Audley, he agrees to find the missing Rutter, who has secretly eloped with Victorine. In the final pages of the novel he finds his friend dying of smallpox and the two are reunited as Victorine deserts her lover. With the double security of a forthcoming marriage to Ann Rutter and the narrative casting of the final words as a deathbed scene, the two friends are permitted a highly emotional exchange:

> 'Kiss me, Hamilton' he whispered.
>   And then – a short, a momentary spasm quivered round his mouth, again there was that glorious smile, and he lay dead in my arms. (364)

This rare moment in Victorian literature, in which one man kisses another (it is not paralleled even in *In Memoriam*), is only rendered possible by its place towards the end of the narration and by the immediate death of the friend who has initiated it. Hamilton recalls sadly that:

> Life has since brought with it many blessings, chiefest of them, the wife now sitting by my side, who mourns a brother in him who was my first friend, but the blessings of these later years have never wholly filled the void left by the great loss I have here recorded. With it, departed the first hopes, the first freshness of my life. what has been can never be again. Such friendships are not twice formed by men, this side of the grave. (371)

But emotional expression between males did not derive its sole authority from the transient codes of schoolboy or undergraduate life. The enabling presence of a wife, who is necessary to the presentation of male friendship but not necessarily able to compete with it, is a theme explored by other sensation writers, most notably Wilkie Collins in *Armadale*, while the complex interplay between male friends and a sister/ wife finds comparable expression in Braddon's *Lady Audley's Secret.*

Perhaps surprisingly, male romantic friendship locates itself not only in the mores of the public school, but also in the tradition of ancient 'Greek love', as mediated through the Victorian imagination. Partly because of this, it opens itself up to being identified, often falsely, with homosexual feeling, if not practice. Working within this tradition, writers took a pair of male friends, or possibly lovers, Pythias and Damon, to exemplify the heroic altruism of romantic friendship. The ambiguous nature of this pairing makes the choice a seemingly unlikely one, but for much of the century an adherence to Hellenism was not necessarily seen as incompatible with the most stringent convention. In *The Victorians and Ancient Greece*, Richard Jenkyns cites numerous clerics and Church adherents who readily declared their admiration of Plato, indeed he argues that: 'A sense of the close alliance between Christianity and the study of the classics, strangely but eloquently blended with an awareness of tension between them, runs right through the nineteenth century' (Jenkyns, 72). It has been suggested by Frank Turner that the nineteenth century simply reinvented Ancient Greece in the light of its own concerns, perceiving similarities in its culture and political concerns. A further explanation for this seemingly unlikely alliance might be the suitability of the Ancient Greeks for contemporary models of manly – or muscular – Christianity. In the Victorian view of classical Greece as implicitly innocent and tied to nature, 'Youth, light and clear southern skies were blent together to represent the Greek genius as a kind of lithe, buoyant athleticism. In the age of muscular Christianity the Greeks became muscular pagans; clean fresh air became a symbol of the Hellenic spirit' (Jenkyns, 171).

Proponents of romantic friendship were quite able to adopt the ideals of Platonic friendship, either by the simple expedient of ignoring the physical side of *paiderastia* or by deprecatingly explaining it away – women, they frequently reminded each other, were not central to the Greek world. As late as 1875, Percival Pickering was able to suggest, apparently with no hint of irony:

> That such friendships in Greece and Rome existed with perfect purity of thought, and inspired a love of fame and noble actions, can hardly be doubted. Woman had not then assumed her true position in society and in the affections of man, and the form that love then so frequently took was in friendship, and there aroused, as in its highest nature it always must, a desire for all that is good and honourable in man. (Pickering, 18)

In her 1873 essay 'In Friendship', Anne Thackeray had observed that the tradition of male friendship was derived from the Ancients and instilled (by implication in the upper and middle classes) through education:

> People say that as a rule men are truer friends than women – more capable of friendship. Is this the result of a classical education? Do the foot-notes in which celebrated friendships are mentioned in brackets stimulate our youth to imitate those stately togas, whose names and discourses come travelling down to us through two thousand years, from one country to another, from one generation to another, from one language to another …? ('In Friendship', collected in *Toilers and Spinsters and Other Essays*, 289–90)

More ingeniously yet, William Alger redeploys the Platonic ideal to support the possibility of friendship between the sexes (notably, he cannot get away from the imagery of sex and procreation):

> Truly understood, the Platonic sentiment does not denote love, in the distinctive significance of that word, but a pure and fervent friendship … Platonic love is a high personal passion, like [ideal love], with the exception that no physical influence of sex enters into it; imagination exalting the soul, instead of inflaming the senses. … Platonic love is the marriage of souls for the production of spiritual offspring, – ideas, feelings, and volitions. (Alger, 12)

As Jenkyns puts it, 'The Hellenic spirit seems to be a sort of 100% pure alcohol, to be distilled, by some unexplained process, out of what the Greeks actually said and did' (Jenkyns, 173).

In retrospect, this appeal to the ancients was not simply invidious, it helped to turn male romantic friendship into a loudly ticking bomb, in that the cultural influence of ancient Greece was the very argument subsequently deployed by liberal apologists for same-sex desire. In *Hellenism and Homosexuality in Victorian Oxford*, Linda Dowling charts the rôle of liberal Hellenism at mid-century in providing a discursive framework for homosexual apologists later in the century. Specifically, she notes the Oxford tutorial as offering at once a site of intense male bonding and a means of promoting platonic ideals, in ways unanticipated by the most influential proponents of Hellenic studies, such as Benjamin Jowett:

> ... so great was the success of Victorian liberal Hellenism in coming to represent all the dimensions of human experience denied under the Calvinist dispensation of religious fundamentalism or starved under the materialists regime of industrial modernity that it would open – in a way wholly unanticipated by the liberals themselves – the possibility of legitimating male love. Liberal partisans of Greek studies had been intent upon deploying Hellenism as a discursive language of sociocultural renewal. ... Precisely as such structures as the warrior ideal underlying classical republicanism came to seem increasingly irrelevant to the actual conditions imposed upon Britain by industrial modernity did the alternative values Victorian liberals located in Hellenism seem to promise the hope of cultural transformation. (35–6)

What Dowling's analysis incidentally makes clear is that romantic friendship and 'male love' were set on a collision course at least from mid-century, when Plato became a prominent feature of the Oxbridge curricula and elevated friendship between men was enjoying a more celebrated and seemingly secure status than it was ever to have again.

The ways in which long-established patterns of male behaviour were registered and assessed would change considerably in the latter years of the century, but the 1890s have traditionally been seen as heralding a particular crisis. It was 1897 when Havelock Ellis's famous study of 'sexual inversion' drew out in some detail the contradictoriness of his contemporaries' response to the ancient Greek ideal of love between men:

> An appeal to the *paiderastia* of the best Greek days, and the dignity, temperance, even chastity, which it involved, will sometimes find a ready response in the emotional, enthusiastic nature of the congenital invert. (*Sexual Inversion*, 146)

This analysis celebrates the purity of Greek sexual aestheticism, but renders an uncomplicated view of ancient culture as simply elevated friendship impossible. The appendix to *Sexual Inversion*, from which this quotation is taken, contains an essay by his late collaborator John Addington Symonds. Himself a practising homosexual, Symonds repudiates the connotations of excessive lust associated with male love, appealing to what he knew to be a widespread respect for ancient Greek culture:

... it was just this effort to elevate paiderastia according to the aesthetic standard of Greek ethics which constituted its distinctive quality in Hellas. We are obliged, in fact, to separate this, the true Hellenic manifestation of the paiderastic passion, from the effeminacies, brutalities and gross sensualities which can be noticed alike in imperfectly civilised and in luxuriously corrupt communities. (appendix to *Sexual Inversion*, 187)

According to Ellis and Symonds, ancient Greece was able to assimilate homosexual practice into an ideal of chivalric friendship; certainly, Pickering's assumption of a purely spiritual relation in this context seems almost determinedly naïve (particularly as he spends much of his essay dwelling on boyish attachments as based on the love of a beautiful male form). Elsewhere, Symonds stresses that Greek love was 'masculine, military and chivalrous' (*In the Key of Blue*, 66). Notably taking the terms 'friend' and 'lover' as being virtually interchangeable, he rhapsodises: 'Passionate friends, bound together in the chains of close yet temperate comradeship, seeking always to advance in wisdom, self-restraint, and intellectual illumination, prepare themselves for the celestial journey' (69). But despite their differing levels of awareness, in each of these four accounts of the Greek aesthetic, the emphasis is placed on enthusiasm or elevated passion rather than on sexuality (acknowledged or not).

In Ellis's and Symonds's accounts, enthusiasm co-exists with sexual practice, but a distinction between the two was, of course, crucial to the Victorian ideal of 'romantic friendship'. If homosexual apologists deliberately conflated friendship and sexuality, taking the ancients as their model and justification for so doing (and this is precisely what Wilde did in his writing and at the Old Bailey), then proponents of romantic friendship had an obvious stake in maintaining clear distinctions and patrolling the boundaries between the two. In this sense at least, they could not have chosen a more ill-advised point of reference than ancient Greece.

But the idealisation of love between male friends, on which the public school tradition was based, could lay claim to two distinct traditions, both of which were accessible to young men with a genteel education. One was based on platonic ideals, as we have seen, but upholders of love between friends could also invoke biblical and religious precedent. In 1896, the Bishop of Winchester offered a series of examples testifying to the importance of male friendship in biblical narrative, concluding that:

> God became man, that he might save and exalt, and bless him with all the blessings of which his being is capable, and for no other reason than because He loved him, and because through taking his nature into fellowship with His own, He could more fully manifest that love, and more blessedly exemplify it, and more persuasively offer it, nay let me be bold and say, more entirely enjoy it than had he been only God – is a witness and voice to us of what friendship in man is meant for, and is capable of in the eternal purpose, whether in the blessing it conveys, the discipline it compels, or the sacrifices it demands. (Thorold, 10)

The image of Christ as friend appears in several Victorian hymns. In 'Thine for ever! God of love' Mary Maude (1819–1913) juxtaposes images of Christ as saviour, protector and specifically friend in the line 'Saviour, Guardian, heavenly Friend'. More famously, John Bode repeatedly stresses the centrality of Christ's role as friend in the popular 'Oh Jesus I have promised' (1868). The word itself is employed in three of the five verses, and the appeals of the speaker in the second verse evoke the concern of romantic friendship with appropriate influence and the encouragement of self-discipline: 'O speak to reassure me / To hasten or control; / O speak and make me listen'.

As Charlotte Yonge argued:

> Friendship has the highest sanction … He, Whose Love is universal had one friend above all, and gave His human affection to those who were with Him; and His type and forefather after the flesh wins our hearts by that noble and unselfish friendship which has been a proverb through all time. (Yonge, 147)

Seemingly less controversially, we have seen how in that it avoided compromising the image of Christ as giving himself for all men, the proponents of romantic friendship repeatedly invoked the Old Testament David and Jonathan to typify their ideal of loving self-sacrifice (as Ouida does, despite her implicit disavowal of romantic friendship, and her substitution of a servant's 'fidelity' for the 'love' of a friend). Indeed, Frederick Roden claims significantly that: 'The importance of this pairing in the nineteenth century may be compared with the legal and emotional power of marriage to be found in the genre of the novel' (Roden, 25). But it is worth noting in passing that this pairing has links with the more tenuous admiration of Ancient Greek culture – Havelock Ellis's disquisition on military homosexuality in *Sexual Inversion* intriguingly cites the story in this context. He remarks that:

> In the lament of David over Jonathan we have a picture of intimate friendship – 'passing the love of women' – between comrades in arms among a barbarous, warlike race. (*Sexual Inversion*, 5)

Ellis goes on to say that: 'There is nothing to show that such a relationship was sexual' but none the less compares it to the exaltation of homosexuality among soldiers in ancient and modern cultures' (5).

In an 1839 translation of a German source, B.B. Edwards invokes the classic spontaneity of romantic friendship in the figure of Jonathan: 'The friendship of Jonathan is not only in its origin, generous in the highest degree, but it springs up suddenly, as if by a stroke of enchantment' ('The Tragical Quality in the Friendship of David and Jonathan', in *Selections from German Literature*, 76). Anticipating Trumbull's later study of friendship rites, in which the identity of one friend is merged with the other, true friendship is defined as requiring 'by its very nature, that every strong and noble feeling in man should be mingled with it' (75). It is 'that delicate connection between two persons … whereby they melt, as it were, into one! But such friendship is wont to be awakened, as certainly in the present case, in a manner one knows not how' (76). Trumbull himself alludes with the confidence of received tradition to '… that most beautiful of all illustrative friendships, the friendship of Jonathan for David, in the Bible narrative' (Trumbull, 27).

The religious status of intense friendship is repeatedly attested to by commentators. Trumbull's wide-ranging study offers exhaustive lists of famous friendships to demonstrate that 'One need not go outside of the Bible record for proof that friendship's love has a place above all other loves; although the concurrent testimony of the ages, earlier and later than that record, is to the same effect' (47). Placing friendship above marriage itself, he argues:

> It can hardly be supposed that it is of carelessness, or without intention, that in both the Old Testament and the New a distinction is repeatedly marked between the mere marriage tie and the highest attainment of friendship, whereby the former is counted of the flesh – the life here in the flesh; while the later [*sic*] is counted of the soul – the very life itself. (49)

In conferring a superior status on friendship and claiming religious sanction for doing so, Trumbull's analysis highlights a potential source of tension in the paradigm he is discussing. While marriage is generally upheld in Victorian writing as the ultimate source of human love, gender ideology necessarily assumed that the greatest sympathy attainable was between members of the same sex.

While fiction of the period incorporates the most detailed portrayals of friendship into the ubiquitous love plot, frequent appeals to the David and Jonathan story are suggestive of the friendship between men at least as exceeding the limits of heterosexual love. At its most obvious, the presentation of close friendship as a symbol of divine love recurs in writing throughout the century. A religious tract of 1858 can argue, seemingly without a sense of controversy, that 'friendship, like all pure emotions, is inspired in its origin, and arises naturally out of love to the divine Creator' (*Thoughts on Friendship*, 7). More explicit in its terms, Walter Miller's poem 'To a Friend at Parting' locates romantic friendship again within a context of divine love, absorbing the personal and temporal in the religious and immanent:

> And now the disuniting pang may prove
> The first vibration of more faithful love –
> As tender vines, in fond luxuriance born,
> Wither, or cling more closely from the storm –
> So be our interest what no shock shall sever
> In each, in Christ, unchanging, and for ever.
> (*Offerings to Friendship and Truth*, 128)

Similarly, Wilde invoked the story of David and Jonathan in order to appeal to the approved ethos of romantic friendship, sidelining the vexed question of sexuality.

Even before the Wilde trials, Victorian commentators were themselves almost certainly aware of the dangers of over-interpretation. The levels of feeling expressed in Shakespeare's sonnets to the young man did not escape censure altogether, despite the iconic status of the writer. The language of passion was deployed in nineteenth-century writing only in carefully regulated contexts, such as the David and Jonathan story was able to provide. Religious sanction was a powerful authority to which the supporter of a precariously balanced ideal like romantic friendship might appeal, and notably, allusions to these biblical friends are much more frequent in discussions of the topic than are more tenuous appeals to the ancients.

But while biblical precedent was invoked as a means of precluding criticism, literal emulation of the ideal was not necessarily seen as practicable or even desirable beyond a certain age. Even before the changes identified by Chandos, the ambiguous status of romantic friendship is underscored by this association with specific life stages and the controls of a pedagogical institution. If its claims as a cultural ideal are to be upheld, its apparent excesses must in fact be carefully regulated, or at least confined within certain understood boundaries. Commentators insisted that such friendships be confined to members of a similar social background, and intense feeling for friends was usually expected to give way at some point to the claims of marriage, just as it was for women. Again echoing the advice given to young girls, writers were often wary of the abrupt intensity associated with romantic friendship, stressing the greater reliability of friendships developed over time. Of the less well-known texts considered in Chapter One, both Henry Jackson's *A First Friendship* and J.H. Wilton's *The First Crime: or, True Friendship* centre on friendships formed independently and outside the regulating context of school or the protagonist's circle of family connections.

In *David Copperfield*, the central friendship between David and Steerforth initiates the theme of relations based on an attraction that attempts – with disastrous consequences – to surmount class boundaries. The naïve David, younger and from a lower social class, is as unable as Emily herself to see past Steerforth's charismatic manner. Only towards the end of the novel is the suitably middle-class and hardworking Traddles reintroduced as the friend David *should* have made in the first place.

All three of the novels considered in this chapter are further concerned, almost by definition, with the demarcation and enactment of gender roles (as is *Armadale*, which will be discussed later). In each case, the necessity for maintaining appropriately gendered behaviour is linked to images of unstable health or nervous illness. The male protagonists all emphasise the difficulty of controlling their physiological responses – the speaker in *In Memoriam* draws repeated attention both to his involuntary tears and conversely, to his inability to cry; David Copperfield wakes from a dream to find Steerforth's name on his lips, and a footstep on the stairs causes his heart to beat faster; Robert Audley's restless activity suggests, both to himself and – as a ploy – to his aunt, the idea that he is susceptible to monomania. The resolution to the dilemma of appropriate behaviour is variously sought in post-mortem unity, marriage into the family of the loved friend, and renunciation of the friendship itself in highly gendered imagery (as I will suggest in the case of *David Copperfield*).

If all three texts are concerned with the tension between expression and self-control, a related feature is the theme of the 'good angel'. Traditionally, this figure would be represented by a woman, and Dickens and Braddon both perpetuate this assumption – at one point David tells Agnes that she is his good angel and she strongly advises him to avoid coming under the influence of his 'bad angel', namely Steerforth. In Braddon's account, Robert Audley is initially motivated by love for his friend, but increasingly he comes to see George's sister Clara as enacting the rôle of good angel, even as he is intermittently troubled by her influence. Of the texts under consideration here, only *In Memoriam* obviates such heterosexual stereotypes altogether, locating the direct source of influence in the dead Hallam. This relationship between death and influence will be central to the following discussion.

The absence or death of one participant in a romantic friendship necessarily alters the perception of that relationship in the mind of the reader, and creates new possibilities for narrative representation. All three of the texts considered here share a specific concern with the death of a friend, although each treats this theme very differently. As a eulogy, *In Memoriam* is perhaps the least inhibited by the prescribed limits of romantic friendship, but *David Copperfield* is similarly retrospective, and the first-person narrator offers forgiveness of his dangerous (but now safely dead) friend as a central moment in his *Bildungsroman*. In *Lady Audley's Secret*, the supposed death of George Talboys directly influences the character of his friend Robert, who makes it the purpose of his life to bring Lady Audley to justice. Robert Audley and the speaker in *In Memoriam* are both inspired specifically by their love for a departed friend, but it is only the former who questions the appropriate limits of feeling itself rather than its outward expression. In the case of Robert Audley, it is absolutely necessary for him to determine the limits of acceptable feeling, as the narrator knows that his friend will return alive at the end of the novel. Of all the texts discussed here, only *David Copperfield* suggests a sinister and direct influence exerted by the friend himself, predicated on the younger character's susceptibility. In this case alone, the death is salutary not for its power over the surviving character, but for getting a dangerous influence out of the way.

The various ways in which images of gender, health and death intersect in *David Copperfield*, *In Memoriam* and *Lady Audley's Secret* will now be considered in detail.

David Copperfield

Critical responses to *David Copperfield* have been quick to identify a disturbing element in the relationship between David and the libidinous Steerforth. Andrew Dowling argues:

> that both Dickens and his character David are more than half in love with this Byronic despoiler of young women. David's eyes water, his heart beats faster, and his face flushes whenever he hasn't seen Steerforth for any length of time. (Dowling, 56)

John Carey unequivocally identifies what he calls David's 'homosexual love for Steerforth – never progressing, needless to say, to the physical' (Carey, 171) as the result of his aversion to the marriage of his mother with the unappetising Murdstone. More recently, Vincent Newey has assumed an erotic basis for the scene where David goes to sleep dreaming about Steerforth on his first night at Salem House, claiming:

> the homoeroticism is all the more evident here for being displaced as hero worship, and becomes a truly open secret in the light of David's being so often associated with the feminine by Steerforth himself ... (Newey, 122)

More cautiously, as exemplified by the profusion of commas and brackets, Lyn Pykett posits Steerforth as:

> An object of David's social and, some would argue, sexual desire, and (perhaps) sexually desiring David ... (Pykett, 119)

Again, Eve Sedgwick distinguishes between the proscribed act of sex itself and the homosocial freedoms enjoined on David as part of a gentlemanly education:

> In short, a gentleman will associate the erotic end of the homosocial spectrum, not with dissipation, not with viciousness or violence, but with childishness, as an infantile need, a mark of powerlessness, which, while it may be viewed with shame or scorn or denial, is unlikely to provoke the virulent, accusatory projection that characterizes twentieth-century homophobia. (Sedgwick, 177)

While this analysis presupposes an erotic element in David's feeling for Steerforth, it strangely ignores the more overtly erotic language of the older and more powerful friend. But the emphasis on powerlessness and childishness will prove central to David's perplexed narrative account.

In dissent from the views outlined above, it has been argued that their relationship should be viewed as 'not homoerotic but a parody of a standard romance' (Barickman, MacDonald and Stark, 95). While Steerforth's predatory appropriation of David surely introduces a homo-erotic element to their relationship – after a separation of several years he resumes their friendship by renaming him 'Daisy', of all things – setting the novel in the context of mid-nineteenth-century enthusiasm and romantic friendship allows a more complex pattern to emerge. A pursuit of the ideal is a defining trait of the young David Copperfield, whose worship of his friend is based on an unabashed romantic enthusiasm. In youthful friendships such as David's for Steerforth, enthusiasm certainly carries connotations of excessive feeling and impetuosity, and yet it is this passionate responsiveness that specifically defines romantic friendship.

That the attraction of Dickens's hero to the untrustworthy Steeforth is not straightforwardly sexual in nature is suggested by the context in which the book was written. *David Copperfield* was written shortly before the publication of Tennyson's *In Memoriam* in 1850 made the celebration of intense male friendship one of the most prominent literary themes of the century. The characterisation of David as innocent enthusiast is determined – in a sense, even made possible – by Dickens's awareness of the dangers inherent in romantic friendship. It is this that necessitates the familiar splitting of characteristics, allowing David's artless passion to be contrasted with his mentor's worldly corruption. As Dellamora notes: 'When Tennyson and others celebrate male friendship, they make careful choices about how to delimit it' (Dellamora, 24). In this case, the limits of the hero's passion are thrown into relief by the greater knowingness and the sexual laxity of his friend, whose coded hints, taken with the response of more aware observers such as Rosa and Miss Mowcher, constantly remind the reader of David's own ingenuousness and comparative innocence of the world. Placed in the awkward position of vindicating his own innocence at the expense of his friend's moral standing, he is obliged to recount dubious exchanges that it is necessary the reader should comprehend – at the same time, it is essential that he himself should be seen to be innocent of worldly knowledge. In a subtle use of narrative obliquity, he delivers Steerforth's more sophisticated innuendo in much the same way as he earlier repeated the Murdstone's joke about Brooks of Sheffield: 'The toast was received with great applause, and such hearty laughter that it made me laugh too; at which they laughed the more. In short, we quite enjoyed ourselves' (*David Copperfield*, 23).

As the narrative unfolds, this lack of prescience is increasingly difficult for the reader to share. Indeed, the status of the narrator at the time of writing, adult and with worldly experience, reminds us that in perpetually reinforcing his own innocence as a young man, the adult David is making a deliberate choice of self-representation. As Newey points out: 'David is not conscious of the catalogue of objections, which are implied rather than stated in his text, but he does go along with them inasmuch as he sets strict limits to his allegiance to what Steerforth represents' (Newey, 124). He chooses to include the erotic hints thrown out by his former friend in the course of the story, as a means of actively disclaiming any erotic desires or even knowledge on his own part, while the seduction of Emily gives him a strong reason for having severed ties with Steerforth on grounds unconnected with the ambiguous element that critics have identified from the earliest stages of their friendship. But David's clear declaration of complex and yet innocent feeling for another man is none the less convincing because it is characteristic both of his age when he meets Steerforth and of the conventions of mid-nineteenth-century romantic friendship. The novel can be placed in relation to a range of fiction and poetry from the same period (I have noted *In Memoriam* as the most famous of these). It may be less than coincidental that the plot of *David Copperfield* is similar to that of 'Early Friendship, or the Slave of Passion', a short story that appeared in *Bentley's Miscellany* in 1840. Dickens had resigned as editor of the journal in 1839; but whether or not he read this particular story, its central premise bears a striking resemblance to the plot of the later novel, and the assumption of shared values contained in both suggests a certain confidence in the response of the contemporary reader: in 'Early Friendship', the narrator remembers his youthful adoration of an older friend who has protected him at school, an infatuation that is later destroyed when the friend seduces a respectable girl. Like Steerforth, Henry Fortescue is a dandy of independent means – he is charismatic and good looking but lacks ambition and, crucially, earnestness. Other parallels aside, what is notable here is the readiness with which each narrator describes his friendship in terms of epic passion, although in retrospect each comes to realise that the object of his passion was unworthy. The writer of the short story portrays the older man, Henry Fortescue, as deeply charismatic, and assumes that:

> With such advantages, it can be no matter of surprise that a lad in all these respects beneath him should be flattered by his notice, and attached by his regard; and, whatever might be his genuine feelings towards me, who had little more than high spirits and good nature to recommend me, his early kindness and subsequent notice bound me to him with a sort of romantic affection, which would have induced me cheerfully to risk my life in his service or defence. (513)

Similarly, David describes his friendship in terms of heroic fantasy, linking it to both the welcome irrationality of dreams and the power of the elements themselves. Recalling his adult encounter with Steerforth at the London inn, their first meeting since Salem House, David recalls:

Here, among pillows enough for six, I soon fell asleep in a blissful condition, and dreamed of ancient Rome, Steerforth, and friendship, until the early morning coaches, rumbling out of the archway underneath, made me dream of thunder and the gods. (*David Copperfield*, 282)

To the twenty-first-century reader, this episode may inevitably suggest a level of eroticism (and it might be acknowledged here that David's first important conversation with Steerforth takes place in the school dormitory, that he is in bed when David says goodbye to him for the last time in the course of their friendship, and indeed, that the reader last sees him as a corpse laid out on a bed). But the possible threat contained in these scenes is far from being perceived by David himself.

David Copperfield is concerned not with questioning the ideal of romantic friendship as such, but with the way in which artlessness on the part of a younger figure may be exploited (in the later *Little Dorrit*, the renegade Tattycoram is similarly manipulated by Miss Wade, and Meagles hints darkly that he has heard of women such as she who wish to corrupt others of their sex). What is in line with Dickens's known sentiments is the distrust of any strong feeling that allows itself only one outlet – Mr Wickfield's obsessive love of his daughter in the same novel is held to be unhealthy and leads to pernicious results – an indication of his redemption lies in his recognition of this, and his new commitment to a more inclusive form of love. The idealism inherent in ardent friendship both reflects the temperament of its proponent and contains threatening elements, as the connection between naïve adoration on the one hand and the predatory interest of an older character on the other, is made increasingly explicit. Standard treatments of romantic friendship require that it should ultimately give way to something with a broader social base (ultimately through marriage and the engendering of a family), and the progress of David's narrative exemplifies this.

When he is first sent to Salem House, it is Steerforth whose approbation he most covets and who protects him from bullying by the other boys. Friendships between schoolboys are presented in comparable terms in more than one novel of the time – in *Vanity Fair*, for example, Dobbin interferes on George Osborne's behalf when he is bullied by an older boy, and in doing so secures his notice. What is notable in Dickens's version is not simply the social inequality of the boys (as a grocer's son, Dobbin is considered inferior to the Osborne banking family), but the element of hero worship on the part of the younger boy. The friendship between Dobbin and Osborne provides a major theme in *Vanity Fair*, but it is restrained and ultimately unromantic, focusing on Osborne's lack of gratitude to his worthier and less worldly friend. David's attachment to Steerforth is consciously romantic, based partly on his sense of his friend's superior accomplishments and his standing in the school, which in turn indicate his upper-class status. This acceptance of his friend's superiority places David in the tenuous position of protégé and acolyte, a dependency that Steerforth is quick to reinforce. Foreshadowing the novel's theme of dangerous sexuality, he immediately appropriates David's personal belongings and changes his name, in much the same way that he will later assume the 'protection' of Em'ly and, in making her his mistress, recast her identity in terms of her relation to him. This protection is in both cases partial and potentially subject to change. Looking back,

David remembers that Steerforth either could not – or at least did not – protect him from the brutal incursions of the headmaster Creakle.

None the less, David's instinctive association of Steerforth with the power to protect is invoked when he finds himself a vagrant on running away from Murdstone and Grimsby's some time later. On the road to Dover, his thoughts turn automatically towards his old friend as he decides to spend the night in the grounds of Salem House:

> I dreamed of lying on my old school-bed, talking to the boys in my room; and found myself sitting upright, with Steerforth's name upon my lips, looking wildly at the stars that were glistening and glimmering above me. (*David Copperfield*, 176)

This reaction is passionate in its intensity, but is also associated with a desire for comfort – as an outcast at this point, David expresses a sense of vulnerability that is somewhat assuaged by the proximity of his old dormitory (though he ruefully acknowledges that Steerforth must have long since left the school).

His dependence on Steerforth's continued interest itself suggests a power dynamic in which the younger figure is vulnerable to the fickle changes of heart associated with the decadent aristocrat. Echoing and extending the stereotype of the pure-minded girl and the roué who proves her undoing, Steerforth himself is irresistibly attracted to what he rightly perceives as David's innocence. As Richard Lettis notes: 'If Daisy for Steerforth is usually a girl – like a plaything, at times he is also a man whose innocence is to be envied' (Lettis, 81) His response to his protégé is suggestive from the outset of attempted seduction – he fantasises that David has an attractive sister, and regards him as 'my property' (*David Copperfield*, 283). The adult narrating David himself both helplessly admires and implicitly condemns Steerforth, through his use of retrospective narration, employing the language of sexual mesmerism to convey his charm and the powerlessness of those who come into contact with it. Perhaps wishing to justify himself in the light of later events, he recalls:

> There was an ease in his manner – a gay and light manner it was, but not swaggering – which I still believe to have borne a kind of enchantment with it. I still believe him, in virtue of this carriage, his animal spirits, his delightful voice, his handsome face and figure, and, for aught I know, of some inborn power of attraction besides (which I think a few people possess), to have carried a spell with him to which it was a natural weakness to yield, and which not many persons could withstand. (*David Copperfield*, 99)

This 'enchantment' not only causes David's identity to be subsumed, it is also morally damaging. Noting David's 'inability to act upon his best moral instincts, a weakness crucial to his subsequent life' (Myers, 111), Margaret Myers notes the power that Steerforth exerts over him from the outset:

> Steerforth is the dominant, experienced, condescending superior in a relationship comfortable in its operating assumption of inequality. Their relationship has only the subtlest of moral content, and the nature of that content explicitly lies within the power of the superior Steerforth. Though founded on genuine love, the friendship of David and Steerforth hints at the corruption of innocence in its best moral impulses. Thus David

represses his sympathy for Mr Mell; thus Steerforth allows the inexperienced David to spend a drunken night on the town. (113)

Reinforcing the sense of Steerforth's falsity as a rôle model, Newey observes that: 'Steerforth is a master of revels, and not at all a mentor in the needful arts of discipline and getting on' (Newey, 122). In other words, he abuses his influence, contrary to the justifying principle of romantic friendship. The idea of fascination persists throughout the text, as David feels himself mesmerised by Steerforth's heady presence. David's love for his friend at this stage of his life leads him to regard him with a jealous possessiveness that he makes no attempt to conceal, admitting that when he is absent with other students from the university – something to which David has not aspired – 'I was so fond of him, that I felt quite jealous of his Oxford friends' (*David Copperfield*, 348). And when he hears Steerforth's step on the stair of his London lodging, the blood rushes to his face in the anticipation of being soon reunited with him.

Despite his acquaintance with what he vaguely describes as 'the meaner phases' of the London streets, David remains naïve about the potential for dishonour in those he loves, and this is in keeping with the ethic of enthusiasm, which, according to Walter Houghton:

> sets up a standard of judgement which may be called moral optimism. The right attitude is one which recognizes and praises whatsoever things are lovely, admirable, and hopeful in human life and human beings. The wrong attitude ... is critical, satiric, pessimistic – even realistic. (Houghton, 266)

David's unwillingness to doubt his friend is mediated through a wiser adult narrating self, who stresses Steerforth's fascinating qualities more than his own susceptibility or – as one might expect – his innocent belief in the validity of youthful friendship. As Rachel Abelow comments:

> David's idealization of Steerforth requires an enormous amount of effort to maintain. Repeatedly, the younger boy witnesses examples of his friend's selfishness and arrogance. And repeatedly, he refuses to accept the most obvious implications of what he sees. (Abelow, p. 25)

Ironically enough, it is the more circumspect and less enthusiastic Agnes who is obliged to warn David in general terms against giving way to the influence of his friend. Tellingly, she denies that her judgement is based on his appearance with an intoxicated David at the opera. Rather:

> I judge him, partly from your account of him, Trotwood, and your character, and the influence he has over you. ... I feel as if it were someone else speaking to you, and not I, when I caution you that you have made a dangerous friend. (*David Copperfield*, 358)

It is this oblivion to possible danger that so attracts Steerforth (as his literary successor Lord Henry Wotton will later be captivated by the initial naïveté of Dorian Gray), and the more knowing narrator implicitly encodes their relationship throughout the novel in veiled allusions to sexual corruption. Tellingly, the friendship between

David and Steerforth is not superseded or modified through the marriage of one party, but dislodged by an illicit liaison on the latter's part. This crisis actually serves effectively to focus the reader's attention on the male friendship in question, where a marriage would have diminished its importance almost by definition.

In place of the sister that David has never possessed, Steerforth seduces his surrogate sister the equally naïve Em'ly, and in a brilliant reversal, David's subsequent assumption of moral authority recasts Steerforth himself as a figure of fallenness. He assures the now dead Steerforth that his reproaches will never bear witness against him, while at the same time positing an uneasy time for him at the judgement seat. The language of this lament echoes the 'Appeal to Fallen Women' that Dickens was circulating at about the same time, warning London prostitutes of the retribution they would incur if they failed to repent of their sexual sins. Disguised in the language of mournful love is the assumption that Steerforth has put himself beyond the pale of social reconciliation at least. Prophetically, David's method of remembering him without guilt is to imagine him 'as a cherished friend who was dead' (*David Copperfield*, 443). Characteristically, he assumes that his reaction is typical of others in his situation, commenting:

> What is natural in me, is natural in many other men, I infer, and so I am not afraid to write that I never had loved Steerforth better than when the ties that bound me to him were broken. ... I believe that if I had been brought face to face with him, I could not have uttered one reproach. I should have loved him so well still – though he fascinated me no longer – I should have held in so much tenderness the memory of my affection for him, that I think I should have been as weak as a spirit-wounded child, in all but the entertainment of a thought that we could ever be re-united. (*David Copperfield*, 443)

This realignment of the power dynamic brings out a 'feminine' susceptibility in Steerforth that stands to reveal this character's complex moral ambiguities. He is ironically cast by David in the same terms Em'ly uses to describe herself, as she urges her family to remember her as one who is dead: 'try to think as if I died when I was little, and was buried somewhere' (*David Copperfield*, 441). Lyn Pykett identifies both masculine and feminine traits in Steerforth from the beginning, arguing that:

> As an indulged and self-indulgent, aristocratic dandy, Steeforth is simultaneously feminized and the embodiment of rapacious masculine sexuality and economic power. (Pykett, 119)

David's attainment of maturity largely depends on his throwing off the influence of his early passion, for his friend as later for his first wife, Dora. In locating Steerforth as an embodiment of fallenness and thereby feminising him, David is able to assert his own masculinity, coming to identify in this with the 'manly' and forgiving Ham, whose love for Em'ly persists while none the less emphasising her feminine frailty and susceptibility to judgement.

Such femininity must be safely externalised if David is to attain manliness and secure the status of a gentleman. James Eli Adams identifies the sense in which:

> Middle-class professionals (including male writers) legitimated their masculinity by identifying it with that of the gentleman, a norm that was the subject of protracted

contention throughout Victorian culture ... throughout the first half of the nineteenth century it was reshaped as an incarnation of ascetic discipline and infused with the fabled Victorian earnestness. (Adams, 6–7)

In this sense, it is important for David to outgrow the enthusiasm of his youth, with its elements of idealistic fervour but also the threat of uncontrolled – or, in the novel's own terms, 'undisciplined' passion. Accepted models of masculine development dictate that in order to attain self-mastery, he must overcome the femininity implicit in his deference to Steerforth and ultimately provide himself with a complementary female figure, who will serve as a repository of feminine virtue, external to himself.

He first attempts to do this in his relationship with the inept Dora Spenlow, who inspires his first real efforts at manly work. But David's chivalrous desire to tire himself out in her service belongs in the province of youthful impulse, rather than professional self-sufficiency. In a chapter appropriately entitled 'Enthusiasm', he recalls with wry amusement how:

> I got into such a transport, that I felt quite sorry that my coat was not a little shabby already. I wanted to be cutting at those trees in the forest of difficulty, under circumstances that should prove my strength. I had a good mind to ask an old man, in wire spectacles, who was breaking stones upon the road, to lend me his hammer for a little while, and let me begin to beat a path to Dora out of granite. (*David Copperfield*, 505)

His very idealism at this stage is symptomatic of a persistent immaturity, represented by the recurring trope of the undisciplined heart. It is only as he gains literary fame that he comes to regard himself in terms of earnestness and masculine achievement, and so becomes a worthy husband for the long-suffering Agnes. As Myers wryly puts it:

> The deaths of Dora and Steerforth are narratively fortuitous. They relieve David of a life-long commitment to erroneous youthful choice, an instance of authorial generosity common in mid-Victorian novels. (Myers, 118)

Tellingly, the deaths of Dora and Steerforth, the inadequate wife and the unsuitable friend, merge in David's mind, as he mourns:

> all that I had lost – love, friendship, interest ... my first trust, my first affection, the whole airy castle of my life ... (*David Copperfield*, 793)

The symbolic expulsion of each figure from the narrative allows David to progress and mature, and in overcoming his double loss, he is finally able to redefine himself with a fully integrated masculine identity.

The very fact that his autobiography is written in the supposedly secret, feminine terms of *Jane Eyre* (David insists that the manuscript is for his own eyes only) serves to differentiate this private account of his early years from the successes of his later life, in which he gains public acclaim and a wide readership for his novels.

As Herbert Sussman explains:

> For the Victorians manhood is not an essence but a plot, a condition whose achievement and whose maintenance forms a narrative over time. (Sussman, 13)

This constant process of self-definition is painfully familiar to Steerforth, who blames his own failure to fulfil his potential on the absence of a paternal role model. Acting up to prescribed roles, as Juliet John has shown, he 'experiences himself from the outside' (John, 177), playing the part of a decadent aristocrat in a melodramatic moral scheme, even as he envies David's transparent – and equally melodramatic – sincerity. The complicating social determinism of the text hints at the inevitability of the actions by which he is condemned. As John explains:

> A consequence of Dickens's increased emphasis on the social construction of selfhood and its ethical exhibitions is that he dilutes, or at least unmasks, his melodramatic art. Dickens appears to dress his characters as either villains or heroes whilst questioning the essentialist ethical scheme which produced them. (174)

For David, this dichotomy remains particularly crucial, as he struggles and finally succeeds in the autobiographical imperative to overcome early humiliations and reinstate himself as the hero of his own life.

In Memoriam

Tennyson's famous mid-century exploration of love and loss in *In Memoriam* is linked to Dickens's *David Copperfield*, published in the same year, both by its central theme of premature death and by its close analysis of the reaction of the bereaved friend, who offers an account of his own response to bereavement, culminating in each case in some level of recovery. Both *In Memoriam* and *David Copperfield* take the narrator or speaker through a crisis of faith, from which a new understanding and a greater strength or 'discipline' can be achieved. Unlike the fictional autobiography of *David Copperfield*, *In Memoriam* is a series of elegiac poems inspired by the actual death of Tennyson's close friend Arthur Hallam. But many of its narrative strategies are comparable to David's, as the poetic voice explores the intensities of a youthful romantic friendship in retrospect. In place of David's ambivalence and somewhat unconvincing forgiveness of Steerforth, which is to some extent conditional on his death, Tennyson expresses an admiration of his friend that is likewise based on unfulfilled potential, but in this case the friend's potential for greatness has been tragically precluded rather than marred by his own corruption. The extent of the poet's own grief is offered as evidence in itself of the perceived worthiness of his lost friend, as:

> … by the measure of my grief
> I leave thy greatness to be guessed.
> (*In Memoriam*, LXXV, *A Critical Edition of the Major Works*, 246)

Elsewhere, Hallam's probable career as a writer or statesman, had he lived, is envisaged in terms that suggest a sense of loss not only to the poet speaker, but to the nation as a whole. In keeping with the traditions of male romantic friendship, the speaker or narrator stresses his own inferiority to his friend, comparing himself in his feelings of inadequacy to a woman who loves a man above her in rank (*In Memoriam*, LX, 238). As the late nineteenth-century scholar Trumbull notes:

> ... envy is forestalled by the very friendship's existence, for envy is a selfish regret that another is in advance of us, while friendship is an unselfish affection for another because he is in advance of us – or ought to be, as we see it. (Trumbull, 39)

The status of the work as poetry in itself allows for more intense expression than is allowed to fiction. Some years later, in 1884, J.C. Shairp, the Principal of St Andrew's University, commented that:

> [the poet] has in his art a safety-valve for the strongest emotion, a medium through which he can express feelings that he would not venture to whisper into the friendliest ear. Much less to commit to the language of plain prose. Perhaps, too, the frigid decorum that dominates English society may serve to intensify by contrast the warmth of pent-up emotion that seeks relief in poetry. (Shairp, 580)

This distinction between the language of everyday speech and the licence allowed to poetry is obvious enough, but the assumption that English society is dominated by a 'frigid decorum' seems on the face of it to be inconsistent with the tradition of romantic friendship to which the poem itself clearly gestures. What the qualifying statement implies is that Tennyson's language is notably emotional even by those standards – what the critic does not say is that language may be seen to derive a greater intensity through its use in a poetic medium, and further that the expression of feeling in poetry is contextualised only with difficulty; the same sentiments in a novel could be enclosed in a clearly outlined scheme involving the development and ultimate marriage of the protagonist.

Tennyson himself had written in a letter of 1846 that 'I wish we Englanders dealt more in such symbols, that we drest our affections up in a little more poetical costume, real warmth of heart would lose nothing rather gain by it' (to Mary Howitt, 20 December 1846, *The Letters of Alfred Lord Tennyson*, vol. 1, 270). In 1892, Trumbull was quoting extensively from *In Memoriam* for his important study on friendship, enthusing: 'In all history there is no fitter illustration of the inspiring power of friendship.' More intriguingly yet in the wake of subsequent events, he goes on to comment on the work as 'in itself a refutation of the charge that friendship has no such potency in the Christian heart of to-day as it had in the heart of the classic Greek' (Trumbull, 364).

Individual poems relate an undefined sense of guilt at the use of passionate expression, 'I sometimes hold it half a sin / To put in words the grief I feel' (*In Memoriam*, V, 206), and this has been read an admission of sexual guilt. However, Dellamora argues with equal validity that:

> A more attentive reading suggests two distinct sets of readers: one a group of loving friends, who will understand what Tennyson half reveals ... The reason for half concealment lies not in the sexual significance of the relationship, which as far as Tennyson is concerned is one of conscious innocence, but rather in an embodied, affective intimacy that so far exceeds normal experience, perhaps especially experience between men and women, that

the bond becomes something for the elect to conceal from the eyes of the mundane. The second group are those who, to understand Tennyson at all, will have to understand him in widow's weeds, ie in terms which restrict devotion like Tennyson's to relations between the sexes. (Dellamora, 35)

Contemporary responses to the work were largely favourable, which suggests that its expression of grief was felt to be comprehensible by its early readers. Charlotte Brontë had by her own confession only read half the book when she wrote to Elizabeth Gaskell that:

> It is beautiful; it is mournful; it is monotonous. Many of the feelings expressed bear, in their utterance, the stamp of truth; yet, if Arthur Hallam had been somewhat nearer Alfred Tennyson, – his brother instead of his friend, – I should have distrusted this rhymed, and measured, and printed monument of grief. What change the lapse of years may work I do not know; but it seems to me that bitter sorrow, while recent, does not flow out in verse. (27 August 1850, quoted in Gaskell, 356)

In this ambivalent response, Brontë implicitly questions the sincerity of romantic friendship, as Thackeray was to do, despite engaging herself in intense friendships to which she gave full expression. Had she read *In Memoriam* more closely and remarked the passages describing Hallam as 'more than my brothers are to me' (*In Memoriam*, IX, 209), this comment would perhaps stand as a more forceful criticism yet of the sorrow that flows out in verse. But more typical of contemporary reactions to *In Memoriam*, is Franklin Lushington's appraisal in *Tait's Edinburgh Magazine*:

> It is one of the most touching and exquisite monuments ever raised to a departed friend – the pure and unaffected expression of the truest and most perfect love … (in Armstrong, 224)

Shairp would concur, in his 1884 article on 'Friendship in English Poetry', that 'English literature contains no other such monument' (Shairp, 593). In our own time, Leonee Ormond has commented that 'Among writers in English, only W. B. Yeats matches the quality and intensity of feeling in Tennyson's poems of friendship' (Ormond, 186). While extracts from Tennyson's most famous work have found their way unscrutinised in later times into the *Penguin Anthology of Homosexual Verse*, the perceived 'purity' of expression identified by Lushington is crucial to the balance maintained throughout between passion and its appropriate form in words and gesture. At its most insightful, criticism that locates a sexualised imagery in Tennyson's work acknowledges that:

> Tennyson's poem speaks of gay sex, but as a figure for a transcendent intercourse that cannot be rendered in words. Sex between human beings can be talked about; it can be described. (Hood, 113)

In this context, 'His startling metaphoric use of sex between men … does give a poetical shock … that jolts readers into an awareness of the spiritual desire expressed in the most starkly vivid terms available' (Hood, 114). Dellamora similarly suggests that:

In *In Memoriam*, erotic sentiment is free continually to expand precisely because – unlike subsequent works like *Leaves of Grass* – the poem is conceived in aesthetic, not sexual-aesthetic, terms. Hence Tennyson can invoke touch, can be tender, even amatory, without connoting perversity. (Dellamora, 39)

While largely agreeing with both accounts of the highly charged imagery and its erotic potential in *In Memoriam*, I would question the sense in which it *must* be read in erotic terms at all, simply because such a perspective does not take into account the considerable licence permitted by the terms of romantic friendship in speaking of a dead friend. Equipped with its own register for enacting mourning, such close friendship does not need to be mediated through alternative imagery, however powerful.

As in *David Copperfield*, the mature perspective and arrangement of the work in itself allows a certain level of passionate expression. Indeed it could be said to emulate the classic form of fiction of the period – as published, the work ends conventionally with a marriage rather than with a straightforward celebration of male friendship. The youthfulness of the subject himself likewise permits a great deal to be expressed that would be unavailable to the presentation of a relationship formed later in life. Summing up the power of early friendships, Tennyson writes tellingly of 'First love, first friendship, equal powers' (*In Memoriam*, LXXXV, 107, p. 255). The status accorded to 'first friendship' here is extreme but permissible, if only because it is paired with 'first love' rather than marriage. The irony here is that first love in the Victorian imagination was likely to be perceived as more passionate, if less durable, than marriage.

The inherent meaningfulness of first friendship is explored throughout *In Memoriam*, despite – and paradoxically, through – its emphasis on inexpressibility or the inadequacy of words. Brontë's wariness of formulaic expression is echoed in several of the poems that deal with precisely this tension between the desire for relief in words and the possible debasement of feeling involved in such expression. Analysing his own fluctuation in feeling on first hearing of Hallam's death, Tennyson compares his 'lighter moods' to the reaction of a houseful of servants to the death of a good master:

> That out of words a comfort win;
> But there are other griefs within,
> And tears that at their fountain freeze.
> (*In Memoriam*, XX, 216)

The image of freezing is a recurring one, as the poet seeks physical relief in tears rather than words:

> Break, thou deep vase of chilling tears,
> That grief has shaken into frost.
> (*In Memoriam*, IV, 206)

In the description of the first Christmas since Hallam's death, tears are associated with the experience of a 'gentler feeling' – the expression of emotion through tears is seen throughout the work as both desirable and consoling, where their absence may suggest either numbness or the threat of forgetfulness.

In an analogy to the bereavement of lovers, mothers and brothers, Tennyson initially envisages a period of indefinite mourning:

> To her, perpetual maidenhood,
> And unto me no second friend.
> (*In Memoriam*, VI, 208)

But within this celebration of male friendship there inheres an anxiety about the proper expression of feeling. The speaker holds it 'half a sin' to express his feeling in words, and he carefully charts his own shifting response to his loss. John D. Rosenberg points out that the speaker's desire to sacrifice his own life for his friend, and '… breathing thro' his lips impart / The life that almost dies in me' (*In Memoriam*, XVIII, 15–16) suggests the laying of one body on another even as it represents 'the love than which there is none greater – to lay down one's life for one's friend' (Rosenberg, 302). This desire is necessarily frustrated, and the speaker is left (like Dickens's David) to invoke the ideal of endurance in suffering that 'slowly forms the firmer mind' (*In Memoriam*, 18). This belief in the power of suffering to strengthen the mind is largely belied by the recurring image of involuntary or inaccessible tears, with their suggestion of nervous malady – the speaker can neither express his feeling adequately in words nor control the response of his body to his acute mental suffering.

But this crisis as the speaker struggles to find an appropriate and sustainable expression of his sense of loss ultimately gives way to a stress on the importance of hope and religious transformation. The governing prologue contains an acknowledgement of mourning as inconsistent with religious belief, 'Forgive my grief for one removed' (Prologue, *In Memoriam*, 204), that anticipates the sense of renewal contained in the final marriage of Tennyson's sister Cecilia. If the period of mourning is implicitly limited and contained by this structure, the ending is none the less removed from the traditional 'plot' resolution in which the narrating hero transfers his affection from friend to spouse – notably, the triumphal marriage celebrated in the poem is that of Tennyson's sister, rather than his own nuptials, which took place in 1850, the same year that *In Memoriam* was first published.

The cultural status of death in the mid-Victorian period allows for strong expressions of intense feeling, as historians have pointed out. The status of *In Memoriam* as an extended elegy places it in the tradition not only of romantic friendship, but of the *ars moriendi*, and this further validates its use of intense language, as the death of the subject implicitly spiritualises the feeling of the bereaved narrator poet. As David Copperfield is free to lament the loss of his friend more fully after his death, so the death of Hallam permits to *In Memoriam* a full and unsparing use of the terms available to romantic friendship. In keeping with the established patterns of romantic friendship, a high level of feeling is expressible in descriptions of youthful passion and particularly in the absence of its object. As Rosenberg expresses it: 'He strains the generic seams of elegy to the bursting point, yet he remains eminently Victorian in mourning at such elaborate length' (Rosenberg, 300).

Paradoxically, this very sense of a rarefied spirituality facilitates a use of more physical imagery than might otherwise be acceptable, but the line is a narrow one. It is the physicality of *In Memoriam* that strains the conventions of not only elegy, but romantic friendship itself, as:

> The most startling effects in *In Memoriam* all have a transgressive quality, a crossing of borders that normally separate the living from the dead, the natural from the supernatural, one sex or species from another. Death in *In Memoriam*, especially in the darker, earlier sections, is not so much the cessation of life as a displaced activity, corpses in motion or embraces underground ... (Rosenberg, 295)

Invoking Sorrow in the image of a wife, Tennyson writes that 'My centred passion cannot move' (*In Memoriam*, LIX, 238), suggesting that the transition from friendship to marriage cannot be fully accomplished, and later he describes his response to the death of his friend in terms of a physicality that could hardly be divorced from the erotic, were it not for the recognisable dependence on religious tropes:

> O days and hours, your work is this
> To hold me from my proper place,
> A little while from his embrace,
> For fuller gain of after bliss:
> (*In Memoriam*, CXVII, 280)

Certainly, 'Bliss' here could stand equally for orgasm or union with the divine, and one could argue, with James Hood, that '*In Memoriam* clearly demonstrates that for Tennyson the imagery of human sexual union provides one of the best poetic means of picturing intercourse within the realm of the divine. In utilizing such sexual figures toward this end, Tennyson of course stands in a long tradition of Western Christian literature ...' (Hood, 112). Elsewhere, the traditional image of Death as reaper is reworked to suggest the consummation of love, giving 'all ripeness to the grain' (In Memoriam, LXXXI, 250).

The removal of the subject of the elegy not only allows a greater emphasis on the physical, but also creates a void in which the desire for identity and reunion can be safely expressed. The loss of self-knowledge that has:

> ... stunn'd me from my power to think
> And all my knowledge of myself
> (*In Memoriam*, XVI, 213)

also suggests a merging of identity, in which the poet's sense of self is dependent on his continuing relation to the idea of his friend. Again, this desire for complete identification one with the other is phrased in religious terminology that gives substance to and endorses the physicality of the expression:

> If thou wert with me, and the grave
> Divide us not, be with me now,
> And enter in at breast and brow
> (*In Memoriam*, CXXII, 283)

The connection between religion and friendship is more fully worked out elsewhere in the elegy, as the tropes of romantic friendship are brought to bear on the experience of bereavement and consolation. The speaker is troubled at least intermittently with the ability of the dead to perceive the sins of the living (*In Memoriam*, LI, 233). But despite their perceived difference in status, Tennyson posits a mutual recognition and reunion between himself and Hallam in heaven, and a mutual influence for good that will transcend their separation in the interim. Not only does he feel 'His being working in mine own / The footsteps of his life in mine' (*In Memoriam*, LXXXV, 253), but:

> Since we deserved the name of friends,
> And thine effect so lives in me,
> A part of mine may live in thee
> And move thee on to noble ends.
> (*In Memoriam*, LXV, 241)

This sense of mutual ennoblement and influence for good is highly characteristic of romantic friendship, is indeed one of its justifying claims. As the essayist Hugh Black was to argue in 1897, with copious accompanying quotation from *In Memoriam*, earthly friendship prefigures and typifies the higher feelings of religion:

> The limitations and losses of earthly friendship are meant to drive us to the higher friendship. Life is an education in love, but the education is not complete till we learn the love of the eternal. Ordinary friendship has done its work when the limits of friendship are reached, when through the discipline of love we are led into a larger love, when a door is opened out to a higher life. (Black, 191)

But while Black cites *In Memoriam* as exemplifying the transience of earthly friendship, the work itself deliberately fuses the temporal and the immanent, suggesting that male friendship can not only prefigure, but be contained in a sense of the divine. Indeed, in his lifetime Hallam is described as having been 'half divine' (*In Memoriam*, XIV, 212) in the eyes of the poet. In death, the prologue states:

> I trust he lives in thee, and there
> I find him worthier to be loved.
> (Prologue, *In Memoriam*, 204)

This fusion of earthly and divine love permits yet further slippage of terms, as a spiritual union with the poet's lost friend is contained within, and becomes synonymous with, his belief in religious influence. The 'inner trouble' and 'spectral doubt' (*In Memoriam*, XLI, 229) lest this hope not be fulfilled is superseded by the transformative power of religious faith, in the sequential arrangement of the poems. The process of mourning is linked to self-immolation and the crucifixion itself, as the crown of thorns borne on behalf of the dead is transformed into leaf, in a symbol of resurrection. The validating grief of the poet is reconciled with the joy of eternal life through the introduction of another voice, that of Christ: 'The voice was not the voice of grief' (*In Memoriam*, LXIX, 243). In the final stanzas directly preceding the epilogue, Hallam's death is negated in the invocation of 'Dear heavenly friend that canst not die' (*In Memoriam*, CXXIX, 287), and his image merges with that of the divine creator and the whole created world:

> My love involves the love before;
> My love is vaster passion now;
> Tho' mix'd with God and Nature thou,
> I seem to love thee more and more.
> (*In Memoriam*, CXXX, 287)

This fusion of secular love with religious worship strongly appealed to a mid-nineteenth-century understanding of the purpose of romantic friendship. As Kingsley enthused in a review:

> Blessed, thrice blessed, to find that hero-worship is not yet passed away; that the heart of man still beats young and fresh; that the old tales of David and Jonathan, Damon and Pythias, Socrates and Alcibiades, Shakespeare and his nameless friend, of 'love passing the love of woman', ennobled by its own humility, deeper than death, and mightier than the grave, can still blossom out if it be but in one heart here and there to show men still how sooner or later 'he that loveth knoweth God, for God is Love!' (in Jump, ed., *Tennyson: The Critical Heritage*, 185)

None the less, this avowal of increasing love for the elegy's subject works against any narrative resolution through marriage, despite the poet's inclusion of verses addressed to his future wife. Rather than moving towards identification with a female figure through marriage, *In Memoriam* employs strategies that vindicate an ongoing commitment to the romantic friendship of the poet's youth.

In so doing, the work implicitly privileges male friendship over heterosexual involvement; the prolonged intensity of mourning is imaginatively confined to friends, as the dead find 'their brides in other hands' and the 'The hard heir strides about their lands' (*In Memoriam*, XC, 260). Justifying the superiority of his own feeling as unchangeable, Tennyson concludes:

> I find not yet one lonely thought
> That cries against my wish for thee.
> (*In Memoriam*, XC, 260)

Later critics have highlighted the gendered terms in which much of this feeling is expressed. A convincing argument for this is that in:

> … *In Memoriam*, [as opposed to earlier poems about female bereavement] new roles are required: Death, by its association with Nature, still retains a female sexuality, but the victim of death is a man, and the elegiac survivor is a man. To represent real death – to invent a form for masculine grief – would take seventeen years of re-vision. (Manning, 210)

But at its most basic, the string of comparisons – the speaker is like a girl awaiting her lover, like the mother of a sailor, like the lover of an absent woman - suggest the all-encompassing self-sufficiency of male friendship. Having once established Hallam's masculinity in the reader's mind through allusions to his logic, 'intellect and force' (*In Memoriam*, CIX, 275), the poetic voice recalls his 'manhood fused with female grace' (275). This balance of masculine and feminine qualities echoes the terms of XXV, in which the language is comparable to that of gendered love. In this formulation, 'with equal feet we fared' (*In Memoriam*, XXV, 219) depends on the capacity of each to bear the burdens of the other. Here, the protective instinct encapsulated in the lines

> I loved the weight I had to bear,
> Because it needed help of Love
> (*In Memoriam*, XXV, 219)

is deeply reminiscent of Victorian romantic conventions, in which masculine love sustains feminine dependence; however this is balanced by the recollection of other times:

> When mighty Love would cleave in twain
> The lading of a single pain,
> And part it, giving half to him.
> (*In Memoriam*, XXV, 219)

Tellingly, Tennyson twice describes himself as 'widow'd' (*In Memoriam*, IX and XVII). Where the intended marriage between Hallam and Emily Tennyson is contemplated, it is largely with reference to the male friendship that it would have served to reinforce:

> I see myself an honour'd guest,
> Thy partner in the flowery walk
> Of letters, genial table-talk
> (*In Memoriam*, LXXXIV, 251)

The next two chapters will treat the potential disruption caused to marriage by the possessive intensity of same sex friendship, in greater detail – the allusion not to Emily but to Tennyson himself as his friend's partner, is certainly somewhat unfortunate in this context. The sense in which marriage becomes simply a vehicle for the strengthening of male bonds, inevitably negates the structural impact of the final marriage in the epilogue. The lack of conviction with which the final stanzas seek to conclude the period of mourning, as one marriage symbolically stands in for another, serves rather to adumbrate the durability of male friendship rather than heterosexual attachment.

In Memoriam, most famous as the great literary exploration of Victorian religious doubt, also conforms in many ways to the accepted contemporary paradigm of male romantic friendship. Like Dickens in his fictional representation of passionate enthusiasm, Tennyson represents youthful love between men as indicative of their moral capacities. In keeping with established literary patterns, the speaker of the poem(s) is intense and seemingly unguarded in his expression of emotion, but this celebration of passion is carefully ordered, and it is vindicated by the youthfulness of its object as much as by his untimely death. In both the novel and the poetic elegy, a mature narrator is able to describe passionate admiration of a lost friend not least *because* the friendship has been abruptly terminated or, in Tennyson's case postponed, during the less restrictive period of the speaker's own youth.

Where David's misplaced love for his friend is subsumed in the more viable conventions of a marriage plot that ends the novel, Tennyson is able to justify a sustained lament for his friend both through an appeal to the nineteenth-century cult of death and through his invocation of specifically religious imagery. Where Steerforth has been proved unworthy, allowing for his convenient removal as a more mature David asserts his independence from external influence, Hallam's influence over Tennyson is increasingly elevated and sanctified through the imagery of religious transformation. The very absence of the friend in question renders this influence less threatening than might otherwise be the case, and the fully articulated response to death so greatly encouraged in nineteenth-century England likewise helps to dispel any anxiety that might otherwise attach to such intense expression of feeling between members of the same sex.

As numerous contemporary writers on the subject make clear, the conventions of romantic friendship allow for an intensity in youth that is carefully repressed or diffused in most literary representations of same-sex relationships later in life. The early death of one participant in such a friendship allows the question of future relations to be obviated, and in this case the cultural status of death permits a spiritual relation to be envisaged that transcends the conventions of earthly friendship between men. The central importance of this relationship determines the relatively ineffectual presentation of marriage offered by the poet in his maturity, even while the status of his early romantic friendship is dependent on its association specifically with his youth.

Towards the end of the century, the more subversive Oscar Wilde would reject the cultural value of marriage and heterosexual involvement altogether, in *The Picture of Dorian Gray*. In its presentation of perpetual youth as calculating and open to corruption, Wilde's novel does much to undermine the innocence associated with the expression of passion between young men, so carefully formulated and protected by Dickens and Tennyson. But this explosive text was still thirty years away. Even the supposedly radical sensation novel of the 1860s kept a close eye on the limits and nature of male friendship – in Braddon's novel, the male hero may come close to breakdown, but he is conscientious to the point of obsession in analysing and upholding the restrictive code of behaviour underpinning romantic friendship.

Lady Audley's Secret

Both Dickens and Tennyson, publishing in 1850, uphold the response of a participant in romantic friendship as elevating (in Dickens's case, regardless of the moral worth of the influential friend). While the 'disciplined heart' is a recurring motif in *David Copperfield* and the speaker of *In Memoriam* likewise sees himself as having been strengthened through his experience of suffering, there is no direct treatment in either work of the need for *rational* self-control. The moral status of romantic friendship in itself is confidently treated, and it teaches, rather than threatening, self-control.

Influenced by Wilkie Collins's psychological sensation novel *The Woman in White*, Mary Braddon's *Lady Audley's Secret* (1862) directly addresses the question of emotion and self-control, not only through the mental aberrations of the eponymous Lady Audley, but equally through the threat of monomania perceived by Robert Audley to himself. The reader is not privy to the early stages of Robert's friendship with George Talboys, as the two are reunited after some years' absence, when the latter returns from speculations in Australia. However, the recurring references to their time together at Eton set up certain expectations, given the intensity of friendship encouraged at the public schools at this time (regardless of their own education, many readers would have been familiar with Disraeli's *Coningsby*, discussed earlier).

The friendship between the two men serves in some sense as the 'rehearsal for life's great drama' that crops up repeatedly in descriptions of female friendship – in himself awakening Robert's passionate responsiveness, George prepares him to love his sister, Clara. As Ann Cvetkovich notes, Robert's emotional awakening is associated with his friend's reappearance from Australia, before his disappearance at Audley Court. As she interprets it:

> At the beginning of the novel, Robert's behaviour, both sexual and professional, is gendered as nonmasculine ... Sexual manhood would seem to require his insertion into a set of relations with a woman, as husband or suitor, yet professional maturity demands that he relate to other men as colleagues. The two processes converge in his attraction to George Talboys, so that a man is the means by which he comes to work and to love. (Cvetkovich, 59)

While I do not see the relationship between the two men as erotic (despite the possibly sexualised language identified by Cvetkovich as imaging Robert's transformation), this analysis is particularly useful here in contextualising the relationship between the friends.

Elsewhere in the novel, female romantic friendship is mocked, even as it involves the sinister Lady Audley's past life. In a book that forms one clue to her identity with the supposedly dead Helen, the narrator makes a wry comment on the inscription by one Miss Bince, 'who presented the book as a mark of undying affection and unfading esteem (Miss Bince was evidently of a romantic temperament) to her beloved friend Helen Maldon' (*Lady Audley's Secret*, 159). This incidental satire is precluded in the exploration of male friendship, which is at once taken more seriously and handled more carefully. Robert himself is persistently portrayed by the narrator as being phlegmatic in temperament, but this very stress on his lymphatic nature paradoxically allows the hint of an intensity in his feeling for his friend, whom he recognises 'with an emphasis by no means usual to him' (35). Throughout the novel, the reader's attention is drawn to this balance – or contradictoriness – in Robert's character. Even before he has real cause for concern about his friend's disappearance, he is seen in an anxious state that the narrator stresses as unusual:

> If any one had ventured to tell Mr Robert Audley that he could possibly feel a strong attachment to any living creature breathing, that cynical gentleman would have elevated his eyebrows in supreme contempt at the preposterous notion. Yet here he was, flurried and anxious, bewildering his brain by all manner of conjectures about his missing friend, and, false to every attribute of his nature, walking fast. (82)

Robert himself is similarly persistent in pointing out the strength of his attachment as uncharacteristic, repeatedly screening expressions of intense feeling through an invocation of his own customary torpidity:

> 'To think,' he said, meditatively, 'that it is possible to care so much for a fellow! But come what may, I'll go up to town after him the first thing tomorrow morning, and sooner than be balked in finding him, I'll go to the very end of the world.' (88–9)

Elsewhere, he disguises the seriousness of his depression through a wry observation on the failure of his appetite: 'I have never eaten a good dinner at this table since I lost George Talboys …' (151). Through these transparent disclaimers of his own energetic love for his friend, Robert (with the help of the narrator) may be setting out to allay any anxiety on the part of the reader, who might be inclined to perceive inappropriate levels of feeling in this determined search. But in repeatedly prefacing expressions of such deeply felt emotion with pointed reminders that this state of mind is alien to him, Robert actually draws attention to the very intensity that his ambivalence seeks to conceal.

Nor is the potential conflict between friendship and marriage addressed, in that George has returned to see his wife's supposed death listed in the papers. In the radical treatment of romantic friendship offered by Wilkie Collins a few years later in *Armadale*, the errant wife is despatched at the end of the novel in order to make way for the male friendship that dominates the text. The more conservative account given here by Braddon deftly bypasses the issue of who will be superseded by whom, in beginning with the supposed death of the wife, and (as in the later text) taking this as a means of strengthening male ties. The account of male friendship in the early chapters of the novel focuses almost entirely on Robert's care of the disconsolate George, who for his own part can think only of the loss of his wife. Emphasising the altruistic nature of male friendship, Robert sacrifices his own comfort and convenience to his friend, whose appointed helpmeet will by contrast later try to murder him. Notably, the dispirited George is at this point as 'submissive as a child to the will of his friend' (51), whose influence is greatly increased by the fact of this assumed bereavement. The allocation of perceived power between the two will shift again at different points in the novel, most obviously in Robert's later perception of his friend as alternately inspiring or haunting him in his quest to bring Lady Audley to justice. Notably, it is George's abrupt disappearance that allows Robert openly to express a sense of emotional loss to others, and so to reveal the depth of his feeling for his lost friend. This emotional reaction is not lost on the jealous Alicia, who sarcastically refers to them as Pythias and Damon, and suggests that one cannot live without the other for more than half an hour (84). Such allusions in literature of the time suggest the self-sacrificial nature of classical friendship, but in this context might also point to a proscribed form of attachment – Pythias and Damon feature as either friends or lovers in different accounts. Robert's response is to take refuge in the conservative but recognisably heartfelt language of schoolboy loyalty. Speaking 'stoutly', he describes George as 'a very good fellow' and admits to being 'rather uneasy about him' (84).

In this rendering of male friendship, the emphasis is necessarily distracted – or displaced – from the interaction of the protagonists, as one is supposed to be dead for much of the novel, and this helps to legitimate the expression of intense feeling (as it does in Tennyson's *In Memoriam*). This expression is further protected, as I have suggested, by its presentation as an aberration, allowing the utterance of highly charged sentiment to be set against a customary reserve and equability. The continually expressed surprise at his own reaction permits Robert to declare that he would give anything in the world to see his friend again, and even to hint at his ultimate importance as a companion:

> 'Who would have thought that I could have grown so fond of the fellow' he muttered, 'or feel so lonely without him? ... I declare that I would give up all and stand penniless in the world to-morrow, if this mystery could be satisfactorily cleared away, and George Talboys could stand by my side.' (*Lady Audley's Secret*, 161)

During his absence, Robert makes repeated references to 'having grown so fond' of his friend, but what these utterances conceal is the strength of his affection long before George's disappearance – he has greeted him earlier with an unusual emphasis in saying that he has not forgotten him, and given him his own bedroom for a year, immediately on hearing of the supposed death of his wife. The elevating effect of romantic friendship is conscientiously stressed by the narrator, as the lymphatic central character becomes purposeful and specifically religious:

> The one purpose which had slowly grown up in his careless nature until it had become powerful enough to work a change in that very nature, made him what he had never been before – a Christian; conscious of his own weakness; anxious to keep to the strict line of duty; fearful to swerve from the conscientious discharge of the strange task that had been forced upon him; and reliant on a stronger hand than his own to point the way which he was to go. (157)

In fact, this increased strength of purpose in one sense serves to rehabilitate Robert from a state of mental instability, in so far as in medical formulations, Shuttleworth suggests, sluggishness might be as suspect as an excess of energy: 'The passivity, so desirable in women, became pathological in men' (Shuttleworth, 50). It is through bringing down the ostensibly mad Lady Audley that Robert is able to display his own powers of self-regulation and secure a social rôle of his own. As Cvetkovich sees it:

> The detective story whose focus is the crimes of Lady Audley masks the narrative of Robert Audley's accession to the world of male power by means of his affective ties to a male friend. Patriarchal culture privileges relations between men in every arena; rather than making him deviant, Robert's homoeroticism seems to fit him all the better to be the bearer of social values. The novel's homoerotic subtext not only reveals his

investments, but intensifies the links between sexuality and work that the novel brings into play. (Cvetkovich, 59)

(I would qualify this statement only by suggesting the anxiety the novel manifests about a homo-erotic interpretation, and the lengths to which it goes in guarding against this possibility.)

Romantic friendship functions, then, to inspire greater earnestness in its proponent, and so to effect his redemption, both socially (Robert will later become distinguished in his profession) and on a religious plane. While all possibility of emotional exchanges appears to be at an end, Robert allows his past relations with his friend to influence his personal development, largely because he believes him to be dead. Again, as in *In Memoriam*, this account allows the absent friend to function as guiding force and good angel (at least until a suitable replacement is provided in the person of Clara Talboys). As in Tennyson and Dickens, memory becomes a powerful force, as past events 'work together' (to use Dickens's own phrase) to strengthen Robert's determination to gain justice in the future. Again, the figure of George is set at one remove, as Robert is moved more by his sense of tragedy – he is determined both to avenge the 'dead', and in so doing, to find repose for himself – and by his complex response to Lady Audley than by the personality of the lost friend himself. The precise personality of this central figure is increasingly obscured in Robert's sorrowful declamations that he had already changed beyond recognition on reading the newspaper that gave him news – falsely, as it turns out – of his wife's death. Even as Robert's new-found motivation is attributed to his friend's influence, that friend comes to seem himself remote and unknowable.

However, Alicia is not the only character to suggest that Robert's reaction is inappropriate to the situation. Lady Audley herself tendentiously hints that his faculties have been impaired by George's disappearance, and Sir Michael is easily persuaded by her, not least because he already perceives Robert's obsession with finding the truth as somewhat eccentric or extreme. In his increasing obsession with solving the putative murder, Robert Audley comes to suspect himself of incipient madness, that ultimate symbol of the failure to exert self-control. This association of obsession with latent insanity is used to great effect by Lady Audley in her efforts to outmanoeuvre her opponent. Victorian mourning rituals allowed for a high degree of emotionalism, but she is able to insinuate that the intensity of Robert's reaction is in this case inappropriate, given the lack of evidence that George has really died and not simply absconded. Lady Audley cleverly undermines her antagonist's claims to sensibility without sacrificing her own feminine status, by assuming a commonsense viewpoint and arguing that there is no need for such despair given that it may have no foundation. But the general uneasiness of the family in this context suggests an underlying anxiety as much as it ostensibly denotes insensitivity; there is a limit to the expression of love that can be bestowed on a friend *in his lifetime*.

Dangerously for himself, Robert actually does begin to show symptoms suggestive of both insanity and, significantly, romantic passion. Predisposed to side with his wife, Sir Michael is easily led to misinterpret his nephew's peculiar behaviour:

He had grown moody and thoughtful, melancholy and absent-minded. He had held himself aloof from society; had sat for hours without speaking; had talked at other times by fits and starts; and had excited himself unusually in the discussion of subjects which apparently lay far out of the region of his own life and interests. (*Lady Audley's Secret*, 331)

Outward signs are carefully recounted and analysed here, suggesting the way in which Victorian medical tracts urged families to observe each other for signs of deviant or unusual behaviour, in an attempt to identify any mental aberration. Robert's inability to control his 'body language' undermines his assumed security, in rendering him susceptible to the malicious interpretations of Lady Audley, who is herself well versed in the outward signs that connote possible insanity. In fact, the suggestion of monomania is never wholly discounted, but the reader is invited to identify with the anxiety that necessitates such careful self-policing. Throughout the novel, the motif of 'sane today and mad tomorrow', linked to the proper control and direction of passion, reminds the reader of the precarious balance of the mental faculties that forms one of its major themes. As Shuttleworth has shown, 'Only the ever-vigilant maintenance of self-control demarcated the boundaries of insanity' (Shuttleworth, 35), a point of which neither the narrator nor Robert himself ever loses sight. But the need for self-control raises difficult questions for Robert, who must constantly strive to balance loyalty to his supposedly dead friend against his love for his uncle, 'perhaps the strongest sentiment of [his] heart' (*Lady Audley's Secret*, 213), as he continually questions the viability of his quest. Not the least pressing issue, as the novel repeatedly suggests, is this question of the level of feeling that can appropriately be bestowed on his friend's memory. Unable to prove that George has been murdered, Robert cannot engage in socially sanctioned mourning rituals, in which context his grief could be more readily understood and condoned. Quite literally, he must prove his friend to be dead before he can be permitted the full range of passionate expression associated with such a loss.

This dilemma is partially resolved through displacement, in the insistence of Clara Talboys that Robert solve the mystery of her brother's 'murder'. Presented as the gendered 'good angel' of Victorian heterosexual romance, Clara is conveniently intense in her own response to those she loves, and readily vindicates Robert's obsession as she concurs with his conclusions and comes to direct his energies herself. In one sense, the quest to solve the mystery is subsumed by this heterosexual love plot, Clara taking her brother's place as the driving force, obliging Robert to continue his detective work against his own professed inclination. Following their first encounter, he periodically expresses a desire to end the search, but is prevented from doing so by Clara's forceful persuasion. Having successfully courted her through his efforts to solve the mystery, Robert is ultimately able to contain his feeling in the approved manner, through marriage to the sister of his beloved friend.

But significantly, the narrator insists on Clara's similarity to her brother, and it is this that initially attracts Robert to her.

As Helena Michie observes:

The text makes no secret of the fact that Clara looks exactly like her brother George, and that much of Robert's fascination with her stems from the fact that when she gazes at him, he feels as if George's eyes are upon him. Clara forms a bridge to, a compromise with, the homosocial economy of the text … (Michie, 70)

It is significant that he has initially felt his domestic hearth to be cheerless, not in lacking a female figure, but specifically in the absence of George Talboys, and that his attraction to Clara should be predicated largely on her resemblance to and love for her brother. At one point he muses: 'If poor George were sitting opposite to me, or – or even George's sister – she's very like him – existence might be a little more endurable' (*Lady Audley's Secret*, 208). This motif of the empty hearth connects Fig Tree Court with the love plot of the soon to be desolate Audley Court – Lady Audley will see her husband for the last time as she symbolically prostrates herself on the domestic hearth – and further emphasises George's central importance in providing a focus for Robert's love and energy. Towards the end of the novel, Clara has apparently superseded him, as Robert imagines himself asking her:

> What would you say to me if I told you that I love you as earnestly and truly as I have mourned for your brother's fate – that the new strength and purpose of my life which has grown out of my friendship for the murdered man grows even stronger as it turns to you, and changes me until I wonder at myself? (*Lady Audley's Secret*, 401)

But this language is strikingly similar to the phrases used to describe Robert's initial transformation – the narrator has first described Robert's love for George as having 'worked a change' in his nature; it is George who is the first to enliven Robert's empty hearth, when he subsequently reappears in Fig Tree Court, and the three elect to live together following Robert's marriage to Clara. As Gail Turley Houston notes, this dynamic is potentially fraught:

> George, Clara's brother, is now truly Robert's blood brother, … This union suggests that Robert takes more pleasure in proving his love for Clara by asserting that he will go to Australia to find George (and not return until he does), than he does in asking Clara to marry him. (in Tromp, Gilbert and Hanyie, eds, *Beyond Sensation*, 28–9)

The closing pages of the novel, however, suggest no tensions in this ménage, and even hint at a future in which George may remarry (what is more likely to evoke unease in the reader is the abrupt reappearance of Alicia as the wife of a man she never loved, or indeed the death by boredom of Lady Audley). Robert's uneasiness at his own perceived failure of self-control and the influence exerted by the memory of his friend is vindicated in the speech George makes on his return. Restoring the balance of control, he cites his own love for Robert as having brought him back to England despite himself – this return to his friend echoes his earlier return for the sake of his wife, on which occasion Robert had likewise been the first to greet him. George now reinforces Robert's own sense of an ineluctable bond between the two of them, and acknowledges his guiding power: 'I yearned for the strong grasp of your hand, Bob; the friendly touch of the hand which has guided me through the darkest passage of my life' (*Lady Audley's Secret*, 444). In this scene, the balance of influence and self-control is restored for each character – Robert has guided George *through* the tragic episode from which he has now recovered, and in the emotional fulfilment represented by his marriage to Clara Talboys, Robert can in his turn safely acknowledge the vicarious influence of his friend, who is now able to assume his place on the domestic hearth with impunity.

In this carefully wrought account of romantic friendship, the ideal is ultimately maintained, as the active party is inspired with the ideals of self-sacrifice and self-discipline, before working towards the closure of marriage that reconstitutes him as his friend's brother. But this resolution is not allowed to eclipse the struggle Robert has undergone to control and direct what he recognises as a potentially dangerous obsession.

Conclusion

Representations of male romantic friendship, in fiction and poetry alike, stress the sense of control or influence exerted by the object of passionate friendship. This may be ambiguous, and in all of the texts considered here, it is either retrospective or predicated on absence (in the supposed death of George Talboys). Paradoxically, though, the experience of suffering associated with this influence is perceived as enabling in so far as it motivates the male figure and encourages self-mastery. This contradictoriness may be expressed through a characteristic splitting, in the trope of good and bad 'angels'. Steerforth is David's 'bad angel' according to the pure and vigilant Agnes, while Clara Talboys must stand in for George if his influence is to be vindicated and not attributed to a dangerous monomania. Only in the case of Tennyson is the object of passion perceived as a wholly positive and inspiring presence, and by the end of *In Memoriam* Hallam has in any case became absorbed into the divine.

Further ambiguities appear in the uncertainty over gender rôles illustrated by each text (and as I will show, by the omniscient narrator of *Armadale*). David's self-esteem increases after the death of Steerforth, who has had a habit of calling him 'Daisy', and whom he promptly casts in the role of fallen woman. Tennyson's adoption of a feminised voice in parts of *In Memoriam* has been attracting the notice of critics since its first publication. Robert Audley is supposedly being accused solely of monomania, but his symptoms include a general rather than localised fitfulness, and a general 'oddness' more usually detected in women. In theory, this apparent instability can be turned to good account in presentations of male friendship, where an allocation of gender characteristics redresses the balance of power and renders the friendship more self-contained (such accounts are careful to display self-regulation and to avoid clashes with the prescriptions of masculine social codes in the wider sense). A balance of power is actively sought in male friendships, and they are rendered tenable by forceful asseverations of mutual influence. That this reciprocal influence is not achievable in *David Copperfield* is one indication of the invidious power Steerforth wields, and suggests a powerful reason for his removal.

The fear of nervous collapse of one form or another is likewise associated with romantic friendship in all three texts (although David's breakdown is attributable mainly to the deaths of his wife and child). While illness is fetishised as a site of intimacy in accounts of romantic friendship, a susceptibility can equally stand as a symbol of unhealthy or diseased emotion (as I will suggest in the next chapter). This underlying ambivalence about passionate emotion informs mid-century texts on male friendship in particular, and the sense in which its proponents are feminised, consciously or otherwise, helps to explain why.

Chapter Three

A Right to Your Intimacy: The Ends of Female Friendship

... can I hurt thee, dear?
Then why distrust me? Never tremble so.
Come with me rather where we'll talk and live
And none shall vex us. I've a home for you
And me and no one else ...
(Elizabeth Barrett Browning, *Aurora Leigh*)

Victorian writers on the subject of female friendship often justified their interest by claiming that there was little available information, and a general unwillingness to believe in the phenomenon at all. Such is William Alger's claim. He insists that:

> Nothing, perhaps, will strike the literary investigator of the subject more forcibly than the frequency with which he meets the expressed opinion, that women really have few or no friendships; that with them it must be either love, hate, or nothing. (Alger, 13)

He notes the dearth of material on historical female friendship and the obstacles to it presented by nineteenth-century society. Tellingly, he takes it as read that 'Husband and children occupy the wife and mother; and marriage is often the grave of feminine friendships' (Alger, 19). Those who claimed that there was little writing on female friendship, and even a refusal to believe in the phenomenon, similarly assumed that friendship was gendered as male. But despite such claims, a reading of the available material actually suggests an almost obsessive interest in the topic of female friendship (I have already suggested that accounts of men's friendships tend to assume a universal as opposed to a *specifically* male subject) on the part of social commentators and writers of conduct literature. In fact, where no explicit division is made between male and female relations, friendship is more often gendered – if implicitly – as female, in its emphasis on strong emotion and a potential for loss of self-control that at its worst involves the threat of madness. Friendship can even lead male figures to become feminised, for instance through the recurring image of fallenness in *David Copperfield* or in the contested ground of *Lady Audley's Secret*, where it is Robert Audley's loving friendship for George that diminishes his right to self-definition and fleetingly threatens to place him in the power of an unscrupulous woman. Conversely, the greater capacity of men for close friendship is set against this association of feeling with femininity.

What is surprising, given the social context, is the similarity in depictions of intense friendships, whether male or female. The putative difference between male and female friendships is nowhere more decisively summed up than in Alger's own study, where he asserts that:

> Man demands action: woman demands emotion. Friendship between two youths is martial, adventurous, a trumpet-blast or a bugle-air: friendship between two women is poetic, contemplative, the sigh of a harp-string or the swell of an organ pipe.
>
> Woman needs friendship more than man, because she is less self-sufficing. (Alger, 18)

The female protagonists in the texts I consider in this chapter cannot be so neatly categorised, nor is the representation of their friendships so uniformly different from that of their male counterparts. In fact, a number of similar conventions govern the pattern of male and female relations before the final years of the century. For instance, literary and other writers concur in emphasising the significance of class within friendship. David Copperfield is seen to be unwise in making an upper-class friend, whose codes of behaviour he is unable to interpret. Similarly, Sarah Ellis expressed uneasiness about female friendship across class boundaries, and an 1891 populist novella by Lanoe Falconer, *Shoulder to Shoulder: A Tale of Love and Friendship*, stresses the element of patronage in its depiction of an upper-class woman who teaches her working-class counterpart how to value a friend in her own station. The young narrator, May, is strongly drawn to her wealthy namesake, May Lyndhurst, who at first predictably ignores her. The first-person narrator comments:

> The fact was I felt drawn to Miss Lyndhurst, whether I would or no; and though I was hurt and disappointed at the way she had treated me, I still thought she was the most charming young lady I had ever set eyes on. Oh, how happy I should have been, if she had given me only one of her bright smiles! (*Shoulder to Shoulder*, 56)

The two are subsequently brought together by common suffering, and the story finishes with a happy ending, and a realisation on Miss Lyndhurst's part that she can empathise with the joys and sorrows of an inferior. Part of May's education, however, is in the importance of her wholly unromantic friendship with her fellow worker, Ellen. The relationship with Miss Lyndhurst remains one of patronage on the one hand and respectful admiration on the other. Notably, this cautionary tale locates the source of inspiration ostentatiously in the upper class – May's admiration for an upper-class woman is acceptable, but a romantic friendship with one of her own background would be inappropriate or simply inconceivable. But if such intense feeling was not available, at least in literary portrayals of working-class life, it was heavily marketed for middle-class consumption. Accounts of close same-sex friendship were appealing not only to novel readers, but to the wider public. Its most public and widely celebrated example in the nineteenth century was the legend surrounding the Ladies of Llangollen in Wales.

The impact of the Ladies of Llangollen, or Ladies of the Vale, on the Victorian imagination was immense. Eleanor Butler and Sarah Ponsonby had run away together in 1780 and overcome family opposition, to spend the rest of their lives together. In *Famous Friendships of Men and Women eminent in politics and literature etc*, one essayist describes their relationship as 'a deep-rooted attachment worthy of the name of friendship' (*Famous Friendships*, 2), and goes on to cast it in the terms of pastoral idyll:

> One really envies them. Amidst beautiful scenery, with intellectual resources, birds for music, trees for shelter, pure air for health, wealth enough for all reasonable wants, and a profound attachment for each other, they are to be numbered among the fortunate of the earth. (10)

But this symbol of female unity, and the admiration it evoked, conceal a more complex reaction among writers on women's lives. Martha Vicinus has detailed the ways in which the Ladies promoted this myth of the pastoral idyll that none the less was not wholly efficient in concealing the erotic nature of their relationship. Appealing to the perceived link between female romantic friendship and the pastoral tradition, the Ladies created a myth around themselves that inspired numerous enthusiasts:

> For over a century their experience of family disapproval, a dangerous escape, and then rural bliss on a narrow income was the paradigmatic narrative of intimate female friendship. ... Single women revered a romanticized version of the Ladies; under the right circumstances, they too could live with a beloved friend in blessed retreat from social and familial responsibilities. (Vicinus, 6)

Vicinus highlights the basis of the Ladies' appeal here, while pointing out that rumours did circulate intermittently about the nature of their relationship.

Moreover, such a relationship sets itself in direct competition with heterosexual marriage (it is an arrangement briefly contemplated and quickly abandoned by a series of Victorian heroines). As I have suggested, the dynamic of female friendship in the nineteenth century is, like its male counterpart, fraught with tensions and apparent contradictions. Apparently unregulated, as Havelock Ellis was quick to point out, it had always been accorded a limited shelf life in advice manuals such as Sarah Ellis's famous series (discussed in Chapter One). Alternatively, a diluted form of romantic friendship could provide a safety valve for those women who 'failed' to marry. Vicinus argues that 'Homosocial and homo-erotic relations were most accepted among bourgeois women if they remained unmarried and within their own all-female communities; they were most threatening if they disrupted heterosexual norms of courtship and marriage' (Vicinus, 79).

I would argue that such friendships were most highly valued as a preparation, and secondarily as a substitute for marriage. At mid-century, the public school system was largely responsible for fostering same-sex attachment among both boys and girls in the name of public morality. With a voyeuristic energy that suggests positively orgasmic rhythms, Alger celebrates the power of schoolgirl friendships in 1868:

> They form one of the largest classes of those human attachments whose idealizing power and sympathetic interfusions glorify the world and sweeten existence. With what quick trust and ardor, what eager relish, these susceptible creatures, before whom heavenly illusions float, surrender themselves to each other, taste all the raptures of confidential conversation, lift veil after veil till every secret is bare, and, hand in hand, with glowing feet, tread the paths of paradise. (Alger, 269)

Indeed, he is enjoying himself so much he seems unable to stop, reverting to the supposed difference between male and female friendships:

> Romantically, warm and generous as the friendships of school-boys are, those of school-girls are much more so. ... Probably no chapter of sentiment in modern fashionable life is so intense and rich as that which covers the experience of budding maidens at school. ... keener agonies, more delicious passages, are nowhere else known than in the bosoms of innocent school-girls, in the lacerations or fruitions of their first consciously given affections. (Alger, 270)

But all-female institutions could pose a particular threat in isolating women from wider social influences (the debate about Tennyson's stance in *The Princess* goes on). In her 1933 educational work *Retrospect and Prospect*, the campaigning headmistress Sara Burstall recalled her own time at Girton College, Cambridge between 1878–81:

> The lack of personal guidance or stimulus, intellectual or moral, from older and wiser women was a serious weakness then in the college it arose not only from the inevitable paucity of staff, but from what seems to have been a definite aim to leave the students free to develop in their own way. Sentimentality was a deadly thing, influence belonged to schooldays, and personal relations at college might lead to these. (Burstall, 67)

This comment (the 'retrospect' in the title of the book is significant in enabling the reader to interpret the carefully controlled awareness of what by the time of publication had long since come to be perceived as a threat) suggests the increasing sense of unease associated with intense female friendship, but at one time it had, of course, appeared to serve a useful – even conservative – social purpose. It could be employed in various strategic ways, not least for purposes of display; Alger's voyeuristic references to the unrestrained contact between women suggest the usefulness of female friendship as a means of conveying passion to male onlookers without sacrificing the demands of propriety. In theory, this could be one reason for the decline in female friendship after marriage, as the passion it served both to regulate and display could now be safely enacted and contained within a conjugal relationship.

Towards the end of the century the representations of the relationship between female friendship and subsequent marriage became more complex and uneasy, as New Woman fiction began to oppose male interference in female relationships as potentially harmful and disruptive. In *The Odd Women*, published in 1893, Gissing's Rhoda Broughton ultimately rejects marriage, and the disappointed suitor's assumed pity as he subsequently marries elsewhere is difficult to reconcile with Rhoda's decisive return to work and the female community. But mid-century writing on female friendship tends to focus not on rejection of the love plot, but rather on marriage as potential resolution. *Bleak House* and *Shirley* both end with a shift in emphasis from friendship to marriage, and even the later *Diana of the Crossways* (1885) features a conventional ending along the same lines; again, it is a sensation story, Sheridan Le Fanu's 'Carmilla', that concentrates most fully on the friendship itself, leaving its narrating protagonist unmarried at its close. That it should be the controversial sensation fiction that gives fullest expression to romantic friendship suggests the subversive potential of the topic itself as it does of the mode of writing.

Shirley and *Wives and Daughters*

It is perhaps ironic that *Shirley*, one of the central female-authored texts studied here, should also be arguably one of the most conservative on the subject of female social relations. Much critical attention has already been devoted to the friendship between Caroline and Shirley, but in revisiting this aspect of the novel, I hope to show how their relationship exemplifies the archetypal patterns of romantic friendship identified in previous chapters, and how it is able, in the middle years of the century, to use such an intense relationship to what are ultimately conservative rather than subversive ends.

The dominant voice is that of Caroline, the more emotionally intense of the two (indeed, as Shuttleworth points out, the reader is never given access to Shirley's inner thoughts). In keeping with the model of romantic friendship offered briefly by *Aurora Leigh*, Caroline and Shirley initially seem to elevate their feeling for each other over the claims of male society, fantasising about a female community where there would be no distracting male presence. Ultimately, these fantasies give way under the pressures exerted by the conventional plot, as each protagonist marries. All question of competition between friendship and family ties is neatly resolved in this novel, as the friends each marry one of two brothers and so create an apparently seamless transition from platonic to familial relations (in fact, this trajectory was earlier damagingly disrupted in Robert's mercenary pursuit of Shirley).

Pauline Nestor has amply demonstrated both the intensity and the ultimate limitations of the novel's central friendship, pointing out that:

> their speculations on living without men are somewhat undercut by the fact that neither Caroline nor Shirley reveal to each other their secret love for Robert and Louis respectively. None the less their relationship is not presented simply as a negative retreat from heterosexual relationships, but as having a value unique to its especially female qualities ... (Nestor, 116)

Gesa Stedman argues that friendship is perhaps one of the most important concepts in the novel, and that is ultimately contained in marriage, rather than giving way to it.

I would like to build on these insights, relating them to the overall pattern of female romantic friendship in particular – the paradigm rather shakily upheld by Brontë here is one that *Bleak House* would quietly subvert, and 'Carmilla' all but destroy, over the next two decades. Even in Brontë's novel, the privileges of friendship can be exercised to what may seem to a modern reader somewhat questionable ends. Nor are the promises of private happiness held out by female intimacy necessarily fulfilled at every stage. The adequacy of female friendship, questioned and undermined by the male writers considered later in this chapter, is here subordinated to a system in which the female protagonists repeatedly enact and impose male views of the rôle of women, even as they ostensibly resist masculine authority.

In common with male paradigms of romantic friendship, the central relationship in *Shirley* offers – or initially appears to offer – emotional rescue (initially seeming to arrest the course of Caroline's illness by diverting her emotional impulses), exclusivity (despite the concurrent heterosexual love plots) and a distrust of incursions from the opposite sex (which do indeed prove disruptive, just as female interference threatens the basis of male friendship in *Armadale* later in the century). Caroline's increasing loneliness as a single and unemployed woman is largely relieved by her rapid intimacy – characteristic of romantic friendship – with the more flamboyant Shirley, a friendship that initially seems capable of superseding the need for heterosexual romantic involvement. Caroline claims that 'I am too English to get up a vehement friendship all at once' (*Shirley*, 263), but her disjointed expressions of regard – 'I esteem you – I value you: you are never a burden to me – never' –immediately undermine this claim to reserve. Similarly, Shirley states, on their first meeting, that she will be guided by Mrs Pryor's estimation of Caroline, but in appealing to the woman who will later be revealed as her friend's mother, she is already conscious of her adviser's liking for her new acquaintance, which she points out to Caroline. Similarly, her apparently cautious ratification, 'if you really are what at present to me you seem – you and I will suit', is immediately followed by the reminder that 'I have never in my whole life been able to talk to a young lady as I have talked to you this morning. Kiss me – and good-bye' (*Shirley*, 220).

The two fantasise about the promise of an Edenic setting in the woods, without the disruptive presence of men, whom they see as coming between the perfect understanding supposedly shared by women. In an uncharacteristically self-conscious literary register, Caroline describes Nunnwood to Shirley:

> … I know all the pleasantest spots: I know where we could get nuts in nutting time; I know where wild strawberries abound; I know certain lonely, quite untrodden glades, carpeted with strange mosses, some yellow as if gilded, some a sober gray, some gem-green. I know groups of trees that ravish the eye with their perfect, picture-like effects: rude oak, delicate birch, glossy beech, clustered in contrast; and ash trees stately as Saul, standing isolated, and superannuated wood-giants clad in bright shrouds of ivy. Miss Keeldar, I could guide you. (*Shirley*, 214)

The stress in this conversation is on a pre-lapsarian, and so by implication sexless, state of being in which women are free to commune freely and unselfconsciously one with another. As Shuttleworth's argument suggests, the female affinity with the natural world assumes an informed choice rather than an ignorance of the supposedly greater possibilities offered by male–female relations: 'In this Edenic world of female love, the fall, initiation into heterosexual love, would constitute a *loss* of knowledge: Nature would then veil herself from their eyes' (Shuttleworth, 213).

But tellingly, the planned visit to the woods never comes off, and as I will argue, it is precisely their sense of being watched or on display that haunts the female characters, even as each consciously collaborates with male figures in order to advance the marriage plot of the other. None the less, male incursions are seen as productive of distrust between women, and this is borne out when Caroline later assumes that Shirley will marry Robert Moore, whom she herself loves. Again. this sense of the opposite sex as vitiating same-sex friendship parallels a central theme of male-centred texts – *David Copperfield* and *Armadale* both base the destruction, or at least suspension, of male friendship on the tempting presence of a sexually desirable woman.

Again in common with traditional views of romantic friendship, serious illness is posited as a site of both intimacy and the trial of affection or moral worth. Caroline, already weakened by her enforced separation from Robert, is made dangerously ill by her conviction that he loves and will marry her friend. It is through their common experience of illness that Caroline and Robert will ultimately be brought together, and this significantly excludes any rôle played by a friend. But given the crucial status of illness in providing a register of moral character – both of the invalid and of the nurse, it is none the less alarming that Shirley fails so utterly to support Caroline during her period of crisis. In fact, she goes on holiday at the very time that Caroline is considered to be in danger of her life. It is left to Mrs Pryor to support and reveal herself to her daughter, and in one of the most subversive moments in the novel, she undermines the traditional role of the mother in preparing her daughter for marriage, claiming that the conjugal state is almost invariably one of misery for the woman. The warning is ignored, but it resonates uneasily through the novel, suggesting an ambivalent subtext to the marriage plot.

The failure of Shirley to engage with the offered intimacy of the sickroom or to sacrifice her own comfort to the exigencies of her friend's physical decline, is deeply disturbing in itself, and by implication, for the value of female friendship as an ideal. But as I have suggested in Chapter One, it is an anomaly common to a number of female-centred texts, although not all. Ada is forcibly excluded from the sickroom in *Bleak House*, while in Le Fan's vision of unlicensed predatoriness, the eponymous Carmilla actually causes and perpetuates Laura's illness in order to gain possession of her soul as well as her body. Despite the perceived value of womanly tenderness and ministration to the sick, female protagonists in these texts are repeatedly found lacking as regards their treatment of each other during illness. Perhaps in an effort to occlude this failure of female relations, *Shirley* falls back on the convention of family ties as the ultimate expression of social unity, even as the novel disrupts this ideal as well, through its ambiguous portrayal of the damaged errant mother, Mrs Pryor.

The whole question of female rôles and relations is then both conventional and unstable. At one level *Shirley* anticipates the New Woman fiction of the end of the century, in its seemingly radical call for female employment and in its stress on the self-sufficiency of female friendship. But even as these questions are raised, they are undermined by the dissident voices themselves as much as by the conventional marriage plot to which the novel ultimately conforms. Caroline demands suitable employment only because she has been rejected in love; Shirley abandons the ideal of friendship, and in so doing shows its inadequacy.

Further investigation reveals ways in which each protagonist responds throughout to a potential male audience, reinforcing masculine expectations of femininity. While the dynamic between the two is not presented as erotic, Shirley's adoption of a masculine role quite literally obviates the immediate need for male protection, as when she takes charge of a firearm and assures Mr Helstone that she will guard Caroline during the riot at Robert's mill. Shirley repeatedly aligns herself with masculine authority, enacting a dominant rôle within what could be seen as a mock marriage with her more conventional friend. This enactment of rôles both forestalls and anticipates the exigencies of the marriage plot, but almost more importantly, its display alerts the reader to Caroline's suitability as a future wife. There is a sense in which Shirley could be seen to collaborate with Robert Moore, as Nestor points out:

> ... Shirley is paradoxically as much Moore's agent as his rival. Not only does she facilitate various meetings of Caroline and Robert, and keep the possibility of a relationship with Moore before Caroline's imagination, she actually substitutes for Moore in a way that gives fundamental significance to the notion of 'rehearsal for the real'. Shirley is the figure through whom Caroline's love is in time transferred to Robert ... (Nestor, 119)

More significantly, Shirley highlights and at times imposes Caroline's womanly attributes, relating her qualities as a friend to her future rôle as a wife. When Caroline sees Robert wounded at the mill and rushes forward as if to go to him, Shirley physically restrains her in order to protect conventions of female passivity and to avoid embarrassing Moore in front of a male audience. Barbarah Leah Harman argues that in this scene, Shirley is reacting with some acuity to the perception of female publicity as inherently sexual, protecting Caroline from a misconstruction of her motives (which in fact would hardly be a misconstruction at all given the nature of her interest in Robert), that Shirley further gains power from her position as witness to a scene in which she herself is unobserved. But in practical terms her knowledge is all but useless, in that it does not further any particular end (unlike her philanthropic manipulation of Mr Helstone, which, as Harman shows, depends for its effect on the appearance of capitulation while a knowing demeanour is preserved for the reader's benefit and behind the men's heads). Shirley is able to protect Caroline from possible misconstruction, but in so doing, she seems to acknowledge the legitimacy of a male authority that defines female action in conventionally narrow terms. Throughout this scene, her arguments are based on the likely reaction of the men to an unexpected female intrusion, and she endorses the validity of Moore's putative embarrassment in such a case, disavowing feminine intervention in such a scene. Notably, Caroline 'cannot bear to be restrained', suggesting both her impatience of Shirley's admonitions and her own lack of self-control, which by implication necessitates such external intervention. Shirley appeals both to masculine ideals of womanly behaviour and to Caroline's interiorisation of those ideals. Caroline is permitted to express solicitude for the reader's benefit, but it is contained by the relentless logic of her friend, who insists that to go to Robert would be 'To teaze and annoy him; to make a spectacle of yourself and him before those soldiers, Mr Malone, your uncle, et cetera. Would he like it, think you? Would you like to remember it a week hence?' (*Shirley*, 347).

Caroline's range of action is circumscribed both by her gender and more crucially, by her status as a single woman. It is this vulnerability to which Shirley is responding when she curtails her friend's passionate determination to act during this scene. Speech itself, either during or after the event, is impossible to her; indeed, the novel repeatedly shows Caroline attempting to conceal her feelings, or risking the condemnation of others. As Tim Dolin summarises her position:

… Caroline, the woman without property, represents a realism that is in effect unnarratable: absolutely without event or the capacity to institute change. All attempts at self-culture are futile, and all attempts at speech frame her as the stereotypical scheming woman with romantic delusions. (Dolin, 28)

But in thus monitoring and controlling Caroline's behaviour, Shirley herself subverts any real sense in which the former at least might be seen as empowered by her position of secret watchfulness. Caroline ultimately submits to this representation of authority, repressing her instinctive desire to assist Moore in the interests of conforming to a culturally endorsed model of feminine behaviour. In this imposition of behavioural norms, Shirley both demonstrates and enforces Caroline's submission, and therefore her eligibility as a wife.

The tension between passionate feeling and its enforced concealment is characteristic of the dynamic identified by Gesa Stedman, in which a difficult balance between emotion and control must always be maintained, and this balance is constantly scrutinised by Brontë in her portrayal of female characters. As Stedman points out:

That Charlotte Brontë uses a gender framework to discuss the emotions in *Shirley* is no idiosyncrasy on the part of a female author, but rather a feature of the discourses on emotions in general. All writers implicitly link emotionality and gender, for instance by making women blush much more often than men … (Stedman, 153)

In this case, blushing or showing signs of emotion is precisely what Caroline must avoid if she is to escape the censure of a knowing audience, although this effort to maintain acceptable behaviour in the face of her emotion will finally make her ill.

Shirley is the sole audience in front of which Caroline may permit herself both the expression of emotion and the visible effort to control it. But if female confidences are less guarded than heterosexual relations can be, such intimacy is none the less made available for male scrutiny as each displays the other's behaviour to a male lover. It is her superior knowledge of her friend's character that Shirley hints to Robert, both implying her greater intimacy with Caroline and suggesting her attractive (because concealed and restrained) capacity for passion: 'The point I wish to establish is, that Miss Helstone, though gentle, tractable, and candid enough, is still perfectly capable of defying even Mr Moore's penetration' (*Shirley*, 363). The sense of dress rehearsal, in which Caroline is displayed in the act of practising her part, is made quite specific in Shirley's half-joking, half-serious comment at another point in the novel, 'And are you so obedient to a mere caprice of mine? What a docile wife you would make to a stern husband' (*Shirley*, 339). No wonder then that Pauline Nestor sees Shirley as being 'as much Moore's agent as his rival' (Nestor, 119). None the less, this reference to 'a stern husband' suggests ambivalent feelings about Moore, whom it immediately suggests.

Indeed, Shirley is also the most confidently defiant figure in the novel, in her refusal to welcome marriage as an unreserved blessing for the woman. Even as she displays Caroline's attractive qualities for Robert's titillation, Shirley expresses mock jealousy of his power over her friend:

> He keeps intruding between you and me: without him we should be good friends; but that six feet of puppyhood makes a perpetually recurring eclipse of our friendship. (*Shirley*, 263)

But this sense of competitive jealousy does not deter Shirley from her 'moral management' of Caroline in preparation for a conjugal rôle, forcibly concealing her emotional state during the riot, only to hint at her presence to Robert the next day. In an equally disturbing act of counter suppression, Caroline at one point interrupts Shirley's declamations on the status of women in much the same way as the misogynistic Jo has done earlier:

> Shirley, you chatter so, I can't fasten you: be still. And after all, authors' heroines are almost as good as authoresses' heroes.

When Shirley protests that on the contrary, 'women read men more truly than men read women' but that she would not find an editor to publish her view of the subject, Caroline retorts:

> To be sure: you could not write cleverly enough; you don't know enough; you are not learned, Shirley. (*Shirley*, 352)

Through such acts of counterpoised intervention and suppression, each character can be seen to impose behavioural conventions on the other, culminating at the end of the novel in Caroline's approval of Shirley's 'taming' by Louis Moore. Feminine watchfulness and subtlety playfully elude the direct exercise of masculine control, but only to transfer immediate control to the female realm itself, as each character constantly watches and comments on the other in collusion with the aims and interests of a dominant male figure. As Shuttleworth expresses it: 'Both women are quick to imprison each other in the straitjacket of male expectation' (Shuttleworth, 215). It is partly this portrayal of female relations as anticipating and preparing for, as well as reflecting, later marriage that obviates the threat of female autonomy the novel might otherwise be seen to raise.

The control and display of feeling are crucial in relation to the dual romance plot that constitutes the focus of the second half of the novel. Caroline believes that Shirley will marry Robert Moore, and the effort to repress her feelings lead to a serious illness from which she only recovers on finding a bond with her mother that she can legitimately express. Only after Robert's experience of a similarly dangerous illness can the plot be resolved with their understanding and marriage. Shirley meanwhile does not divulge her own feeling for Robert's brother Louis, thus perpetuating the misunderstanding.

In these scenes, the intimacy previously shared by the friends is redirected into intense relationships with others, which neither initially discloses to the other. As Caroline moves from intimacy with her newly discovered mother to the fulfilment of her relationship with Robert Moore, Shirley independently locates her own shift in loyalty from family to husband; it is her uncle whose influence she must withstand in expressing her love for Louis, and again Caroline is excluded from these scenes.

This division is emphasised as each protagonist is seen developing an understanding with Robert and Louis respectively.

Barbara Harman has demonstrated the ways in which Louis Moore appropriates Shirley's personal belongings as a means of fusing intimacy and display, or rather the way in which this appropriation figures intimacy *as* display. In these final scenes, Shirley reveals herself directly to her lover, not through the mediation of her watchful friend. Once this process has been completed and Shirley has confessed her feeling for Louis, the relations between the two friends can be to some extent safely restored, as Caroline and Robert collaborate with Louis in the 'taming' of Shirley. Responsibility for watching and restraining Shirley now passes to her husband, as Caroline approvingly notes the futility of her efforts to postpone the wedding itself.

Caroline's greater tractability has been made explicit throughout the text, in her deferral to Robert even before her engagement – such education as she has enjoyed has taken the form of lessons from his sister Hortense, often under his eye.

The misunderstandings having been resolved and the double marriage plot concluded, Caroline and Shirley are able to adopt familial roles towards each other, and any possible conflict between the demands of friendship and the superior claims of marriage and family are thereby sidestepped. The symbolic status of friendship is maintained, as Gesa Stedman suggests:

> After working through friendship, marriage of convenience without love, and benevolence as compensation for love, [Brontë] finally arrives at a concept of heterosexual love-as-friendship which has left passion behind and carries with it the promise of private and public happiness for all. (Stedman, 79–80)

But the absorption of friendship into marriage and family relations does not provide a convincing resolution to the tensions within female friendship, in its relation to patriarchal control. Rather, *Shirley* raises a series of questions that it does not fully confront, as Caroline's call for female employment and Shirley's desire for independence give way to a conventional marriage plot.

In the terms of romantic friendship, this transfer of feeling and energy is consistent with a scheme that locates female (and indeed male) development within just such a pattern of transfer. According to the conventions held up by Sarah Ellis and other popular writers on the social rôle of women, friendship is both valuable as a rehearsal for marriage and fragile in its transience. Brontë's novel, far from questioning this assessment, offers female friendship as both invaluable in itself and as a means of internalising male authority in the absence of any particular male figure. The ultimate worth of such friendship, and the status of its claims, are left open, as friends become sisters and so obviate the need for such a question. A later female-authored text, Elizabeth Gaskell's *Wives and Daughters*, offers an account of friendship between women that, while compromised from the start, is for that very reason presented as less problematic and apparently unambiguous.

Published serially in *The Cornhill* between 1864 and 1866, Gaskell's last novel works towards marriage in quite straightforward and conservative terms, despite its repeated stress on the feeling between pairs of women. Like Brontë's *Shirley*, it is set some decades before the time of writing (the action takes place in the 1820s), and again as in Brontë's novel, two female friends are rivals for the same man, who is initially attracted to the charismatic newcomer in preference to the woman with whom he has a longstanding relationship and with whom he is shown to be more compatible. In another parallel with *Shirley*, it is this newcomer who is a source of attraction not only to the hero Roger Hamley, but also to the central female protagonist, Molly Gibson.

Molly's capacity for romantic friendship is suggested from the outset, in her appeal for the emotional invalid Mrs Hamley, the mother of the man Molly will ultimately marry. Molly fulfils the rôle of both daughter and companion to Mrs Hamley, but from the beginning her readiness to fall in love with the older son, Osborne, purely on the basis of his questionable poetry, complicates the status of the romantic ideal embodied by the older woman. The absent Osborne indeed functions almost entirely at this point as a medium for Molly's projection of romantic feeling, a function that is superseded after his return home by the interest surrounding Cynthia. This new focus for romantic curiosity screens Molly from the suspicion of having indulged in a fancy for the wrong brother, altering the current of her thoughts and the reader's attention together.

As the daughter of Mr Gibson's second wife, Molly looks forward to forming a sibling relationship with Cynthia. But in the mysterious, quasi-heroic stature she assumes, she also takes the place of the newly returned – and somewhat disappointing – Osborne in Molly's imagination. Cynthia's arrival from France, continually put off by her jealous mother, is anticipated for nearly half the novel. Accounts of her suggest simply that she is beautiful and accomplished, and the first images of her are derived either from Molly's direct questions or from her initial impressions when Cynthia finally arrives. In the first moments of her arrival, the reader is offered a physical description of a highly attractive girl, reinforced by the classic insignia of romantic friendship, 'Molly fell in love with her, so to speak on the instant' (*Wives and Daughters*, 224). She feels that she wants to serve this new sister, and this response is immediately justified by the narrator:

> A school-girl may be found in every school who attracts and influences all the others, not by her virtues, nor her beauty, not her sweetness, nor her cleverness, but by something that can neither be described nor reasoned upon. … A woman will have this charm, not only over men but over her own sex; it cannot be defined, or rather it is so delicate a mixture of many gifts and qualities that it is impossible to decide on the qualities of each. (225–6)

It is her failure to fulfil Molly's expectations in the understood terms of romantic friendship that undermines Cynthia's moral status soon after her arrival in the Gibson household. She confesses herself to be lacking in emotional responsiveness, a failure that she imputes to a lack of motherly care during her childhood and early youth. Even when she engages herself to Roger, she is unable to reciprocate his love, tellingly confessing that her greatest affection is for Molly herself. By her own account, her capacity for romantic affection is so limited that she is able to take her love for Molly as the standard by which any passion should be measured – this odd admission, far from introducing an erotic element into their relations, further underlines the sense of Cynthia's passionlessness:

... I've often told you I've not the gift of loving; I said pretty much the same thing to him. I can respect, and I fancy I can admire, ... but I can never feel carried off my feet by love for any one, not even for you little Molly, and I am sure I love you more than – (396)

But this refusal to engage with Molly's fervid admiration or to exchange expressions of affection, is used to mark her as shallow, and increasingly, secretive as it becomes obvious that Cynthia has a past she is unwilling to indulge. This lack is repeatedly contrasted with Molly's own straightforwardness (made easier by the fact that she has no past to reveal, her first love letter having been intercepted by her father and Osborne Hamley having been less appealing in person than she had expected) and strength of feeling; it is from Molly's point of view that the story of their relationship is seen by the reader.

At one level, Cynthia's lack of responsiveness and her indiscriminating desire to attract others (particularly men) render the question of necessary boundaries in friendship all but redundant. She repeatedly comments that while she is more attached to Molly than to her own mother, she is not capable of any deep feeling for another person. Despite the reference to falling in love, Molly herself is not shown to be particularly intense in her relations with her new sister – rather, she is dreamily poetic, an aspect of her character that has already been revealed in her predilection for reading poetry with Mrs Hamley. None the less, the narrator loses no opportunity of stressing Molly's girlishness, and her growing attraction to Roger Hamley has been made clear to the reader, if not to herself, before Cynthia's arrival. The appearance of Cynthia is well placed to cover the transition of Molly's interest between the two brothers, as well as offering the notorious 'dress rehearsal' and displaying her superior qualities. The conventions of romantic friendship are particularly useful in displaying Molly's predisposition to strong feeling as against Cynthia's inability to love, but there is no overt passion in the friendship between the two girls, and their relationship is enabled more by this notable lack of intensity than by any obvious awareness of boundaries.

Indeed, despite Molly's romanticism, effusive expressions of sentiment are shown to be untrustworthy, being associated predominantly with the affected Mrs Gibson. Feigning surprise to Mr Gibson when he proposes, she follows this up with the memorable 'Call me Hyacinth – your own Hyacinth' (109), only to be embarrassed by Lady Cumnor's revelation that this outcome has been discussed between them only that morning. She will later discourage Roger Hamley as the younger son from visiting her house, only to countenance his engagement to her daughter when she learns of Osborne's mortal illness, and finally encourage Cynthia to marry to advantage elsewhere when her husband tells her that there is disagreement about his diagnosis.

Mrs Hamley is similarly given to romantic outpourings; more sincere and ingenuous than Mrs Gibson, she is no more reliable an arbiter of character, and persistently undervalues Roger, who turns out to be a scientific rather than a literary genius. The moral standard for the novel is set not by literary figures, but by Roger himself and by another scientist, the doctor Mr Gibson. Both Mr Gibson and Roger urge reticence and restraint, even at the cost of repressing difficult feelings altogether. As Emily Blair points out, the narrator similarly:

[expresses] anxiety concerning the direct expression of feelings. Repeatedly, the narrator assigns words the power to express and to define feelings, to give them a distinctness they otherwise might not have. Perhaps more importantly, the narrator warns that when a character acknowledges feelings by putting them into words, the character will be forced to face painful, unpleasant realities. (Blair, 587)

It would appear that Molly's simplicity of motive and action is more valued in the scheme of the novel than the suspect emotionalism she initially seems to endorse, to which the often laconic speech of her father and Roger (specifically described as her mentor from an early stage) stands as a corrective. The capacity to love and be worthy of Roger is linked to the straightforward dutifulness urged by Mr Gibson and Roger himself. Indeed, Roger's passionate declaration of love to Cynthia before leaving on a dangerous expedition overseas is justified partly by his efforts to restrain his emotion and leave it unexpressed. Molly similarly controls her own love for him rather than give it inappropriate expression. As Blair suggests, 'Gaskell's narrator fears what an expression of feelings might do to the lives of the healthy characters in the novel – Mr Gibson, Molly Gibson, and Roger Hamley' (Blair, 588).

But equally, the capacity for female love is foreshadowed by the muted version of romantic friendship represented by Molly. It is Cynthia's failure to meet her friend's expectations that marks her faultiness as a potential wife, even as it ironically points to her fulfilment of a particular ideal – continually described as 'passive' in her response to others, in her seeming plasticity and instinctive subduing of her own personality to fit male expectations and desires, she embodies the ideal of the pliable woman. This apparent passivity is counterbalanced by a vivacious charm, exercised to effect upon her step-father as well as Molly herself. As Terence Wright comments: 'Even the sceptical Mr Gibson, whose daughter's reputation has been threatened by Cynthia's exploitation of her step-sister, cannot resist her for long' (Wright, 55).

In Roger's absence, it is Mr Gibson and the faithful Molly who will supervise Cynthia and attempt to impose standards of conduct which she is unable or unwilling to adopt. She confesses:

> 'I've never lived with people with such a high standard of conduct before; and I don't quite know how to behave.'
> 'You must learn,' said Molly, tenderly. 'You'll find Roger quite as strict in his notions of right and wrong.'
> 'Ah, but he's in love with me!' said Cynthia, with a pretty consciousness of her power. (*Wives and Daughters*, 430)

In yet a further echo of *Shirley*, Molly attempts to control Cynthia's behaviour and protect her reputation (she disentangles her from the blackmailing Preston at the cost of incurring suspicion by her own clandestine meetings with him). She specifically links this function to the absence of Cynthia's future husband, on whose behalf she sees herself as operating. With a telling confusion of motives, she pleads with her father:

'And Roger, – for Roger's sake, you will never do or say anything to send Cynthia away, when he has trusted us all to take care of her, and love her in his absence. Oh! I think if she were really wicked, and I did not love her at all, I should feel bound to watch over her, he loves her so dearly. And she is really good at heart, and I do love her dearly.' (*Wives and Daughters*, 547)

Roger and Cynthia appear all but interchangeable here as objects of earnest affection. The appropriateness of Molly's feeling is underlined by her father's response and implicitly justified by the withholding of maternal care by Mrs Gibson:

'Go to Cynthia' he whispered, and Molly went. She took Cynthia into her arms with gentle power, and laid her head against her own breast, as if the one had been a mother, and the other a child. 'Oh, my darling!' she murmured. 'I do so love you, dear, dear Cynthia!' and she stroked her hair, and kissed her eyelids; Cynthia passive all the while, till suddenly she started up stung with a new idea. (578)

Cynthia has in fact broken off her engagement with Roger without consulting Molly or her father; her 'new idea', that he will end by marrying her friend, is predicated on a desire for her own convenience rather than any intuition of the truth. The insouciance with which she predicts the effortless transfer of his affection suggests that she has been unworthy of the moral guidance offered by her adoptive family. Notably, her passivity under Molly's caresses reinforces the manner in which she habitually receives love she has no intention, or even means, of returning.

But the juxtaposition of Molly's apparent transparency and consistency of behaviour with Cynthia's flightiness thus creates another layer of ambiguity. It is after all Molly, not Cynthia, whose reserve causes her to hide her own love for Roger and pretend to a feeling of simple friendship, ultimately (like Caroline Helstone) making herself ill as a result; Cynthia admits quite candidly that she is incapable of strong feeling, and her coquetting is misinterpreted by the men who fall in love with her in line with their own preconceptions. It is with some insight that she says of herself, 'I am not good, and I never shall be now. Perhaps I might be a heroine still, but I shall never be a good woman, I know' (229). Her deception of men largely depends on their collaboration, while her candour to Molly shocks by its very completeness, refusing to hide behind the language of feminine romanticism. It is unclear whether Cynthia is ultimately to be judged on her concealment of certain facts – her previous engagement to Mr Preston the land agent – or her open avowal of her own inconsistencies.

She is in one sense a female Steerforth, blaming her absent mother for her foibles very much as he blames the lack of paternal guidance when comparing himself with David:

Oh, how good you are, Molly. I wonder, if I had been brought up like you, if I should have been as good. But I've been tossed about so. (344)

Again like Steerforth, she sets out to attract whatever company she finds herself in, with no regard for consequences. But there are no sinister undertones in this case.

When Molly is ill, Cynthia is not given an opportunity to recover moral status by nursing her back to health, because her mother has deliberately concealed the seriousness of the situation rather than curtail her daughter's London visit. She does, however, return immediately on learning the truth. And when Roger terms her 'the false Duessa', Mr Gibson is quick to modify his criticism: 'Come, come! Cynthia isn't so bad as that. She's a very fascinating, faulty creature' (677). Unlike the predatory Steerforth, she is accorded an appropriate marriage rather than a narrative punishment – her 'fascination' is not the destructive power embodied by Dickens's villain, and she is permitted to find her own level in the text rather than being expelled from it. This very absorption, though, denies her any claim to heroic stature; as Wright points out, she 'escapes more or less unscathed, her moral evasiveness rescuing her from the kind of confrontation of the self Mrs Gaskell usually reserves for her heroines' (Wright, 55).

Romantic friendship in this account is used then as a test of moral worth and an index to character, rather than being closely scrutinised as a phenomenon in itself. None the less, it conforms to established paradigms in two key respects: the viewpoint is taken from the more intense or loving figure; marriage is contemplated from the outset, and the central friendship is deployed to safeguard rather than threaten this. While Cynthia's lack of emotion might allow a greater level of emotional expression to Molly, this licence is not implied – in fact, the reference to 'falling in love' is almost the sole indication of a passion after they actually meet. The relationship between the two enacts, and is a necessary part of, Molly's progress towards love, but it is Cynthia's coquetting that dignifies Molly's own – initially unreciprocated – passion for Roger.

The prescribed boundaries of intense same-sex friendships are respected, but this account is largely unproblematic because the aloofness of one party is never exploited to give scope to the passion of the other in a text that disavows passion as tending to be transient or affected. This keynote allows the narrator to avoid the kind of questions that haunt *David Copperfield*, with its loving victim/hero and charming villain. Cynthia is not overburdened with Molly's passion and is untroubled by any such feeling of her own – for both these reasons, there is no real question of narrative punishment, allowing her to be absorbed, seemingly effortlessly, into the text.

Neither the subversive potential of female solidarity nor the dangers of intense friendship between women are fully explored by either Brontë or Gaskell in these novels to which the theme of friendship is so central. Later in the century, the New Woman novel would explore the first idea. The second threat is one to which male writers such as Dickens and Sheridan Le Fanu were fully alive, as their portrayal of female romantic friendship demonstrates.

Bleak House

In keeping with the approved social model of its time, *Bleak House* is structured, at least superficially, by the move of female protagonist from intense same-sex friendship to marriage. The beautiful Ada Clare is set up by Esther's narrative as the heroine of this conventional plot, as Esther herself repeatedly denies her own importance to the story she tells, and focuses on Richard's courtship of Ada even as she rhapsodises about her own friendship with her. As Barickman, Macdonald and

Stark explain, Esther perceives herself as unmarriageable because of her illegitimacy, and her romantic friendship with Ada provides an appropriate outlet for her intense need for love:

> Esther cannot follow the pattern of courtship and marriage allowed a heroine like Ada. So the one deep attachment she does feel free to express, her love for Ada, assumes many of the qualities of romantic love, a version of the role she unconsciously desires, the role she would ordinarily assume in this society, the role that could most easily and fully give her the love and sense of identity she needs. (Barickman, MacDonald and Stark, 80)

But a closer reading of the text throws up certain tensions and inconsistencies within this putative model. Firstly, friendship survives marriage in both senses, as Richard Carstone dies leaving his young wife to be represented by Esther's controlling narrative. The structure of this narrative itself contains the story of Ada and Richard's marriage, and so subtly stresses the governing importance of female friendship, in opposition to the expectations that narrative itself has raised. Secondly, the marriage that has been set up as the assumed resolution is not the one with which the novel ends; Ada is left a widow at the end of the book, and it is Esther who assumes the coveted role of wife and mother, while Ada herself takes on Esther's original function as John Jarndyce's housekeeper.

In its passionate expression and its insistence on the inherent selflessness of Esther's feeling at least, the central friendship between her and Ada is a paradigmatic romantic friendship as outlined by Sarah Ellis or Dinah Mulock Craik – Esther herself describes it as having been, significantly before her own marriage, 'that sisterly affection which was the grace and beauty of my life' (*Bleak House*, 638), although on further analysis this statement proves to be problematic. That this relationship is intended as a recognisably romantic friendship is clear from its defining features, many of which it shares with the David/Steerforth and Caroline/Shirley models. While Esther is remembered by generations of readers for her overpowering mode of expression, her characteristic outpourings are reserved almost entirely for her female friends, and Ada in particular – when her mother disappears, it is the quiet practicality noted by other characters throughout the novel that is confirmed by an approving Inspector Bucket.

A perceived similarity of social status and experience is fundamental to such a relationship, where the affinity between the characters is based not least on shared class values that allow the description of their affection as 'sisterly' or familial. Sarah Tytler (Henrietta Keddie) and other writers of mid-century conduct manuals, stress the advisability of keeping intense friendships between members of the same (by implication, middle) class; in theory at least, this shared status secures an equal distribution of power and entails similar expectations on either side.

It is interesting to compare Esther's effusions on meeting Ada with the more restrained tone she adopts in talking to Caddy Jellyby, who is of a lower social class and to whom she stands in the relation of patron. In conversation with Caddy after several meetings, she proffers the relatively cautious invitation, 'I begin to have a great affection for you, and I hope we shall become friends' (*Bleak House*, 214).

By contrast, Esther and Ada are mutually attracted at their first meeting, and Esther rhapsodises:

> I saw in the young lady, with the fire shining upon her, such a beautiful girl! With such rich golden hair, such soft blue eyes, and such a bright, innocent, trusting face! ... She came to meet me with a smile of welcome and her hand extended, but seemed to change her mind in a moment, and kissed me. In short, she had such a natural, captivating, winning manner, that in a few minutes we were sitting in the window seat, with the light of the fire upon us, talking together, as free and happy as could be. (38)

In a passage deleted at proof stage, Ada blushes as she fantasises about their possible life together, speculating about how much they would need to live on in the case of an adverse Chancery judgement. Female fantasies of a life together are not unusual in Victorian writing – Elizabeth Barrett Browning's Aurora Leigh posits a secluded life with the ruined Marian before a convenient plot convention allows her to marry her cousin Romney after all, while Marian renounces romantic love altogether; Caroline and the eponymous Shirley indulge briefly in the same wish, suggesting Charlotte Brontë's attraction to the idea of purely female communion. In Dickens's novels, however, such desires are potentially transgressive – most obviously in *Little Dorrit*, the relationship between Tattycoram and the unrestrainedly passionate Miss Wade has lesbian implications, and Tattycoram must be rescued from this implied 'fall' by the paternalist Meagles. The relationship between Esther and Ada then must be protected from this possibility if it is to be upheld as an ideal, a necessity which creates its own peculiar problems within the constraints of a first-person narrative. If the genuine feeling of a participant in romantic friendship is to withstand possible misinterpretations that that narrator, by definition, cannot openly acknowledge, the most obvious strategy is to define this innocence against a more ambiguous figure. But where David Copperfield is insulated by his own innocence from the insinuations of the more worldly Steerforth, both Esther and Ada are clearly intended to be seen as 'pure', and their friendship develops under the auspices and close supervision of a benevolent male guardian. In the first half of the novel, their relationship is not superseded by a heterosexual romance, as in *David Copperfield*, but is carefully constructed in relation to the Richard/Ada marriage plot against which it is held in tension. Esther repeatedly introduces the theme of romantic love between the cousins, even as she emphasises her own centrality – Richard's status as active agent in the marriage plot means that he is removed from the domestic sphere fairly early on in order that he may earn a living sufficient to support his future wife. Paradoxically, this removal places him in much the same position as a more subversive character such as Steerforth, effectually expelling him from the site of same-sex friendship just as Steerforth is expelled in reverse to make way for a heterosexual love plot. This concentration on female domestic space, facilitated by the insistent voice of a consciously feminine narrator, further problematises the suggestion that friendship will ultimately be superseded by marriage – at this stage, heterosexual romance faces an unequal competition with same-sex friendship. The delicate balance Esther has resolutely and subtly upheld throughout her narrative begins to fracture with Ada's marriage, and is finally overthrown in the final pages, where Esther herself creates a new household with Alan Woodcourt, and so emphasises Ada's questionable status as a surplus woman in the old Bleak House.

Esther's narrative – as a succession of more or less irritated critics have pointed out – is highly tendentious in places. Her evangelical upbringing is itself, in the context of the novel, enough to undermine her constant declarations of unworthiness, as this assumption of personal sin is associated with Christian humility, and by extension, worthiness. In other contexts, Dickens mercilessly satirises this tendency – not the least famous of his evangelical hypocrites is Chadband in *Bleak House* itself, whose professions of humility are designed to point attention to his supposed religious virtue, and who ends the novel by attempting to blackmail the genuinely upright Sir Leicester Dedlock. In more serious vein, Dickens repeatedly stresses the damage inflicted on children by an evangelical upbringing – Esther and Arthur Clennam in *Little Dorrit* are, psychologically speaking, two of his most maimed characters. Like Eliot's Maggie Tulliver (herself drawn to evangelical asceticism), Esther feels a deep-seated craving for affection, famously striving to *win* love through her manner towards others, and hoarding evidence of the high regard in which she is held by those around her.

This underlying anxiety about her relations with others further undermines her account of her friendship with Ada, as her insistence on their exclusive feeling for each other comes to appear obsessive and perhaps one-sided in a novel that is overtly concerned with the inclusiveness of family life. With no apparent resentment, Esther rehearses the list of more or less unappealing names she is accorded in Bleak House – 'Old Woman, and Little Old Woman, and Cobweb, and Mrs Shipton, and Mother Hubbard, and Dame Durden, and so many names of that sort that my own name soon became quite lost among them' (*Bleak House*, 111) – as a proof of the love she has managed to secure; meanwhile, she herself names Ada, calling her 'my pet' or 'my darling girl' from an early point in the narrative.

If this friendship appears consciously intense and even possessive in its bearings, it is Esther, then, who presents it in her chosen terms, telling the story and implicitly casting rôles. Notably, Esther's nicknames are accorded to her by the household in general, while the more intimate endearments she bestows on Ada denote their personal relationship, as signified in the constant use of the possessive pronoun 'my'.

There are certainly some grounds for doubt about the reciprocity of such exclusive feeling. While Esther directly glorifies Ada, the latter's compliments in return are often mediated through conversations with others, as when Ada praises the way in which it 'rained Esther' at the Jellybys', in talking not to her but to Jarndyce. Such use of indirection repeatedly testifies to the other characters' sense of Esther's worth, but she is not above attributing sentiments to them that are not expressed in any verifiable way, as when she recalls an early walk in the flower garden of Bleak House:

> with my darling at her window up there, throwing it open to smile out at me, as if she would have kissed me from that distance. (106)

Elsewhere, positive feedback is directly relayed to the reader with characteristic expressions of reluctance – a seemingly evasive strategy that serves effectively to focus the reader's attention on what is being said.

It is in keeping with the pattern I have identified as being characteristic of literary romantic friendship that it should be Esther, the more intense character, whose point of view is so insistently offered directly to the reader, Ada's comments being mediated through her friend's first-person narrative. As other critics have noted, however, Esther is not necessarily a reliable narrator, and the very structure of her narrative – the red herrings, the supposed uncertainty about whose story she is meant to be relating – exemplifies this textual instability.

As I have suggested, the first-person narrative incorporates the first – Ada's – romance plot, within a governing pattern of female friendship. Ada's romantic attraction to her cousin Richard is seemingly pre-dated by her equally loving response to Esther, where the status of both women as middle-class and inherently pure, allows a fuller and more immediate expression than is possible to the conventions of a love plot. But again Esther employs her power as narrator in the way she chooses to tell her story, deliberately concealing the ending as it works towards an unexpected conclusion.

In the early stages, she presents herself as indispensable to the progress of Richard and Ada's courtship, despite the possibility raised by the Chancellor's possible misapprehension – on hearing that 'a suitable companion' has been provided, he completes the sentence with 'For Mr Richard Carstone?' (40). It is not clear whether he is referring to Ada, to whom he has just been introduced, or to Esther, who is hastily brought forward with the explanation that she is to be a companion for Ada. This ambiguous suggestion that Esther might be a suitable wife for Richard is duly reported by the narrator herself, but tellingly, any such contingency is overlooked by the group at Bleak House, and she herself channels any resentment she might be supposed to feel into furthering Richard's relationship with her friend.

Much of her importance in this respect is conveyed through her personal observation alone, rather than being supported by the remembered comments of the lovers themselves. In one scene at the theatre she asserts confidently:

> As to escaping Mr Guppy by going to the back of the box, I could not bear to do that; because I knew Richard and Ada relied on having me next them, and that they could never have talked together so happily if anybody else had been in my place. (184)

This statement is not supported by any comment from either Richard or Ada themselves, and this lack of evidence for her centrality in the love plot suggests that contrary to what she says, Esther's function may be largely self-serving. In recounting events in her own terms, she continually pushes Richard to the confines of his own story, placing herself figuratively as well as literally between the other two. When she is told that Richard has finally declared himself, Esther recalls how:

> They brought a chair on either side of me, and put me between them, and really seemed to have fallen in love with me, instead of one another; they were so confiding, and so trustful, and so fond of me. (194)

It is such flashes of humour that alone make this narrator bearable to some readers, and yet the ironic comment is worth noting for another reason – arguably, Esther may covet Ada's position, and in drawing attention to her own importance as mediator, she covertly undermines the subordinate role to which she has in theory been relegated. When Richard later succumbs to the 'curse' of the Chancery suit and distances himself from Jarndyce, Ada is left to the sympathy of Esther, and when the cousins ultimately marry, Esther ghoulishly listens at the door of their new home, as if reluctant to relinquish her rôle as chaperone and confidante. Richard dying shortly afterwards, the friendship between the two women is in theory fully recovered, but it is just at this point that Esther herself leaves the Jarndyce household for her own marriage with the more eligible Alan Woodcourt. Jarndyce comments that both houses are now Ada's home, but that his must take precedence. In a complete volte-face, this development instates the now penurious Ada as de-sexed housekeeper to Jarndyce – though she is spared the final humiliation of a daughterly marriage, the very fact of her unattended residence with him precludes the possibility of the narrative representing her in sexualised terms. Emphasising the point, Ada is instructed to address Jarndyce in future not as 'Cousin John', but as 'Guardian', Esther's own name for him. The disturbing effect of this volte-face is significantly increased by the structure of Esther's narrative, which withholds this information even as she details her own reluctance to live alone with Jarndyce as his wife, and appears to be moving towards the final resolution of Ada's union with Richard.

Ada, then, is ultimately denied the fulfilment of a loving marriage that, according to Sarah Ellis, could alone provide satisfaction for a woman in adult life. Indeed, it cannot necessarily be assumed that her friendship with Esther has ever been sufficient in itself, having been always contained within a family circle. As Ellis put it in *The Daughters of England*:

> Friendship, which is narrowed between two individuals, and confined to that number alone, is calculated only for the intercourse of married life, and seldom has been maintained with any degree of lasting benefit or satisfaction, even by the most romantic and affectionate of women. True friendship is of a more liberal and expansive nature, and seldom flourishes so well as when extended through a circle. (337)

It will be remembered that Ada's naming of Esther is a shared activity, in which other members of the household participate, and that her declarations of regard are as often made to either Jarndyce or Richard as to Esther herself. It is not the plot outcome alone, then, that complicates the status of this central female friendship.

If it is possible to question the authority of Esther's pronouncements, it is likewise possible to doubt the integrity of her motives in her presentation of friendship. In his study of *Bleak House*, Alexander Welsh identifies a latent hostility to Ada embedded in Esther's narrative, and suggests that her propounded sentiments do not necessarily accord with her actions. He points out that, tellingly, Esther does not allow Ada anywhere near her during her illness, or even when the danger is past – given the central importance of nursing in Victorian fiction, as identified by Miriam Bailin, and its place in romantic friendship, this rejection undermines the very capacity for love and moral heroism that Esther so perseveringly attributes to her friend.

At the moment of crisis, Ada is withheld from the offices of self-sacrificing friendship that would justify Esther's representation of her as the model heroine – instead, she is placed in an invidious position, necessarily failing to afford such attentions as Charley is able to offer, and so simultaneously emphasising Esther's loving concern in protecting her from infection:

> I had heard my Ada crying at the door, day and night; I had heard her calling to me that I was cruel and did not love her; I had heard her praying and imploring to be let in to nurse and comfort me, and to leave my bedside no more, but I had only said, when I could speak, 'Never, my sweet girl, never! ... (514)

Notably, Ada's response to her friend's illness is highly charged and emotional, but her desire to risk her own health is upstaged by Esther's equally determined refusal to let her enter the sickroom.

But, Welsh notes, there is a long interval of convalescence during which Esther refuses to see Ada at all, giving as her reason, somewhat unconvincingly, that she does not want to be seen until she has first accustomed herself to her altered appearance. Welsh's point is that this prevarication on Esther's part serves to protract Ada's anxiety unnecessarily. In the wider context of literary heroines and their sacrificial response to illness, such a refusal to accept the offices of friendship further deprives Ada of her angelic status (indeed, it recalls the somewhat uneasy moment in *Shirley* when Caroline becomes ill and Shirley goes on holiday). Once again, Esther could be seen as tendentiously realigning rôles, drawing attention to her own virtuous behaviour in contradistinction to Ada, who is obliged to remain passive long after the infectious phase of the illness has passed.

This suspicion of hidden motives once aroused, Esther's liking for window seats takes on more complex shades of meaning, and it becomes difficult to read a passage such as the following with an entirely easy mind:

> [in the bedroom at Bleak House] there was a hollow window-seat, in which, with a spring-lock, three dear Adas might have been lost at once. (78)

Ultimately, the plot does carry out this fantasy, allowing Ada to be 'lost' in Bleak House, as her self-sacrificial role in caring for her husband is subsumed, after his untimely death, in her sexless care of her guardian's depleted household. Denied both a socially endorsed sexual destiny and the heroic status achieved by Esther (who loses her looks in selflessly caring for Jo, only to regain them, as the last lines of her narrative imply, while she is forgetting to look in the mirror) – Ada is rendered almost useless as well as sexless and voiceless at the end of the novel.

Certainly, the importance of romantic friendship to *Bleak House* is apparent in its very structure, in which Esther's fixation with Ada is only superseded by her feeling for Alan Woodcourt towards the end of the novel, and Ada's courtship and marriage is contained within a narrative of female friendship. But militating against any simplistic reading of this friendship as conventionally desirable is the reversal of the expectation Esther's narration has raised in the reader. When she marries the eligible Woodcourt and Ada is left as a dependent widow, the final pages of the book firmly reinforce the triumph of this ostensibly marginalised figure by humiliating her potential rival, seemingly justifying Welsh's reading of the central friendship as more fraught than Esther herself would have the reader believe.

Esther's self-abnegation and service of those around her leads, the outcome seems to suggest, to a well-deserved attainment of the very goal she has ostensibly denied herself – marriage to a suitable man. This renunciation of a desired object in order ultimately to gain it is typical of Dickens's narratives. Ironically, it is also a formula associated with evangelical writing, and as such, it is a device that he was prone to ridicule elsewhere for encouraging sanctimonious hypocrisy. In this context, it is important to remember that Esther's story is not related by an approving third-person narrator, but is almost entirely self-told. Where the third-person narrator of *Bleak House* is famously difficult to pin down, the ambiguity in Esther's relation of events can be located not in the tone of her narration, but in the status of the narrator herself.

Aurora Leigh

Elizabeth Barrett Browning's major verse novel *Aurora Leigh* has one significant parallel with Tennyson's *In Memoriam* of 1850 – it celebrates an intense friendship with a woman who by its end describes herself as to all intents and purposes dead, and specifically dead to earthly love (other than for her child). In its treatment of romantic friendship, *Aurora Leigh* encapsulates many of the themes treated by fiction of the time: it stakes out its ground on gendered terms; the displacement of passion onto a female friend is reconciled with the heroine's love for her male cousin in the final denouement; false sentiment is purveyed by the fashionable for their own purposes (a theme explored in the satire of Thackeray). More radically, the fantasy of a female Utopia is briefly fulfilled, as Aurora crosses class boundaries and rejects the insidious Lady Waldemar to form a community with the working-class Marian Erle and her illegitimate child.

In most accounts of romantic friendship, its defining sensibility is heavily dependent on class and education, but *Aurora Leigh* successfully challenges such assumptions. Even if, as Helen Cooper and others suggest, Aurora finds strategies for feeling 'charity toward a poor sufferer while scorning her class' (Cooper, 165), the text none the less places the innate goodness of a working-class woman above both the acquired manners of an upper-class rival and even the intellectual commitment of the saintly Romney, who must learn to value human love before he can finally marry his female counterpart, Aurora.

But despite such radical elements, friendship in this account largely conforms to mid-century ideals. Significantly, it is located specifically in the natural realm, being associated with the Italy of Aurora's idyllic childhood; through a recurring trope of maternity to the exclusion of the father, it is further clearly gendered as female. Aurora makes it clear from the outset of her friendship with Marian that female solidarity is more sustainable than the fraught relations between men and women. When Romney insensitively states that his intended marriage to Marian is motivated by his socialist agenda and not personal love, Aurora recalls:

There I turned
And kissed poor Marian, out of discontent.
The man had baffled, chafed me, till I flung
For refuge to the woman, – as, sometimes,
Impatient of some crowded room's close smell,
You throw a window open and lean out
To breathe a long breath in the dewy night.
(*Aurora Leigh*, Fourth Book, 345)

Although their first meeting is in an insalubrious area of London, Marian is associated from the outset in Aurora's mind with the natural world in which she will not see her until several years later, and she will later think of her as 'Poor Marian Erle, my sister Marian Erle, / My woodland sister, sweet Maid Marian (*Aurora Leigh*, Fifth Book, 1 095–6). This pastoral imagery is strongly associated with female friendship. The importance of a specifically female pastoral becomes clear when Marian's drunken father burns down Leigh Hall, which Romney has intended as a rural sanctuary for the poor.

But the contemporary fashion for the supposed simplicity of romantic friendship can itself render it suspect in another context. Romantic friendship as perceived in London can act both as an antidote to, or conversely as a means of serving, social expectation. Marian stands for pre-lapsarian innocence despite her harsh upbringing and her situation as an unemployed seamstress in one of the poorest areas of London (this status will be magnified when Aurora comes across her as an unmarried mother in Paris, some time before the creation of their self-sufficient household in Tuscany, the land of Aurora's own idyllic childhood). Significantly, as several critics have commented, Aurora initially imposes her own voice on the telling of Marian's story, very much as Romney attempts to impose his socialist values on his own relationship with her. Even when Marian takes up the story in her own words, when she meets Aurora in Paris, it is the literate poet who writes it down and contextualises it. This retelling may function both as an appropriation of Marian's voice, but also, as Angela Leighton points out, it constitutes a powerful defiance of prohibitions on female speech:

> Although Marian tells her own story, with challenging moral assurance, it is Aurora who writes it. The relationship between them thus reflects on Aurora's purpose as a poet. Not only does she take up with the other woman, and without the man for whom they should be rivals; she also takes up Marian's story as her own. That the story is a forbidden one throws into relief Aurora's consciousness of being a woman poet whose purpose is to break the rule of silence. In Marian she finds a subject which the world denies and which convention prohibits her from telling. She tells it, therefore, with crusading energy. (Leighton, 151)

But if Marian represents an attempt at escape from class antagonism, associated by Aurora with the fresh air from a window in the midst of a claustrophobic city, London also contains the false sensibility of the fashionable poseuse. The unscrupulous Lady Waldemar defies etiquette in speaking to Aurora of her unrequited love for Romney, not because she is artlessly affectionate, but because she wishes to appear more ingenuous than she is – in love with Romney, she attempts to gain Aurora's friendship in order to enlist her aid against Marian, and Aurora later reminds her:

> did I ever ink my lips
> By drawing your name through them as a friend's,
> Or touch your hand as lovers do? Thank God
> I never did …
> (*Aurora Leigh*, Seventh Book, 289–92)

Here, social standing is no guarantee of genuine feeling, and it is rather Marian who is influenced by passionate sensibility – lured away by Lady Waldemar's accomplice, she writes to Romney on what would have been their wedding day, telling him that Aurora resembles him and has been of comfort to her; the implication is that what she could not with propriety have taken from Romney himself, she has been able to accept safely from the feminine Aurora. Even this comment is complicated by Aurora's own feelings for Romney. Stone points out that:

> Lady Waldemar is linked to Aurora through a complex series of plot and character parallels and contrasts that bring into relief both Aurora's limitations and her growing strengths. Thus Aurora climbs up Marian's garret for much the same reason that Lady Waldemar has climbed up to her third-floor Kensington flat. (Stone, 166)

Unlike her aristocratic rival, Aurora finds fulfilment initially in her relationship with Marian rather than pursuing Romney himself. She will later reiterate the gendered terms of their friendship when she realises that she has wrongly accused Marian of sexual transgression (she has in fact been lured into a brothel and raped):

> … I, convinced, broken utterly,
> With woman's passion clung about her waist
> And kissed her hair and eyes – 'I have been wrong,
> Sweet Marian' (weeping in a tender rage)
> (*Aurora Leigh*, Sixth Book, 778–81)

Romantic friendship is explicitly linked by both participants to the experience of a religious conversion, as Marian recalls her response to Aurora in terms reminiscent of Tennyson's *In Memoriam*, 'She kissed me mouth to mouth: I felt her soul / Dip through her serious lips in holy fire' (*Aurora Leigh*, Fourth Book, 940–41). In her turn, Aurora will make increasing use of religious imagery in her appeals to Marian when they are reunited abroad. Having heard Marian's story, she sets out her own ideal of a female Utopia, in which no father will be necessary to bring up Marian's child:

'Come with me, sweetest sister,' I returned,
'And sit within my house and do me good
From henceforth, thou and thine! ye are my own
From henceforth. I am lonely in the world,
And thou art lonely, and the child is half
An orphan. Come – and henceforth thou and I
Being still together will not miss a friend,
Nor he a father, since two mothers shall
Make that up to him. I am journeying south,
And in my Tuscan home I'll find a niche
And set thee there, my saint, the child and thee ...'
(*Aurora Leigh*, Seventh Book, 117–27)

This proposal appears to supersede the role of men. It is significant, however, that after ten years of failure to recognise her love for Romney, Aurora acknowledges that she made a mistake in refusing him not only when she believes him to be newly married to Lady Waldemar, but at the moment when she begins her new life of communion with Marian. As Aurora takes on Romney's role with regard to Marian, it seems momentarily as if marriage may be superseded by romantic friendship (the similarity between Aurora and Romney has been stressed by both Lady Waldemar and Marian herself). But this brief idyll is enabled largely by Marian's perception of herself as dead to earthly love, a claim that subtly pre-empts any suspicion of the erotic – in these final scenes, she is presented as virtually disembodied, a device which will also allow her to reject Romney's renewed proposals at the end of the poem, and so bring about the traditional resolution of marriage between the central figures.

But Aurora's transient communion with Marian has been crucial in reconciling her poetic vocation with Romney's philanthropy. Certainly, her social benevolence is exercised by her engagement with Marian after learning of the rape. Helen Cooper suggests that:

> transformation from imagining the child as a 'thing' to determining to help both mother and child is Aurora's first altruistic move. Until this point, survival for her in a society that demanded woman's self-abnegation necessitated Aurora's absorption in her own affairs. ... Aurora's growth into a harmonious selfhood is achieved through love as well as art, and through a compassionate sympathy for Marian's situation on Marian's terms, not according to convention. Marian is the instrument of this transformation. (Cooper, 172)

But the offer of help is not entirely one-way. Early in the poem, Marian has been allowed the lines:

'Ah you,' she said, 'who are born to such grace,
Be sorry for the unlicensed class, the poor,
Reduced to think the best good fortune means
That others, simply, should be kind to them.'
(*Aurora Leigh*, Fourth Book, 53–7)

Aurora may be recalling these words years later, when Marian leaves her child to comfort her:

'But now,' I said, 'you leave the child alone.'
'And you're alone,' she answered, – and she looked
As if I too were something. Sweet the help
Of one we have helped! Thanks, Marian, for such help.
(*Aurora Leigh*, Seventh Book, 511–14)

It is this key moment of humility in accepting help from one to whom she has been charitable that suggests the most important lesson Aurora will learn from her romantic friendship – from offering patronage, she has progressed to the sharing of an equal relationship with a woman socially removed from her by both class and misfortune. As Angela Leighton notes:

> It is interesting that, although Aurora takes the philanthropist Romney's place in her relation to Marian, it is really Marian who finally saves *her*. … The quest for Marian is a quest to go on living and writing, in spite of and even, now, careless of, the seductive, haunting memories of the dead. (Leighton, 155)

Aurora Leigh is more far-reaching than Brontë's novel *Shirley*, idealising the physical embraces of female friends as tending to sanctity or at least lead to religious inspiration, in contrast to the failures of its central male figure, who is initially ill-equipped to respond to or direct individual passion. But the speaker is aware of the limits imposed on female friendship – Aurora and Marian briefly achieve the pastoral idyll aspired to by the women in *Shirley* (whose wood is subsequently razed to make factories). But at precisely the point where they create a female-centred community, the references to passion and the spontaneous 'holy fire' of female kisses must be cut off. This idyllic communion appears tenable precisely because it is of short duration, and the last lines celebrate not the relationship between the two women, but the final understanding between Aurora and Romney. It is this heterosexual embrace that resolves the final scene, as Marian literally disappears into shadow and Aurora is restored to social usefulness in her complementary relationship with Romney. Romantic friendship, having served to rescue her from the loneliness of existence as an 'old maid', will finally propel her back into a heterosexual plot as Marian firmly rejects Romney's proposal to marry her rather than his cousin. This denouement allows full play to the traditionally conservative ends of romantic friendship – in this 'rehearsal', Aurora is permitted an outlet for passion that rescues her from the dread alternatives of sexual fall or the degeneration so feared by Caroline Helstone in *Shirley*; the friendship finally ends on the entrance of the successful suitor, as Aurora looks forward to marriage.

'Carmilla'

Like *David Copperfield*, 'Carmilla' is narrated some time after the expulsion and death of a subversive figure by the intended victim. But unlike the authoritative narrative voice proffered by David, Laura's status is ambiguous – she is not herself the judge of the events she narrates and her narrative is contained within a medical treatise, the overarching framework of Le Fanu's *In a Glass Darkly*. This mediation places her in the position of a medical case rather than a governing voice – the inclusions of such anecdotal case studies are familiar from medical text books of the time, and invite the reader to participate in a narrative judgement of the histories being related.

The relation of Laura's 'case' in the archives of Dr Heselius in some ways anticipates the work of Havelock Ellis, in that her exposure to female erotic influence renders her listless and ill, even as the unsuitability of her friendship with the dangerous Carmilla is obscured by the conventions of mid-century female intercourse. The familiar themes of obsession, loss of control, and the splitting of characteristics between two central protagonists, are crucial to this governing perspective. This story constitutes a highly critical view of romantic friendship, as Le Fanu's vampire subverts the ideal of self sacrifice, attempting literally to sacrifice Laura rather than herself.

Although the story is judged within the terms of a scientific/medical discourse, the older judgement according to religious principles is concurrently maintained. Where romantic friendship traditionally makes an appeal to religious precedent, Carmilla's telling rejection of Christian ritual identifies her as an opponent of accepted moral values. One instance is her carefully conveyed horror of funeral rites, as she expresses repugnance at the procession of a villager's coffin, having herself killed the girl in question. Laura later recalls:

> If it had not been that it had casually come out in one of our careless talks that she had been baptized, I should have doubted her being a Christian. Religion was a subject on which I had never heard her speak a word. ('Carmilla', 277)

This lack of interest in religion serves as an index to moral character, even as the scientific study of the vampire phenomenon will ultimately serve to identify and explain the lesbian element in the story. In maintaining a dual framework for judgement, both medical and moral, 'Carmilla' is therefore able to locate its radical critique of romantic friendship within the traditional spectrum, while anticipating the later terms of *fin de siècle* sexology.

The subversively sexual element in the story is contained, as in *David Copperfield*, through the simple technique of splitting traits between two central characters, but its continuing power remains recognisable despite the climactic resolution, in which the threat is eliminated presumably without the Laura of the time of the story being aware of what precisely has been at stake. Regina Barreca sees the equation of sexuality and death represented by Carmilla as characteristic of vampire fiction in the most crucial sense:

> The vampire's combination of death and sexual activity brings one of the nineteenth century's major public preoccupations – death, the dead, funerals, tombs – together with its major private and secret preoccupation, sex and sexuality. One could be talked about and celebrated incessantly; the other could not be talked about at all, except by thus combining it with death and so disguising it. The vampire story supplies a metaphoric vocabulary to represent certain obsessions and anxieties not otherwise admissible into literature … (Barreca, in *Sex and Death in Victorian Literature*, 35)

Significantly – in terms of the paradigm I have identified - Ken Gelder further argues that:

> ... same-sex desire between women is licensed, then managed or regulated (by 'eliminating' its object) – but continues to be licensed even after this, through Laura's 'reveries'. (Gelder, 61)

I would argue that the status of lesbian attachment introduced by Carmilla is never licensed, although it is pervasive. Certainly, it is disturbing to Laura, as her divided response and careful analysis, despite her admission of a continuing responsiveness, demonstrates. Victor Sage notes that Carmilla's invitation to Laura to die 'as lovers may' assumes her acquiescence, as 'Predation is glossed over: in this rhetoric, all is mutual' (Sage, 196). As Laura's apathy increases in response to Carmilla's influence, this mutuality becomes more obviously real – at the end of her story, Laura recounts how, many years later, she sometimes starts from a reverie, thinking she hears Carmilla's step at the door.

The continuing fascination for Laura, as for her earlier counterpart, David, lies in the very ambiguity of her friend's nature, which allows for a series of responses. Though rather unhelpfully conflating romantic friendship with the embodiment of physical desire (Auerbach, 51), Nina Auerbach stresses both the eroticism of Carmilla's feeling for Laura and its essential lovingness. Pointing out that in vampire literature as in more conventional representations, female relationships contained more scope for affection than their male equivalent, she reminds the reader of Le Fanu's story that:

> In the nineteenth century, vampires were vampires *because* they loved. They offered an intimacy, a homoerotic sharing, that threatened the hierarchical distance of sanctioned relationships. Generally contorted and vicarious, that love expressed itself most fully through men's imaginations of women, those licensed vehicles of intimacy. (Auerbach, 60)

Despite her apparent languor, Carmilla is decidedly intense in her expressions of affection, although Faderman points out that at the time of writing (1872), 'it was still conceivable that, aside from Carmilla's most extravagant utterances about hating, her behavior might be considered appropriate within the framework of romantic friendship – apparently Laura sees it as such' (Faderman, 288). Faderman goes on to suggest that Le Fanu 'may have been somewhat confused in his intent' (Faderman, 288–9), but this seems unlikely given Laura's retrospective insistence on her own rejection of her friend's extravagant advances. Disrupting the pattern of naïve complicity set up by Dickens in *David Copperfield*, Laura repeatedly draws attention to her own discomfiture at Carmilla's excessive displays of feeling. She herself is highly idealistic, and participates fully in the conventions of romantic friendship, from her first interview with Carmilla in the latter's bedroom:

> I took her hand as I spoke. I was a little shy, as lonely people are, but the situation made me eloquent, and even bold. She pressed my hand, she laid hers upon it, and her eyes glowed, as, looking hastily into mine, she smiled again and blushed. ('Carmilla', 259)

Notably, this interchange, reminiscent though it is of a heterosexual courtship scene, can be accommodated within the limits of an intense female friendship. Laura's insistence on her friend's beauty, which recurs throughout her recollections, is deployed to suggest not an erotic temptation, but an acceptable reason for her trust in this mysterious stranger. Dickens's Lizzie Hexham and Bella Wilfer are similarly drawn together in *Our Mutual Friend*, as are the male protagonists in Ouida's *Under Two Flags*. Playing on this convention, Carmilla herself claims to trust Laura for the same reason. Each girl expresses herself as reassured by the other's beauty, despite a mutual recognition from a disturbing childhood vision; Carmilla claims:

> If you were less pretty I think I should be very much afraid of you, but being as you are, and you and I both so young, I feel only that I have made your acquaintance twelve years ago, and have already a right to your intimacy ... ('Carmilla', 260)

Like other predators, Carmilla is quick to enlist convention on her side, but as Sage shows in his discussion of the story, her success is based on a constant mirroring of Laura's own concerns; she both reflects and appropriates her victim's reactions in order to gain her trust and direct her responses:

> It is brilliant theatre, especially the idea of 'Carmilla' being 'afraid' of Laura ... And the idea that they dreamed each other before they met is of course the traditional Platonic 'affinity' of romantic friendship which we can regard as persuasive on Laura. (Sage, 185)

But at this stage, the victim actively resists any erotic invitation. While Laura, as the hostess, takes a dominant role, taking Carmilla's hand while the latter blushes, this is quite consistent with the terms of romantic friendship. In fact, such heightened feeling on both sides as is suggested here is distinguished from, and actually serves to draw attention to, the inappropriate emotion expressed in Carmilla's later appeals. Significantly, Laura, although immediately drawn to her new friend and impressed by her beauty, is always perturbed by the uncontrolled intensity of her 'raptures', as she terms her friend's outbursts, and this serves to distinguish her own innocently romantic response from the erotic advances of the vampire.

For this reason, I would differ from Sage in his assessment of Carmilla as 'one of the great seducers in literature' (Sage, 195) – seduction is not accomplished through her ability to play on Laura's fears, or her admittedly clever use of rhetoric. It is only through supernatural means that Carmilla gradually overcomes Laura's distaste, a response that Laura herself, having learned the cause of her own fascination, candidly admits, and even analyses with scientific accuracy:

> In these mysterious moods I did not like her. I experienced a strange tumultuous excitement that was pleasurable, ever and anon, mingled with a vague sense of fear and disgust. I had no distinct thoughts about her while such scenes lasted, but I was conscious of a love growing into adoration, and also of abhorrence. This I know is paradox, but I can make no other attempt to explain the feeling. ('Carmilla', 264).

As both Gelder and Auerbach imply, Carmilla attempts to use the conventions of romantic friendship as a vehicle for sexual persuasion. The constant references to her blushing and to her expressive eyes and drooping head testify to her embodiment of feminine erotic invitation, and she deliberately uses the language of desire in her appeals to Laura. Although the precise boundaries between the conventions of romantic friendship and the threat of sexual possessiveness are necessarily identified almost entirely from the evidence of Laura's reaction, there are moments where Carmilla's tone clearly transgresses acceptable limits. Notably, she makes much of the fact that she relies on having her bedroom door locked from the inside every night, only to claim at one point that she is too weak to get off her bed and lock it herself – the invitation to Laura to join her in the bed is transparent enough, even before Laura hastily removes herself from the room.

While Carmilla assumes a pointedly feminine, even passive rôle, drawing attention to her own languid state and luxuriating in her status as a ladylike invalid, she seeks a physical consummation of her love for her victim and repeatedly indulges in displays of energetic emotion. Drawing attention herself to this paradox, she insists:

> You will think me cruel, very selfish, but love is always selfish; the more ardent the more selfish. How jealous I am you cannot know. You must come with me, loving me, to death; or else hate me and still come with me, and *hating* me through death and after. There is no such word as indifference in my apathetic nature. ('Carmilla', 276)

Jealousy can be portrayed as a sign of intense feeling within the ideal of romantic friendship, but in blatantly stressing her own selfishness, Carmilla undermines the very terms on which love between friends can traditionally be celebrated in the nineteenth century. One of the defining and justifying features of this ideal is its emphasis on self-sacrificial love.

The vampire repeatedly assumes and exploits the values of romantic friendship, only to disrupt them through an unacceptable intensity or through such use of paradox. In her vocabulary, love is cruel, as humiliation is rapture. Despite her possessiveness, she foresees Laura's love for others than herself, once she too has been made a vampire:

> In the rapture of my enormous humiliation I live in your warm life, and you shall die – die, sweetly die – into mine. I cannot help it; as I draw near to you, you, in your turn, will draw near to others, and learn the rapture of that cruelty, which yet is love … ('Carmilla', 263)

Laura is aware in her narration of events that she herself is expressing her relationship with her former friend in paradoxical terms, remembering a consciousness of growing adoration mingled with abhorrence.

Tellingly, she describes her failure to govern her own reaction, as she daily loses control over her body, in the terms of insanity. It is not entirely clear whose condition she is describing in her response to the 'increasing ardour' with which the vampire gloats on her as her resistance wanes – 'This always shocked me like a momentary glare of insanity' ('Carmilla', 281). The way in which this epicurean protraction of torture is carried out is suggestive of a complex interplay of control. Carmilla describes herself as having no control over her own vampiristic or, by implication, sexual imperatives – she does, however, seek to dominate her friend mentally and emotionally rather than contenting herself with a mere physical seduction or attack, and Laura appears powerless to resist such a process of assimilation.

This obsessive behaviour and the loss or abandonment of rational self-control on both sides in turn highlight one of the perceived dangers of romantic friendship – Laura's letter to the female friend who is the supposed recipient of this confidence stresses the loneliness of her position, and by extension, her vulnerability to manipulation by a friend living in such close proximity. In addition to the unconstrained nature of her advances, I have suggested that Carmilla's lack of interest in religion is suspect in itself, although an older Laura admits in retrospect that she might have found this less shocking had she known the world better.

Again indicating her vulnerability, she gives her age at the time of these events as 19, making her both the right age for a romantic friendship to be socially sanctioned and also young enough to be susceptible to external control by an older friend. Ironically, Carmilla turns out to be over a century older than Laura, although she has retained the appearance of a young girl.

As a stranger mysteriously left with the family by a mother who will give no clue as to her identity, Carmilla's lack of knowable antecedents is ambiguous in itself, as in so many accounts of romantic friendship. However, the vampire's status is further complicated in this version by her previous incarnation as the human Countess Millarca. In this previous existence, she was involved in a heterosexual attachment (she later claims that she has never been in love and never will, unless it be with Laura), but the narrator stresses repeatedly that the family of Karnstein, now extinct, was in its time an evil one. As Laura herself is descended from the Karnstein family on the mother's side, this places the vampire in the place of ancestor as well as sinister interloper – this technique of heightening the terror felt by both reader and protagonists by locating it actually within the family circle is perhaps the most famous characteristic of sensation fiction from the 1860s onwards.

But the subversion of the family circle here also draws on earlier concerns about the abruptness with which romantic friendships are formed, as attention is repeatedly drawn to Carmilla's mysterious introduction both to Laura and to her predecessor, Bertha Rheinfeldt. In each case, the father or guardian is injudicious in his willingness to accept the new friend of his daughter or ward, respectively, as an inmate of his house. In recounting his own experience, the General bitterly recalls his ward's impulsive welcoming of a new friendship, and his own failure to remonstrate, ungoverned as it is by a conventional introduction:

> I never saw anyone so taken with another at first sight, unless, indeed, it was the stranger herself, who seemed quite to have lost her heart to her. ('Carmilla', 298)

The sincerity of Carmilla's feeling is not, of course, in doubt. Indeed, this emotional intensity serves to distinguish her from earlier, more insouciant male villains such as Steerforth – in one sense, her conflation of intensely felt friendship and sexual love anticipates Wilde's more celebratory arguments in *The Portrait of Mr W.H.* and *The Picture of Dorian Gray*, although the vampire's experience of love quite literally depends on the death of its object. In explaining the obsessive feeling displayed by the vampire, as opposed to her own reciprocal attachment, Laura herself collapses the boundaries of romantic friendship and sexual desire, distancing herself from the vampire through her use of generic and non-gendered terms:

> The vampire is prone to be fascinated with an engrossing vehemence, resembling the passion of love, by particular persons. In pursuit of these it will exercise inexhaustible patience and stratagem … ('Carmilla', 317)

In this account, the 'fascination' has ostensibly been exorcised with the summary execution of the vampire herself, but its uneasy influence over Laura remains (as David continues to be affected by his love for Steerforth at the time of writing his autobiography). In Le Fanu's account, as in Dickens's, the intended victim narrates events while allowing a powerful retrospective voice to the more subversive figure. But in a reversal of the norm, it is the less intense figure who is celebrated here and who is allowed to tell the story. In this later version of transgressive friendship, the threat to innocence is located not in the tempter's thoughtless dissipation, but – perhaps more logically – in the dangerously obsessive feeling that the ideal of romantic friendship actively sought to exclude.

In many ways, then, 'Carmilla' conforms to traditional patterns in its treatment of romantic friendship. The central protagonist is highly responsive to her new friend, being taken with her almost at first sight, and largely on the grounds of her pleasing personal appearance. The purity of this reaction is carefully conveyed and protected through the detailed first-person narrative. While the reader's suspicions are quickly aroused, the very innocence of the narrator limits her perception of the threat posed by her friend – this intrusion, and the ultimate expulsion of the threat through other means than the victim's agency, is recognisable from the mid-century *David Copperfield*.

However, the complexity of Laura's relationship with Carmilla comes under more precise scrutiny than is common in earlier treatments of romantic friendship. Anticipating the arguments of later medical writers such as Havelock Ellis, Le Fanu incorporates an overt sexual element into this friendship, which, while it is confined to the subversive figure or justified as part of an insidious supernatural influence, is none the less treated scientifically. Laura's increasing sense of lassitude as she gives way to the fascination she feels for another woman is related to her vulnerability as both lonely and youthfully ingenuous – that she does not lack self-awareness is shown by her minute observation of her own reactions, and the controlling male narrator retrospectively praises her intelligence. Her illness and her inability to resist her own disintegration again anticipate Ellis's warnings about the wasting effects of indulgence in lesbian relations, but effectually pre-empt his claim that sexual responsiveness is dangerous primarily because of women's lack of awareness in pursuing this suspect ideal.

What separates 'Carmilla' from earlier treatments of romantic friendship is not, then, its suspicion of obsession and excess – earlier narrators constantly patrol their texts to ensure against this – but its engagement with transgressive relationships as potentially fascinating. Initially imposed upon, Laura is later made complicit in her own victimisation, as she loses the will to resist her infatuated assailant. Notwithstanding the controlling perspective of medical science, and the presence of a loving father, she is seen to participate in her own 'seduction', resisting all attempts to save her until it is almost too late. Comparing this scenario to the similar story in Coleridge's 'Christabel', Martha Vicinus notes the ambiguity surrounding the victim in each case, as both writers:

> titillate the reader about the degree of complicity involved. ... These preternaturally innocent girls serve as a warning to fathers: pretending to maternal love, a sexually experienced woman can steal a girl's affections and destroy her appetite for marriage. (Vicinus, xxvi)

In Le Fanu's account, as in the earlier poem, Laura is saved the full implications of this responsibility for her own destruction by the text's insistence on supernatural agency. Her complicity is, however, far removed from the conventional mutuality of Caroline Helstone's pre-marital friendship with Shirley, or even Esther Summerson's possessive appropriation of Ada, both of which friendships are seemingly sanctioned by their authors.

The dangers of excessive friendship culminate here in the near death of the narrating protagonist, a threat that is only exceeded in the murder of Wilde's Basil Hallward by his too easily trusted friend Dorian Gray. It is notable that in either case the radical nature of the plot depends on a supernatural element that allows for the final destruction of the murderous party. Such explicit treatment of the threat contained within romantic friendship, based as it is on the expression of strong feeling, does not in itself deny the appeal of such relationships. Indeed, it is the very allure of this level of intimacy that makes it so dangerous in these later texts.

In these accounts of female friendship, the intimacy generated by youth and close proximity can be seen almost as an illness in itself, requiring regulation and control. Indeed, if death was a unifying theme in the male-centred texts explored in the last chapter, it is illness that provides a common ground for the pairs of friends in *Shirley*, *Wives and Daughters*, *Bleak House* and 'Carmilla' (in Dickens's later novel, the unsuitable spouse is killed off not in favour of a long-suffering replacement, but rather to usher in a new phase of the pivotal female friendship). But despite its ostensible status, illness in both *Shirley* and *Bleak House* highlights the tensions or inadequacies inherent in the female friendships under discussion, while *Wives and Daughters* withholds the status that nursing would bring, from an unrepentant Cynthia. In 'Carmilla', more disturbingly still, the vampire literally causes and celebrates the illness that will at once draw her victim closer to her and suggest her diseased state of mind. Although nursing is culturally associated with women, illness here simply exposes flaws in each friendship (in the male-focused *Armadale*, conversely, friendship will be initiated through the nursing of a mysterious stranger).

But if loyal service between women is not always assured, neither is there the anxiety about gender reversals that threatens to undermine male friendships. Despite her assumption of masculine habits (which are in any case fully independent of her relationship with her friend), Shirley is ultimately reducible to a feminine role, a process in which the already feminine Caroline is thoroughly – even complacently – complicit. Esther and Ada are both presented in the stereotypically feminine terms of gentleness and domesticity. Even Carmilla effects her seductions not through assuming a masculine persona, but through an appeal to mutual femininity (her privileged access to her victims' bedrooms itself testifies to this).

If unregulated emotion was perceived as the natural state of women, this would explain why romantic friendship was implicitly feminised in some accounts, and why accounts of male friendship are so anxious to stress self-regulation and stability. As *fin de siècle* sexology retrospectively makes clear, the laying out of boundaries and the stress on self-control (constantly threatened by suggestions of the erotic and the exertion of control by the object of passionate regard) were absolutely necessary to the maintenance of the ideal in both its masculine and feminine forms. This anxiety about self-control is interpreted by some critics, such as Martha Vicinus, as evidence of sexual feeling. In her analysis of boarding school friendships and crushes, Vicinus argues:

> Although a religious vocabulary effectively masked personal desires, a woman who loved another girl or woman always spoke of this love in terms that replicated heterosexual love. … commentators would probably not have argued so forcefully for the control of these emotions if they had not recognized their sexual source' ('Distance and Desire: English Boarding School Friendships, 1870–1920', in Duberman, Vicinus and Chauncey Jr, eds, *Hidden from History*, 212).

The available evidence suggests, as I have been arguing, that commentators were certainly aware of an erotic *potential* in the conventions of romantic friendship, and that the comparisons with marriage made it imperative to have some means of distinguishing friendship from sexual love. Literary texts find various discreet means of doing this, but the underlying insecurity identified by Vicinus in this context helps to explain why – as the next chapter will show – feminine changeability might be available for satire, but the excesses of genuine (particularly male) passion had to be treated with a degree of caution.

Chapter Four

Tenderest Caresses: Romantic Friendship and the Satirists

> 'How dull you are tonight!' sneered Miss Squeers.
> 'No, indeed,' replied Miss Price, 'I am in excellent spirits. I was thinking *you* seemed out of sorts.'
> 'Me!' cried Miss Squeers, biting her lips, and trembling with very jealousy; 'Oh no!'
> 'That's well, 'remarked Miss Price. 'Your hair's coming out of curl, dear.'
> (*Nicholas Nickleby*)

If romantic friendship was widely upheld as an ideal in the nineteenth century, it was also subject to a tradition of satire, and was indeed an easy target for ridicule. Ironically, the assumption that women were more pure, and indeed more given to emotional responsiveness, did not preclude their being satirised as incapable of genuine friendship. As Trumbull tactfully puts it, before slipping in yet another list of famous friendships in support of women's capacity:

> Between man and man, all admit the possibility of the highest friendship. It is there that friendship has found its most notable and traditional illustrations. … Few, again, would question the reality of abiding and exalted friendship between woman and woman, although classic writers were not always willing to admit its possibility, and many modern writers have adhered to the classic skepticism on this point. (Trumbull, 106)

Mary Mitford argues for the value of genuine friendship among women, while satirising mercilessly what she saw as its cheap imitation. In her story 'Rosedale', two young women renounce male society in emulation of the renowned Ladies of Llangollen, and:

> Juxtaposition laid the corner-stone of this immortal friendship, which had already lasted four months and a half, and cemented by resemblance of situation, and dissimilarity of character, really bade fair to continue some months longer. (in Broomfield and Mitchell, eds, *Prose by Victorian Women*, 22)

In what is presumably an ironic misreading of the relationship between the famous Ladies of Llangollen, Mitford was quick to disclaim:

> any intention of casting the lightest shade of ridicule on the remarkable instance of female friendship to which I have alluded in the text. … Such a friendship is the very poetry of life. (22)

But other writers were less careful in making such distinctions between the real and the superficial. The best-known of the Victorian satirists, Thackeray, addressed the question of the validity of female friendship in two major novels, *Vanity Fair* and *The History of Pendennis*. Thackeray had himself had an intense relationship with Edward Fitzgerald at Cambridge, involving a series of effusive letters. As Catherine Peters describes their relationship at this time:

> The few letters and fragments of letters of their youth that survived are a mixture of fooling and fantasy, and an outspoken emotionalism that seems almost lover-like to modern eyes. Young men today would hardly dare to write to each other in such terms, unless they were having a homosexual relationship, which Thackeray and Fitzgerald certainly were not. They called each other by pet names, and wept at parting. Life without the other seemed to each dreary and blank; their friendship the only thing which gave it savour … They openly referred to their feeling for each other as love. (Peters, 55–6)

But despite this personal experience, he went on to portray male friendship in his fiction as restrained to the point of taciturnity. It is female expression that is critically examined in both *Vanity Fair* and *Pendennis* (notably memories of Edward Fitzgerald's naïve poems to 'my Willy' did not deter him from satirising the supposed excesses of female friendship).

One explanation for this inconsistent treatment may lie in the anxieties raised by female relations in the nineteenth century. Crucially Lisa Moore points out that although romantic friendship:

> is invoked to render relationships between women transparent and accessible to the purposes of bourgeois patriarchy – heterosexual companionate marriage, class and colonial relations, the disciplinary rule of law – it surfaces again and again as an ambiguous term that raises anxieties in the act of attempting to contain them. At this crucial juncture in the emergence of modern notions of sexual identity and the self, women's texts (often novels) and women themselves are linked in the representation of romantic friendship. Both are seen as dangerous and hard to read … (Moore, *Dangerous Intimacies*, 500–501)

If Lydia Gwilt and Lady Audley defy their critics to locate their sins in their beautiful faces, then male friendship is by contrast reassuringly transparent.

Certainly, satire of male friendship is less common, but a few years before the start of Victoria's reign, Maria Edgeworth had questioned the validity of romantic friendship for both sexes. Her novel *Helen*, popular throughout the century (Thackeray's daughter Annie was to write an introduction to a new edition of 1896) features two pairs of friends, and in each case one friend is unworthy of the other. It becomes obvious at an early stage that Granville Beauclerc and Helen are destined by the novelist to marry. Significantly Beauclerc lavishes money on repairing his friend Beltravers's estate because the latter had once done him a service at Eton, and in his mind this justifies their having become intimate in the space of three weeks, on meeting again some years later. Helen herself is manoeuvred into a false position in agreeing to conceal her friend's pre-marital attachment, an affair which she has never confessed to her husband, and which he now assumes to be a love affair of Helen's own that she obdurately refuses to admit to his ward Beauclerc. As the deception becomes increasingly complex, it transpires that Beltravers had hoped for a match between his sister and Beauclerc – when this fails to happen, he first schemes to ruin Helen and ultimately gambles away his newly repaired estate. The narrator comments wryly, 'Yes, this man of romantic friendship, this *blasé*, this hero oppressed with his own sensibility, could condescend to write anonymous scandal, to league with newsmongers, and to bribe waiting-women to supply him with information'. (*Helen*, 436) The treatment of Helen's friend Cecilia is more forgiving, ending with her voluntary confession and reformation. The moral however seems to be that truth in the abstract can too easily become the prey of a romantic sensibility, one that takes the form in Helen's case, of something like an addiction to self-sacrifice. Notably she is not praised for her loyal silence, rather her mentor (Cecilia's mother) reiterates a point she has made throughout the novel about Helen's weakness and cowardice, before saying that she will not remonstrate with her when she has suffered such punishment already.

Vanity Fair and Pendennis

Perhaps the most highly respected satirist of his age, despite periodic accusations of cynicism, Thackeray was an unflinching and close observer of social behaviour, and in that sense well placed to query the gap between the ideal and the quotidian mechanism of social relations. His most celebrated novel, *Vanity Fair* works largely within a recognisable satirical tradition in its treatment of the issues raised by romantic friendship. Most notable is the way in which it scrutinises the very viability of friendship as the romance plot develops, offering a sceptical view of the female capacity for lasting friendship in particular. In its exploration of the conventions governing social relations, the novel repeatedly undermines the sincerity, or at least the reliability, of female expressions of attachment. More urgently, it uncovers the danger of romantic friendship as being vulnerable to exploitation. Catherine Peters captures the duality of this presentation, in which female relations are at once ridiculed by, and a source of concern to, the narrator:

> Where women are concerned … the friendship is attacked, or condescended to as being a second-class, temporary kind of emotion which will disappear with marriage. This is, of course, part of Thackeray's attack on the sentimentality of debased romanticism; such exaggerated responses are not warranted by the circumstances. There is, too, a more sinister side to them: a trusting and innocent girl is being manipulated by a more sophisticated and unscrupulous one. (Peters, 56)

Speaking from an insistently male viewpoint, the narrator introduces Amelia with the ambivalent comment on her popularity at her school in Chiswick, that 'She had twelve intimate and bosom friends out of the twenty-four young ladies' (*Vanity Fair*, 7). The subsequent decline in her status with other women is attributed to the presence of men in her social circle once she leaves school – unlike Brontë's Shirley, however, the narrator of *Vanity Fair* does not hesitate to blame the jealousy of women themselves for any such disruption to their mutual goodwill.

This intrusive narrator is at once knowing and self-incriminating – drawing attention to his own fictionality through implausible accounts of his knowledge of each character, he deliberately assumes a place in the world of 'Vanity Fair' even as he satirises its questionable scheme of values. From this position of assumed complicity, he is able to direct the reader's response to a series of conventions governing the relationships he presents. Both male and female friendships are based on a knowledge of these conventions, which differ according to age and gender. The conventions of female friendship are implemented at school, and responsiveness is expressed both physically, through tearful embraces, and by the interplay of stock theatrical phrases. Letter writing is an integral part of the way in which relationships between women are later perpetuated, and the tone and regularity of correspondence offer some guide to the depth of feeling between them. Male friendship is shown to depend on rather different forms, such as duelling and the facilitating of love affairs – that this code is not wholly borne out by external accounts suggests the extent to which the narrator of *Vanity Fair* is prepared to fictionalise male friendship norms in order to make a point. But as in *Coningsby* or *Tom Brown's Schooldays*, its conventions are determined by the ethos of the public school, where honour is established through an adherence to particular ideas of conduct.

Knowledge of the rules of friendship, in both its romantic and more restrained forms, allows manipulation of feeling by an opportunist such as Rebecca, who points up the artificial construction of effusive expression in her mocking emulation of Amelia's behaviour. The expression of strong feeling can be either superficial – Amelia quickly forgets her friend in her anxiety about her love affair with George Osborne – or deliberately manipulative, as in Rebecca's case. It can also act as a mask for more covert social and economic concerns, as norms of conduct reveal membership of the gentry or an expensive education; similarly, the expression of sudden attachment between women can facilitate the mercenary marriages of male family members. As the engagement between George and Amelia is vetoed by Mr Osborne on the failure of Mr Sedley's business concerns, for instance, the wealthy Miss Swartz is introduced as a replacement and the narrator comments wryly that:

> ... the major part of the Osborne family, who had not, in fifteen years, been able to get up a hearty regard for Amelia Sedley, became as fond of Miss Swartz in the course of a single evening as the most romantic advocate of friendship at first sight could desire. (*Vanity Fair*, 249)

Such exploitation of fashionable expression of feeling between women informs much of the satire on its status as dispensable or simply expedient. Certainly, it is female rather than male friendship that comes in for most of the dismissive commentary in the novel, as the two central friendships are played out.

The close friendship celebrated is that of Dobbin for George Osborne, rather than the questionably effusive tenderness displayed by Amelia for Rebecca. Notably, this friendship is largely one-sided – characteristic of the novel is the way in which the more worthy party considers himself to be the other's inferior. The intrinsic worth of characters is tested through comparison with each other, as Dobbin's selfless behaviour is contrasted with the self-indulgent egoism of his friend (and Amelia herself). The male friendship explored is not intrinsically romantic, as this feeling is deflected onto female objects; however, it has begun with the hero worship of approved school convention, although in a reversal of tradition, it is the heroic Dobbin who first rescues his younger compatriot from bullying and then worships him accordingly:

> Even before they were acquainted, he had admired Osborne in secret. Now he was his valet, his dog, his man Friday. He believed Osborne to be the possessor of every perfection, to be the handsomest, the bravest, the most active, the cleverest, the most generous of created boys. (*Vanity Fair*, 56)

Interestingly, the narrator claims that this is 'such a love and affection as is only felt by children', ignoring the fashion for romantic friendship among women that he criticises so pointedly elsewhere in the novel.

Dobbin's continuing love for his friend is shown through repeated acts of self-sacrifice, most notably when he orchestrates the marriage with Amelia that signals the end of his own hopes. This conflict is finally resolved when George dies, having planned to elope with Rebecca – significantly, Rebecca first prepares to divulge this not out of friendship for Amelia, but out of respect for the rejected Dobbin, towards the end of the novel.

The relationship between Amelia and Rebecca is more ambivalent. It too begins in youth, although the two seem only to be spending an initial holiday together because they are leaving school on the same day. By implication, Rebecca is not among the twelve intimate friends named by the narrator, and the development of their friendship is as limited as it is rapid:

> as for the girls, they loved each other like sisters. Young unmarried girls always do, if they are in a house together for ten days. (*Vanity Fair*, 34)

The emphasis on friendship as depending on the absence of men is crucial to the narrator's satire here – where Dobbin sacrifices his own romantic aspirations for the sake of his friend, female characters are shown to replace one form of affection with another as marriage supersedes their friendships with members of their own sex. During her friend's visit, Rebecca is able to combine friendship with the pursuit of marriage simply because the object of her schemes is Amelia's own brother. As in *Shirley*, a marriage that would incorporate friendship in marriage has an obvious appeal, and Amelia:

> warmed into a most tender friendship for Rebecca, and discovered a million of virtues and amiable qualities in her which she had not perceived when they were at Chiswick together. For the affection of young ladies is of as rapid growth as Jack's beanstalk, and reaches up to the sky in a night. ... women are not commonly satisfied until they have husbands and children on whom they may centre affections, which are spent elsewhere, as it were, in small change. (*Vanity Fair*, 41)

The possibilities of a lasting friendship between women depend, then, on a further relationship through marriage, and this is forestalled by the manoeuvring of George Osborne, who wishes to avoid a family alliance with a governess.

The subsequent parting between the women is the direct result of this disruption, as Rebecca's presence becomes embarrassing in the face of Jos's sudden departure for Cheltenham. Their leave-taking itself reveals the mechanisms of female romantic friendship as made up of directionless sensibility on the one hand and deliberate manipulation of convention on the other, as:

> after a scene in which one person was in earnest and the other a perfect performer – after the tenderest caresses, the most pathetic tears, the smelling-bottle, and some of the very best feelings of the heart, had been called into requisition – Rebecca and Amelia parted, the former vowing to love her friend for ever and ever and ever. (76)

But despite these protestations, Amelia predictably allows her friendship with Rebecca to subside; as she enters the social, economic world of her parents, her preoccupation with George and romance replaces her callow attachment to female society. A more active and aware participant in the competition for social advancement, Rebecca likewise loses interest in the Sedleys once she has ingratiated herself with the family of a peer. With heavy irony, the narrator notes the fulfilment of his earlier insinuations:

> During the months of Rebecca's stay in Hampshire, the eternal friendship had (must it be owned?) suffered considerable diminution, and grown so decrepit and feeble with old age as to threaten demise altogether. The fact is, both girls had their own real affairs to think of: Rebecca her advance with her employers – Amelia her own absorbing topic. (168)

The character of each is shown through their reaction to meeting again, the only notable difference being that Amelia feels a level of self-reproach, while Rebecca again draws attention to the conventional nature of her greeting in a way that verges on parody:

> When the two girls met, and flew into each other's arms with that impetuosity which distinguishes the behaviour of young ladies towards each other, Rebecca performed her part of the embrace with the most perfect briskness and energy. Poor little Amelia blushed as she kissed her friend, and thought she had been guilty of something very like coldness towards her. (168)

The allusion to Rebecca's 'performance' is not incidental – throughout the novel she will undermine the sincerity of conventional expression through performance and mimicry. At various points she caricatures types of behaviour for the benefit of an audience on whom she will later practise it. The readiness of Miss Crawley to be swayed by sentimental performance, having joined in the laughter at Brigg's copious tears, is a case in point.

This satire of female sensibility and capacity for friendship is contained within the larger plot of romance, which is itself coloured by the overall satire of social values. Meanwhile, the conventions of both friendship and marriage are seen to be implicated in wider considerations of economic and social status. Individuals such as Miss Crawley, as her treatment of Rebecca shows, are as well able as that character herself to distance their practice from their own expressions of sentiment. Social connections are paramount, and the novel itself tends to focus on the wider social implications of individual relationships rather than on the individuals themselves.

Miss Swartz herself only visits Amelia on her return to the more fashionable part of London:

> Swartz would have liked her always if she could have seen her. One must do her that justice. But, *que voulez-vous?* – in this vast town one has not the time to go and seek one's friends; if they drop out of the rank they disappear, and we march on without them. Who is ever missed in Vanity Fair? (781)

Indeed, the enthusiastic display of passion, in its susceptibility to theatrical posturing, is presented as potentially suspect throughout the novel, and the most moral figure, Dobbin, is significantly restrained in his expression. The less sympathetic George is driven by an undisciplined indulgence rather than by genuine passion; similarly, Rebecca's passions are for good society, and later for whisky and gambling, rather than for any particular individual. Amelia appears initially to be driven by passion, if not for her friend, for her husband, and later her child; however, her self-indulgence is remarked on by the narrator as well as by other characters, and Dobbin comments in the final pages of the novel that she is incapable of an elevated response to genuine feeling. Paradoxically, it is this containment of a real passion that marks Dobbin as an authentic 'gentleman', according to the narrator. In this ambiguity Thackeray embodies the dilemma identified by Stedman as pertaining to all expression of emotion in Victorian literature:

> In the 19th century, individualisation had advanced significantly and the cult of privacy – albeit a highly organised privacy – had reached new heights. Being too open-hearted and willing to express one's emotions without any restraint whatsoever was not in keeping with this cult. But since the absence of all emotional expression not only implied the unhealthy absence of all feeling, but also rendered it impossible to judge what kind of class an individual belonged to, and what type of character he or she represented, the Victorians found themselves confronted with an almost unsolvable dilemma. This dilemma is the reason why authors of texts on the emotions oscillate between the call for total emotional control and the sometimes only grudgingly admitted individual and social necessity of emotional expression. (Stedman, 55)

This analysis, while it fails to account for the prevailing fashion for the highly emotional cult of romantic friendship, is none the less useful in the light it casts on Thackeray's individual position as his narrator vacillates between admiration for Dobbin's self-control, and criticism of the ill-bestowed passion it is designed to conceal.

Ambivalent about both marriage and female friendship, the narrator bases Dobbin's moral status largely on his supportive but non-romantic, adult friendship for George Osborne. Famously condemning the novelistic practice of ending with a marriage, the narrator of *Vanity Fair* in fact leads up with a high degree of inconsistency to the final marriage of Dobbin and Amelia in the closing pages. The satire of female friendship and rivalry – Rebecca openly flirts with George on his honeymoon with Amelia – is contained within the initial marriage plot. However, this in turn hinges on Dobbin's friendly and self-sacrificial intervention, while the more important romance plot leading up to Amelia's declaration of love for Dobbin is inhibited throughout by male loyalty. Having first orchestrated the marriage of the woman he himself loves to his friend, Dobbin later protects George's memory by concealing his involvement with Rebecca, even though this perpetuates Amelia's illusions about the worthiness of the husband she has lost. Characteristically approving of the potential for male friendship, the narrator draws attention to Dobbin's energy in assisting his friend:

> What is the secret mesmerism which friendship possesses, and under the operation of which a person ordinarily sluggish, or cold, or timid, becomes wise, active, and resolute, in another's behalf? (*Vanity Fair*, 269)

The parallel relationship between Amelia and Rebecca is based, on the contrary, on rivalry and competition for George's attention – even Rebecca's belated intervention on Dobbin's behalf proves to be redundant, as Amelia has already written to recall him before learning of her husband's proposed desertion.

Describing itself as 'a novel without a hero', *Vanity Fair* purports to expose the inconsistencies of socially regulated individual behaviour through the commentary of a narrator whose very complicity in false values renders his satire the more easily digestible. Through a series of parallels, individual characters' response to their situation exposes them to the judgement of the reader. But the novel locates false displays of feeling almost entirely in the female realm, while advocating the steadfast friendship shown by Dobbin to a friend whose lack of credibility ceases to be an embarrassment with his death halfway through the novel. In constantly displaying female inconsistency against this resolute male loyalty, the narrator implicitly questions the status of female relations in general.

It is through the presentation of Amelia's behaviour, as both the epitome of approved feminine standards, and weak dependence, that female codes of behaviour are most closely questioned. The deliberately formed product of her education, much as Eliot's Rosamond Vincy would later be presented with heavy irony as the pride of Miss Lemon's school in *Middlemarch*, Amelia is at once the embodiment of feminine virtue and the sentimental purveyor of false standards. Her enactment of the code of romantic friendship is not a sign of genuine passion, but simply an acceptable social demonstration of feminine feeling, and her development throughout the novel is discussed in the language of stereotype. As Barickman, MacDonald and Stark astutely comment: 'Through his own ambivalence the narrator reveals the stress of stereotypic responses that have deformed Amelia's character' (*Vanity Fair*, 36).

Amelia's own dependence on conventional stereotype is both parasitic and self-destructive, but in his ambivalent response to such unwitting victims of social convention, the narrator implicates both himself and the reader in the tendentious perpetuation of stereotypes. This narrative dilemma leads to high degree of ambivalence in the presentation of female codes of conduct. Indeed:

> The extremes of satire and sentiment are … in continual conflict in Dickens's novels, as in Thackeray's, not because they are actual polarities but because they have a common origin in the narrator's ambivalence. (Barickman, MacDonald and Stark, 45)

This ambivalence extends to Amelia's continuing devotion to her husband's memory, but it is in their relations with each other, rather than in their adherence to male authority, that female characters are most vulnerable to narrative satire. Ironically this satire, which is able to maintain a discreet distance from its object, itself depends on a tradition of stereotype.

In its celebration of unsustainably high levels of emotion, romantic friendship can be presented as reductive, depending on conventions that are only tenable within the confines of school. Where male friendship matures and develops through the extension of codes of honour laid down in youth, female friendships are increasingly rendered suspect by their continued dependence on conventional emotionalism. Exploiting this anomaly, it is such performers as Rebecca who are best equipped to survive in a opportunist society, by presenting herself in the false terms of effusive naïveté even as she effects her schemes for social and economic advancement. This satire of female superficiality exposes the brutal underlying mechanisms of polite society even as it condemns those like Rebecca who manipulate those mechanisms for their own ends.

Twenty years later, a first-person female narrator would articulate a compelling defence of such opportunism, commenting scathingly on the assumptions surrounding feminine conduct, in Wilkie Collins's *Armadale*. Thackeray himself offers no such defence, although Becky Sharp has proved popular with generations of readers despite her unscrupulous behaviour. In his next novel he would return to the theme of self-seeking hypocrisy as both masquerading behind and literally embodying the prescriptions of approved feminine behaviour, through a parodic treatment of female romantic friendship.

Serialised at the same time as *David Copperfield*, *Pendennis* is, like Dickens's novel, semi-autobiographical. Thackeray himself admitted to having been influenced by his rival's work, and claimed that Dickens had learned a level of restraint from him – a series of letters to his mother during this period show him making close and anxious comparisons between the two works as they appeared in the press. But despite the similarities – the hero of each has a close relationship with another man, and fails to recognise the appropriate female love interest until it is seemingly too late – the tone and thematic treatment of Thackeray's novel are markedly different from *David Copperfield*. Continuing the satire of female romantic friendship begun in *Vanity Fair*, Thackeray juxtaposes this against the more restrained expression of Pendennis and Warrington. While the narrator makes poignant reference to male romantic friendship, it is not a feature in the development of his central character, and love for the same woman actually unites the male friends, suggesting a fairly seamless transition when Pendennis ultimately marries Laura (in Dickens's account, this issue is bypassed as sexual licence abruptly ends the friendship with Steerforth some time before David meets his first wife).

The presentation of same-sex friendship is at times inconsistent and contradictory. Recalling the intense relationships traditionally enjoyed at university, the narrator wistfully comments:

> What passions our friendships were in those old days, how artless and void of doubt! How the arm you were never tired of having linked in yours under the fair college avenues or by the river-side, where it washes Magdalen Gardens, or Christ Church Meadows, or winds by Trinity and King's, was withdrawn of necessity, when you entered presently the world,

and each parted to push and struggle for himself through the great mob on the way through life! (*Pendennis*, 206)

Notably, such intense friendships between men are perceived as ending when each begins a post-university career, or 'the race', as the narrator repeatedly terms it. Female friendship is explicitly assumed to be a temporary substitute for marriage, and despite the narrator's own nostalgia elsewhere, he affects a tone in describing it that suggests the sentimental and vaguely contemptuous response of an observer to whom this tradition is entirely alien:

> [Laura] devoted herself to Helen with the utmost force of her girlish affection – such affection as women, whose hearts are disengaged, are apt to bestow upon a near female friend. It was devotion – it was passion – it was all sorts of fondness and folly; it was a profusion of caresses, tender epithets and endearments, such as it does not become sober historians with beards to narrate. Do not let us men despise these instincts because we cannot feel them. (229–30)

The contempt contained in this aside is almost palpable. In fact, these gendered friendships appear remarkably similar, despite the narrator's proscriptive disclaimer; however, where female friendship in this account waits to be displaced by a superior affection, its male equivalent is necessarily at odds with the individualist agenda of a competitive career.

But in a novel concerned with the transience of passion, depth of feeling is repeatedly belied by overt expression. It is a sign of the narrator's unease that he insistently genders romantic friendship as feminine – Pen's friendship with Warrington begins only after they have left Oxbridge, and is carefully detached from any romantic connotations. The reader is explicitly addressed as being masculine and encouraged to identify both with the male characters and with the almost abrasively male narrator (us men). This careful demarcation allows female friendship to be scrutinised from an ostensibly safe distance. But as in *Vanity Fair*, it is not friendship itself that is satirised; rather, the narrator undermines the female capacity for strong feeling, locating passionate expression within specifically female friendship, only to treat it at its best much as he does Pen's adolescent love for the Fotheringay. Female characters do not preserve or form friendships after adolescence, although men are implicitly given more leeway, reserving the right to form new friendships even where they lack the capacity; 'As you can seldom fashion your tongue to speak a new language after twenty, the heart refuses to receive friendship pretty soon: it gets too hard to yield to the impression' (*Pendennis*, 641–2).

While Laura's most passionate relationship in the novel is with her adoptive mother Helen, she enters into a briefly intense friendship with Blanche Amory before her marriage. For Laura, it is specifically her 'first experience in friendship' (265) (it will also be her last), and she is initially taken aback by Blanche's apparent enthusiasm. Her lack of awareness of the conventions of romantic friendship allow her to appear, however momentarily, as a satirical commentator in her own right. Her response to Blanche's tendentious questioning about her relationship with Pen exposes the falsity of her friend even as it suggests her own blunt sincerity:

> 'Tell me everything. I already love you as a sister.'
> 'You are very kind,' said Miss Bell, smiling, 'and – and it must be owned that it is a very sudden attachment.'
> 'All attachments are so. It is electricity – spontaneity. It is instantaneous. I knew I should love you from the moment I saw you. Do you not feel it yourself?'
> 'Not yet,' said Laura, 'but I dare say I shall if I try.' (247)

This new friend is presented as both shallow and self-deluding:

> Blanche had had hosts of dear, dear, darling friends ere now, and had quite a little museum of locks of hair in her treasure-chest, which she had gathered in the course of her sentimental progress. ... But it is the lot of sensibility to suffer, and of confiding tenderness to be deceived, and she felt that she was only undergoing the penalties of genius in these pangs and disappointments of her young career. (254)

From her initial moment of naïve insight, Laura herself is soon relegated by the narrator to a more invidious role, as she becomes aware of Blanche's subsequent relationship with Pen and persists in her expressions of affection in order to hide her jealousy. Her status in the narrative is ultimately rescued not by the constancy of her friendship to Blanche, but by her renunciation of what has been shown to be a romantic illusion:

> And so Laura, with a sigh, was obliged to confess that the romantic part of her first friendship was at an end, and that the object of it was only worthy of a very ordinary sort of regard.
> As for Blanche, she instantly composed a copy of touching verses, setting forth her desertion and disenchantment. It was only the old story, she wrote, of love meeting with coldness, and fidelity returned by neglect; and some new neighbours arriving from London about this time, in whose family there were daughters, Miss Amory had the advantage of selecting an eternal friend from one of these young ladies, and imparting her sorrows and disappointments to this new sister. (269)

In magnifying her friendships through appeals to a heroic tradition (the old story), Blanche deliberately appeals to a social context that justifies and elevates romantic friendship. But her calculated appeal to a wider social context is satirised as she accords herself a poetic status based on her own substandard verses.

Nor is she as ingenuous as she wishes to appear, using her awareness of convention to further her prospects in a competitive marriage market. In this sense, the relationship between Laura and Blanche is comparable to that between Amelia and Becky in *Vanity Fair*, in so far as Blanche uses her friendship with Laura as an excuse to visit Pen, whom she plans to marry despite suspecting Laura's own attachment. As in that case, the friendship is disrupted partly because Laura resents her friend's flirtation with the man she herself loves. Again, Blanche is the medium for a narrative satire on female correspondence – towards the end of the novel she covers her retreat from her engagement by writing affectionately to Laura for information, while addressing Pen with deliberately opaque but passionate reproaches. The narrator pointedly alludes at this point to the greater candour of men's letters.

But more damagingly, in her professed sensibility and indulgence in sentimental bathos, Blanche is also a natural successor to Amelia herself, who begins *Vanity Fair* with twelve intimate friends out of a possible twenty-four.

This evident suspicion of passionate expression informs the narrative treatment of Pen's relationship with Warrington, which constitutes the central friendship in the novel. In sharp contradistinction to Dickens's Steerforth, Warrington exerts a salutary influence over Pendennis as well as being his acknowledged mentor; this despite his being, like Steerforth, of a higher social class and slightly older than his friend. His taciturnity is itself offered as proof of sincerity, as the concept of English reserve is brought in to play against a supposedly European, and by implication suspect, effusiveness:

> his enthusiasm is too coy to show itself, even to his closest friend, and he veils it with a cloud of tobacco. He will speak more frankly of confidential evenings, however, and write ardently and frankly about that which he is shy of saying. (*Pendennis*, 720–21)

This willingness to communicate frankly in writing what cannot be openly said contrasts pointedly with Blanche's evasions in writing to Pen. It is also reminiscent of Thackeray's own youthful correspondence with Edward Fitzgerald, in which both allude to the greater freedom of expression that writing permits. None the less, Warrington is compromised at certain crucial points in the novel, where Pen faces moral and bodily breakdown. Absent from London during Pen's pursuit of Fanny Bolton, Warrington does not return in time to nurse him through his near fatal illness – this office is carried out first by Fanny herself, and later by Helen and Laura. Again, he advises Pen to end his ill-advised engagement to Blanche on the grounds that she has turned out to be the daughter of a convict – it is the altruistic Laura who urges him to behave honourably.

While Thackeray's narrator largely succeeds in establishing a male friendship that is both nostalgic and credible, it is not sufficient to replace the marital relationship that Pen attains at the end of the novel. True to the conventions of nineteenth century realism, the most lasting form of love can only be achieved with a female counterpart and within the confines of marriage.

Armadale

If Thackeray's writing on female friendship is inconsistent in presenting it as both risible and exploitative, Wilkie Collin's *Armadale* would leave no doubt as to the manipulative power of its engaging criminal adventuress, Lydia Gwilt. Like Dickens in *Bleak House*, Collins employed what is effectively a first-person narrative in the form of Lydia's diary, which militates against the supposedly more objective third-person narrator of the body of the text. Like *Vanity Fair*, *Armadale* contains a scathing satire of the hypocrisies of female romantic friendship – unlike Thackeray's urbane third-person narrator, however, the parodic commentary in *Armadale* proceeds from a criminally complicit female character. Pre-empting the type of dismissive commentary purveyed by the male narrators of *Vanity Fair* and *Pendennis*, Lydia herself rejects the false rhetoric of feminine sentimental friendship, and reverses the terms of satire by destabilising the relationship between two male friends.

Lydia Gwilt herself has troubled and disconcerted a succession of critics. Summing up her effect on many readers, Donald Hall comments:

> ... Lydia's narration is wholly trustworthy and even indispensable, for she knows more about what is happening than anyone else; the men of the novel are particularly confused and inept at interpreting the actions of others.' (Hall, 165)

However, 'the inside of Lydia's head is sometimes a rather frightening place to be. Determined, intelligent, and adept at playing roles, she is also thoroughly corrupt' (165). Adept at rôle-play she may be, but unlike Becky Sharp, who is seen as a consummate actress in her enactment of feminine sentiment, Lydia overtly mocks the conventions of female friendship, refusing to comply with Mrs Oldershaw's euphemistic treatment of what is essentially a criminal business alliance. It is this preference for honesty that differentiates Lydia from a Becky Sharp, and an insight from John Kucich is useful in assessing her claim to administer satirical justice:

> ... Collins tried to distinguish the special social deserts of those who could negotiate the moral gap between honesty and lying in ways that seem to advance the administration of social justice. Legitimate claims to insiderhood come to rest, not simply on moral grounds, but on the logic of *transgressive* moral authority. (Kucich, 85)

Both *Vanity Fair* and *Armadale* contain the threat of intrusion by at least one stranger whose antecedents are concealed or in some way mysterious, and both exploit class anxiety in their treatment of lower-class female adventurers who plot advantageous marriages for themselves. Where Becky Sharp manipulates the transient interest of the Sedley family and the romantic conventions adopted by Amelia, Lydia Gwilt similarly makes use of her dramatic personal appearance and the limits imposed on enquiry by polite breeding to inveigle her way into respectable society. Both protagonists expose the tendentious imperatives concealed by the rhetoric of romantic friendship in their plots to marry wealthy men, Becky through her manipulation of Amelia, and Lydia more ostentatiously in her mockery of the inaptly named 'Mother' Oldershaw's insincere effusions. Where Mrs Oldershaw addresses letters to 'My darling Lydia', Lydia taunts her in return with such forms of address as 'Mother Jezebel', deliberately drawing attention to the status of their correspondence as ruthlessly practical rather than tenderly feminine. This parody of the traditions of friendship parallels the development of the intense relationship in the second generation of Armadales, discussed for the sake of clarity as Allan and Midwinter.

But where the intelligent satire of Lydia Gwilt undermines the status of female relations, suggesting an inherent distrust as she and Mother Oldershaw attempt to outwit each other, the novel offers a far more positive treatment of romantic friendship in its celebration of this feeling between the central male characters. As in *Vanity Fair*, this important central friendship features two very different characters: Armadale himself is robustly healthy and socially confident, while the more complex and passionate Midwinter is shy and generally fails to make a favourable impression on strangers. Like Dobbin, Midwinter is deeply grateful to his superficially more engaging friend, and like Dobbin, it is Midwinter who is in fact made to appear the more remarkable of the two in the eyes of the reader.

On the face of it, the relationship between the two young men in *Armadale* conforms to a familiar pattern of male romantic friendship, although in an incisive account of the intense bond between the two, Maria K. Bachman and Don Richard Cox have noted the hysteria Midwinter is at such pains to control as signalling an unease about his own response to his friend. They point out that Armadale's family see the relationship as 'perverse', and that while the source of their anxiety is never named, Midwinter's outbursts correspond to the assumed symptoms of 'homosexual panic': 'Thus, throughout the novel, Midwinter hovers on the brink of hysteria as he struggles not only to conceal his mysterious heredity, but also to separate himself from the man he most desires' (Bachman and Cox, 328). Midwinter does indeed question the legitimacy of his friendship with Armadale, but his feelings of guilt can be directly traced to the childhood experiences which he himself submits to the Rev. Brock for his judgement – first appearing as a confident toddler, Midwinter recounts his later sufferings at the hands of a Calvinistic stepfather and his abrupt fall down the social scale when he runs away. It is this social taint, exacerbated in his mind by the psychological torment he has already endured, that Midwinter sees as rendering him an unfit companion for a gentleman. Social parity, as we have seen, was deemed crucial to the suitability of an intense friendship in particular, where the level of influence exercised was known to be potentially immense.

In the case of the two Armadales, there is an immediately acknowledged attraction of one to the other, although the very frankness of this avowal militates against a sexualised interpretation, and Midwinter's rapture in his new-found friend is carefully explained (Allan is almost the first person to be kind to him), while Midwinter himself is set against a character who is suitably impulsive, but lacks his passionate responsiveness; the early stages of the friendship are presided over by the clergyman Mr Brock. Allan is clearly responsive to women, and Lydia stresses Midwinter's appeal for her own sex. None the less the course of the narrative points to the perceived dangers of this romantic friendship in the disruption of social structures it entails, as the two Armadales are left to travel alone together, and so develop their individual relationship far from the constraints of a watchful family.

The doubling of these characters suggests a familiar trope in Victorian fiction, and Helena Michie's detailed discussion of this theme shows that difference in such pairings is often reproduced as sexual or moral difference, allowing a virtuous (often female) character to redeem a fallen counterpart or even rival.[1] But while the redemptive and forgiving hero/heroine was a powerful focus of narrative idealism, texts likewise suggest a level of anxiety associated with the figure of the transgressor or stranger. Midwinter sees himself as having been redeemed by his love for Armadale, while a misleading precedent is set in the first generation, in the mysterious appearance of Allan's father in the West Indies. In his deathbed letter, Midwinter's father recalls his own readiness to trust a stranger as showing a culpable lack of restraint:

---

1   See Helena Michie's *Sororophobia* for a fuller discussion of female pairings.

My impulses governed me in everything; I knew no law but the law of my own caprice, and I took a fancy to the stranger the moment I set eyes on him. (*Armadale*, 32)

The folly of giving in to such an impulse without further enquiry is revealed when the identity of the stranger is discovered and his machinations revealed, too late to prevent his vengeful marriage to Miss Blanchard under false pretences. This suspicious appearance of a stranger is ironically re-enacted in reverse in the second generation, as Allan first encounters Midwinter in a state of dangerous illness, and with no clues as to his identity. In this context, Midwinter is perceived as potentially threatening, both by Allan's mother and by the Rev. Brock, who depend on family relations or acquaintance in order to judge the suitability of a new acquaintance (such precautions will later be ironically undermined by Lydia, who gains access to Major Milroy's family, and so to Allan himself, by means of a false reference, before screening her anonymity behind a conventional appeal to 'family troubles').

At the same time, it is Midwinter's illness and his very friendlessness that appeals to Allan, whose constancy of purpose in ministering to his new friend is implicitly compared to his romantic vacillations between Lydia and Neelie later in the novel. Significantly, Allan is described as showing resolution for the first time in his life in his championing of Midwinter, and it is his readiness to nurse him through a potentially infectious illness that gives a moral impetus to this impulsive adoption of a stranger despite cautions from his mother and his mother's adviser.

The straightforward attachment of the two is favourably compared both to the hypocrisy of female alliances and the inconsistency of Allan's own feeling for women, throughout the novel. Barickman, MacDonald and Stark note that 'Male rivalry in *Armadale* is brutal almost to absurdity. The entire novel is engendered by one initial male rivalry over a woman and money' (131). But this analysis, valid as it is in its emphasis on rivalry in the first generation of Armadales, does not account for the novel's theme of atonement in the male impulses of the second generation, as one character repeatedly attempts to sacrifice his own interests to those of his friend. Ironically, such self-abnegation is associated primarily with feminine behaviour in the nineteenth century, but it is also a means by which the depth and sincerity of male romantic friendship can be tested. Where Lydia despises Mrs Oldershaw, who alternately threatens and pacifies her in the interests of a potentially lucrative association, Midwinter's genuine love for Allan leads him to sacrifice his own feeling on a number of occasions. Tellingly, he is willing to leave Allan for what he sees as his own good, rather than be the cause of further suffering arising, as he fears, from his father's original crime in murdering Allan's father.

Midwinter himself is unashamedly passionate in his grateful response to Allan as the one person who has been kind to him, and he is at moments unable to contain his feeling within socially sanctioned limits. In talking to the Rev. Brock, he attempts to restrain his expressions of emotion, only to break out finally with:

I do love him! It *will* come out of me – I can't keep it back. I love the very ground he treads on! I would give my life – yes, the life that is precious to me now, because his kindness has made it a happy one – I tell you I would give my life – (*Armadale*, 122)

This hysterical response is certainly suggestive of a lack of appropriate control, but Midwinter recovers himself almost immediately, and the narrator repeatedly draws attention to his powers of self-restraint as he suppresses the expression of his own feeling in deference to the expectations and convenience of those around him. As the friendship between the two young men develops, both assume and interchange rôles: Midwinter is first described in terms of feminine nervous sensibility, despite the constant references to his physical hardiness; Allan himself is described in terms of robust animal health, but he too will later be feminised through his vulnerability to nervous sensation on the wreck of the *Grace de Dieu*. Such assumption of feminine rôles is not uncommon in literary romantic friendships between men. Perhaps most famously, Tennyson imagines himself as a widow at various points in the course of *In Memoriam*, while also according feminine attributes to Hallam. Such rôle-allocation may suggest status (Tennyson's admiration for his friend as a superior is reflected in his play on gender, but this does not preclude an invocation of the best qualities he perceives as belonging normally to women). Again, *David Copperfield* shows David's changing status through his rejection of a feminine rôle and the violent death of the friend who renamed him Daisy. In *Armadale*, the use of gender stereotypes contributes to the sense of reciprocal love between the two friends, as each is able to nurse or minister to the distress of the other. Furthermore, the attribution of feminine status to each in the face of ill health or nervous shock subtly relegates the standard picture of tender female nursing, as women are excluded from these initial scenes, despite the popular associations of illness with feminine care.

The scene on the *Grace de Dieu* typifies this interchange of gender rôles within same-sex friendship. It is Midwinter's persistent superstition and knowledge of past events that govern the reader's response to the discovery of the wreck. In keeping with his perceived nervous sensibility, it is Midwinter who first shows signs of distress when he realises where he is – fainting on the deck of the boat, he has to be revived by his friend as he will later be revived twice in succession by his wife. But in an unlikely turn of events, the prophetic dream is accorded to Allan, who then suffers a nervous reaction from which Midwinter relieves him. The magnetic response of one to the other is suggested in this interchange of care, as:

> Midwinter laid his hand gently on Allan's forehead. Light as the touch was, there were mysterious sympathies in the dreaming man that answered it. His groaning ceased, and his hands dropped slowly. (*Armadale*, 164)

Midwinter's later refusal to accept a rational explanation of the dream, and his altercation with the doctor, align him once again with feminine intuition rather than masculine reason, but it is also significant in upholding the value of the seemingly irrational, through its suggestion that friendship may be capable of insight where medical science is necessarily inadequate. Despite the recurring associations with feminine weakness and the irrational represented by a belief in the meaning of the dream, the conventions of male romantic friendship are ultimately upheld through this mutually supportive relationship between Midwinter and Armadale.

What is satirised in the novel is not the male responsiveness between these two, but rather the expected transfer of female loyalty from friend to future spouse, as the marriage plot is based on a mercenary conspiracy between criminal associates rather than friends. While Bachman and Cox identify the tensions between the two Armadales and Lydia as 'a love triangle that may very well be unique in Victorian fiction' (Bachman and Cox, 320), this mutual jealousy of friends and potential marriage partners actually lies at the very heart of romantic friendship, and operates as a driving force in several of the novels considered here.

In more traditional renderings of the theme, notably in *Shirley*, female characters gradually withdraw their strongest feelings from each other as each attaches herself to a future husband. As Tess Cosslett observes of Victorian depictions of female friendship in general, an interchange between seemingly antagonistic female characters often serves to advance the marriage plot of one or the other (just such an exchange, although it proves unnecessary, occurs between Amelia and Becky towards the end of *Vanity Fair*), but '… very rarely is a female friendship set up as a substitute for or in competition with a male–female relationship …' (Cosslett, 3). No such moment of solidarity is even contemplated by female characters in *Armadale*. In the novel's parodic enactment of female relations, Lydia's irate threat that Neelie will regret interfering with her plans does lead indirectly to the advance of the latter's marriage, but only because Allan is moved to protect her from her rival, and in doing so, to declare his own revival of interest in her as the sole adherent to his cause after the abrupt departure of his friend. The alternative, and false, 'romance' plot has hinged on Lydia's scheming with her accomplice Mrs Oldershaw to marry Allan as the inheritor of the Thorpe Ambrose estate and fortune, at which point the association between the women would presumably come to an end.

Mrs Oldershaw's insistence on addressing Lydia as her 'bosom friend', and her previous position as a false mother to her, draw attention to this parody of female friendship, by emphasising the expectation that if marriage supersedes the ties of family and friendship, such ties have at least been valued by young women up to this point. More obviously even than Becky Sharp in her sentimental posturing, Mrs Oldershaw draws attention to the uses of romantic expression as a cover for mercenary exploitation. Having failed to intimidate Lydia with her threats of arrest for debt, she retracts them and appeals instead to traditions of female friendship as both deeply felt and fallible. With heavy irony, she emphasises their distance from each other even as she humorously appeals to their shared status as the objects of (implicitly male) satire:

> How cruel of you, if your debt had been ten times what it is, to suppose me capable (whatever I might say) of the odious inhumanity of arresting my bosom friend! Heavens! have I deserved to be taken at my word in this unmercifully exact way, after the years of tender intimacy that have united us? But I don't complain … Let us expect as little of each other as possible, my dear; we are both women, and we can't help it. (*Armadale*, 494–5)

Lydia refuses to respond to this letter in similar vein, but she herself will later exploit the tradition of perceived feminine inadequacy in order to manipulate Midwinter, protesting: 'How I like your anxiety for your friend! Of, if women could only form such friendships! Oh you happy, happy men!' (464).

Both in her correspondence with Mother Oldershaw and in her diary, Lydia unhesitatingly exposes the basis of female collaboration as self-serving, in direct opposition to the self-sacrificial nature of Midwinter's deeply felt love for Allan. Again, this exposure deliberately undermines the tradition of romantic correspondence and diary writing, wherein women were traditionally held to express their feminine sensibility. Perfectly capable of exploiting social norms when they suit her purpose, Lydia also serves as an ironic commentator on, and judge of, the very conventions she uses to protect her position at Thorpe Ambrose.

If the male friendship explored is more sincere, Lydia's machinations apparently expose it as equally vulnerable to intervention. The conventions of romantic friendship assume that it will at some point be susceptible to the greater demands of a love plot, and it is his love for Lydia that causes Midwinter's temporary estrangement from Allan. Initially disposed to sacrifice his own feeling for her when he believes that his friend will marry her, Midwinter champions the woman against his friend when he learns that enquiries have been set on foot in violation of her privacy. This conflict between romantic love and friendship creates the tension on which the plot revolves in the second half of the novel. Notably, the parallel rivalry between Neelie and Lydia shows none of the heroism involved in Midwinter's renunciation – Lydia seeks revenge on Neelie for having destroyed her own material prospects, while Neelie is jealous of the woman whom she believes to have stolen he lover as she was earlier jealous of Midwinter as her lover's friend. This jealousy provides a further parallel after Lydia's marriage to Midwinter, as she comes to feel resentful of her husband's continuing love for Allan. Indeed, his marriage itself has been interpreted as an act of sacrifice, albeit unconscious, on his friend's behalf. William Marshall suggests that: 'He thereby takes upon himself ... the suffering and perhaps the destruction intended for his friend' (Marshall, 74).

There is, then, no simple progression from the exploration of friendship to the exigencies of a marriage plot. Lydia marries Midwinter for love, only to convince herself within a matter of two months that he no longer loves her. This belief is almost certainly unfounded, as at least one critic has noted:

> She is confused about the change in their relationship, especially about the control Midwinter maintains over his former passion for her; and she fears that either he loves her less or that he suspects the truth about her character. None of her speculations is validated by his behaviour. (Schroeder, 14)

But it is at this point that Allan reappears and asserts his claim to the attention of his friend. The resulting resentment on Lydia's part jeopardises the assumed resolution whereby she will be redeemed by her love for her husband, as she once again plots to take Allan's life. The continuation of a close male friendship within the marital domain is shown to be deeply problematic, as contemporary essayists suggest it to be – Lydia complains with some justification that her husband gives time to his friend that he cannot spare for her, although Allan appears blithely oblivious to the deepening rift for which he is at least partly responsible. That Lydia is too hasty in her suspicions is confirmed by the narrator, who implies that Allan has in fact become secondary in Midwinter's affections since his marriage. Meeting Bashwood at the railway terminus in London, he is reminded of 'the old grateful interest in his friend which *had once been* the foremost interest of his life' (*Armadale*, 783; my italics).

But with Lydia's subsequent abandonment of Midwinter and her entrapment of Allan in Dr Downward's sanatorium, the claims of male friendship are fully restored. Midwinter almost dies for his friend by changing rooms with him, so fulfilling the claim made to Mr Brock that he would give his life for Allan. He is only saved by the intervention of Lydia, who writes to him in similar terms that it is easy for her to die knowing that he will live. Re-enacting the scene on the *Grace de Dieu* in which Allan revived Midwinter from his faint, she now restores him to consciousness before herself entering the room containing fatally poisoned air. In this act of atonement and self-sacrifice, she both validates her own superior love for Midwinter and at the same time relinquishes her claim to him, allowing his loyalty to remain with his friend rather than with his unsuitable wife. As Allan accompanies his friend to Lydia's funeral, the restoration of male ties is shown to be complete.

Reversing the trend in which an unsuitable or inconvenient friend dies to facilitate the marriage plot, *Armadale* depicts the initial remorse of a woman who abandons her criminal purposes for love, only to resume her plotting when she comes to feel that her husband's attention is reserved for his friend. At this point, it is not the friend but the wife herself who is sacrificed to the exigencies of plot. In this uneasy resolution to the novel, male friendship is shown to be ultimately more durable than heterosexual involvement, as Lydia is redeemed by dying in place of her husband at the right moment and Midwinter's heroism is brought out by an almost equally intense love for his friend. In case the reader has missed the point, the novel concludes with a conversation between the two friends on the morning of Allan's wedding day, in which Midwinter justifies his belief in the significance of the dream:

> I once believed that it was sent to rouse your distrust of the friendless man whom you had taken as a brother to your heart. I now *know* that it came to you as a timely warning to take him closer still. Does this help to satisfy you that I, too, am standing hopefully on the brink of a new life, and that while we live, brother, your love and mine will never be divided again? (*Armadale*, 815)

The ending of the novel is traditional in so far as it ends with a marriage between the eponymous hero – although Midwinter has an equal claim to this status – and his innocent female counterpart. However, the marriage at the end of the novel is made subordinate, as it is in *Bleak House*, to the theme of romantic friendship. The ambiguous status of Lydia herself, and her timely death, further complicate the status of friendship and marriage respectively, as Allan is restored to the foremost place in Midwinter's affection. It is telling that this relationship, and not the conventionally satisfying marriage between Allan and Neelie, is made the focus of the final lines of the novel.

Both *Vanity Fair* and *Armadale* work within a discernible tradition of satirising female friendship, but both go beyond simple mockery to suggest the ruthless exploitation that this fashion for passionate expression may disguise. In drawing attention not only to the falsity, but to the calculated manipulation of free expression between women, each novel offers a social critique extending far beyond the sometimes complacent remarks of the characters themselves. In each novel the presence of an enduring male friendship, and an unsatisfactory marriage, suggests a greater faith in the efficacy of male relationships. None the less the resolution of *Armadale*, in its very dependence on male bonds, suggests an instability caused by such intense feeling, as friendship seemingly competes with the tradition of the marriage plot.

At the end of the century, both male and female friendship would come under increasingly close scrutiny, but relations between women would prove – despite being more closely 'studied' – to be more resilient than the romantic register previously available for friendship between men.

In both *Vanity Fair* and *Pendennis*, the ingenuousness of the heroine is favourably – if laughingly – contrasted with the sentimental outpourings of her calculating and highly manipulative competitor in the marriage market. The tendentious possibilities of romantic friendship are fully brought out in such appropriation of its language by skilled adventuresses; nor does the more innocent party escape unscathed, as the narrator repeatedly undermines the depth and solidity of female passion. This irony – that the female capacity for feeling at its best should be seen as both pure and ultimately superficial – is never fully addressed; Laura is given brief moments of satirical insight, but both Becky Sharp and Blanche Amory remain the objects, or instruments, rather than the agents of narrative satire.

But if the insincerity and transience of female friendship is available for satire, its erotic potential is clearly not. The intense friendship between Limping Lucy and Rosanna Spearman in *The Moonstone*, for instance, raises the possibility of sexual jealousy as an element in Lucy's hostility to Franklin Blake. It is his disruptive influence that leads to Rosanna's suicide, overthrowing Lucy's plan that she and her friend should live and work together in London. This friendship is treated seriously, but the negative impact of Rosanna's love plot on her relationship with Lucy is not examined at any length; meanwhile, Dickens virtually demonises the possibly lesbian Miss Wade in *Little Dorrit*, but spares her the satire he so often accords to 'strong-minded' female characters.

If Thackeray's realist satire insistently privileges the marriage plot and denigrates female relationships, Collin's sensation fiction make some attempt to redress the balance. In *Armadale*, the clear-sighted Lydia Gwilt takes the narrator's place to become an agent of satire, offering a wry commentary on the central male friendship, even as she parodies traditional perceptions of female flightiness. Her sarcastic ripostes to Mother Oldershaw satirise both the idea that women are incapable of lasting friendship, and the hypocrisy of those who profess feeling too effusively. None the less, by the end of the novel Armadale has been reinstated as the prime focus of Midwinter's love, while the former's marriage to Neelie Milroy is accorded a less central place in the scheme of events than this restoration of male friendship.

Satirical accounts of romantic friendship can act either to explode cultural myths or to perpetuate stereotypes. In treating the conflict between marriage and friendship apparently without giving serious attention to the object of satire, these satirical narrators partly conceal their own interest in the accounts they offer. In her resentful animosity towards Armadale, Lydia has a more obvious reason for doing this than Thackeray's third-person narrators, which does threaten to compromise her status as 'detached' observer. But in Thackeray's texts the satirical mode, appealing to stereotypes of female caprice and shallowness, allows a threatening picture of exploitation and betrayal to emerge, without being fully acknowledged within the terms of the text itself. Such a strategy is characteristic of mid-century fiction, in which a carefully constructed picture depends for its success on the appearance of transparency.

As the stakes became increasingly high, *fin de siècle* texts would treat the power struggles of romantic friendship with overt seriousness, whether these conflicts arose between the friends themselves, between friendship and marriage, or even where the struggle was more simply a battle for appropriate definition.

Chapter Five

Sinister Meaning: Crises at the *Fin de Siècle*

Yet when the glow of friendship's warmth
Sheds halo over mind and senses
'Tis somewhat hard to ascertain
Where friendship ends, and love commences!
(Lucilla Hamilton, 'Love or Friendship?')

The *fin de siècle* is historically a time of nostalgia, but also of crisis and re-evaluation (resurgent fears about the end of the world throughout the 1990s confirm a latterday susceptibility to just such cultural anxieties). It is almost unavoidable, then, to see in the Oscar Wilde scandal and the emergence of the New Woman signs of a deeper crisis of identity in Victorian society as a whole. Towards the end of the century, the nature of romantic friendship itself came under increasingly severe scrutiny. The possibility of a sexual element was increasingly likely to be acknowledged in treatments of romantic friendship that, coupled with its social implications, rendered it doubly suspect to its more sceptical commentators (and as Faderman has shown, the opponents of women's emancipation). Sheila Jeffreys has discussed the process by which lesbianism was constructed as a category by Ellis and others, a process which she sees as having constituted friendship as sexual through a process of assimilation:

> In order to fit women's passionate friendships into the category of lesbianism, it was necessary to categorise the forms of physical expression quite usual in these relationships as homosexual behaviour. So Ellis asserted that the commonest form of sex practice between women was 'kissing and embracing' and that genital contact was rare. (Jeffreys, 109)

This process of definition depended, then, on problematising certain behaviour, not because it was seen as intrinsically sexualised, but because it was associated with an ethos that was in itself coming to be viewed with suspicion. In the course of the next century, the behaviour itself would gain significance as a register of proscribed feeling.

Notably, New Woman fiction is characterised by its attention to the intensities of same-sex friendship, but despite anxiety about control or possible seduction by an influential and unscrupulous friend, female romantic friendship can still be presented unapologetically. As Margaret Jackson has pointed out:

> There were also many strong, independent women who were only peripherally or not at all involved with the Women's Movement, and whose relationships with women could be described as 'passionate', 'romantic', or 'lesbian'. The question of the distinction between 'passionate friendship' and lesbianism is an extremely complex one, not least because of the difficulties in defining the word 'lesbian' in a historical context. (Jackson, 17)

Indeed, romantic friendship retains some of its force for conservatism, even as the potential for radical departures becomes increasingly clear. It is precisely here that the ground is contested in nineteenth-century accounts of the phenomenon.

Although parallels between male and female friendship are discernible in literary treatments throughout the century, the stakes became much higher for male friendship as behavioural norms were radically adjusted at the *fin de siècle*. The trial of Oscar Wilde was famously both a symbol and a catalyst for the anxiety surrounding what Eve Sedgwick has called a 'homosexual panic' in late Victorian England.

As Richard Dellamora puts it:

> Wilde-as-dandy provided something of an early warning signal that the combined prescription and proscription of intense male bonding at public school and the older universities was vulnerable to changes in masculine self-identification. ... Hence the need to separate the gentlemen from the dandies, to retrench, to generate scandals ... (Dellamora, 208)

Alan Sinfield clarifies the particular element of upper- and upper-middle-class education that the Wilde trials threatened to bring into view. Specifically, he posits a relationship between the public schools and the Uranian poetry that was deliberately vilified at the time of the trials:

> ... public schools were crucial in the development of homosexual identity because, despite the official taboo, they contributed, in many instances, an unofficial but powerful cultural framework within which same-sex passion might be positively valued. The poetry of boy-love, towards the end of the nineteenth century, presents the virtues of same-sex passion as elaborated and eroticized versions of the standard public-school virtues – service, physical vigour, hero-worship, and personal loyalty. (Sinfield, 65–6)

The perception of just such a potential eroticism had been leading from the second half of the century to a diminution in the transparent language so greatly celebrated by mid-century writers in their treatments of male friendship. The shift in attitude is clear from a comparison between earlier and later texts, as the openness of romantic feeling so notable at mid-century is largely irreconcilable with *fin de siècle* literary treatments of concealment and secrecy. But even in the 1890s, some kind of compromise could be effected and the transparency of male friendship norms could be discreetly upheld as the mainstay of 'ennobling genius'. George du Maurier's *Trilby*, published in 1894, locates dangerous fascination not in uncircumscribed male language, but in the hypnotic powers of a charismatic male musician on a hitherto tuneless but impressionable girl. Svengali's famous mesmerism of Trilby in order to bring out her singing voice is the very antipathy of the open manner in which the central male friendship is seen to operate. But in order for this dichotomy to work, du Maurier is obliged to construct a carefully regulated context in which his characters' emotion is mediated through narrative comment, much as Trilby herself acts as a cipher for the greater genius of her mentor.

The bestselling *Trilby* deploys many of the strategies used by mid-century writers to justify intense friendship between men, although he expediently locates the important scenes of his story in Paris and characterises the bohemian lifestyle of the central characters as a youthful aberration, as ideal in its romanticism as it is ultimately unsustainable. Still, he stresses the centrality of Little Billee's genius more even than his character as a reason for his friends' admiration and love; the English characters return to their own country separately, and so avoid the difficulties that a representation of such a ménage in London would have presented. (Even so, the setting of the story in the 1850s allows the 'innocence' of the youthful artists to remain uncontested by a supposedly more knowing readership of the 1890s. Although no direct comparisons of friendship norms are made, this forty-year time lag is a point that the narrator reiterates throughout the novel, even as he uses playful anachronism to comment on art and literature as being intrinsically universal.)

The ostentatious boyishness of Taffy, the Laird and Little Billee constitutes a form of special pleading from the outset, and the narrator repeatedly anticipates the diminished passions of middle age, with apposite quotation from Thackeray:

> Oh, ye impecunious, unpinnacled inseparables of eighteen, nineteen, twenty, even twenty-five, who share each other's thoughts and purses, and wear each other's clothes, and swear each other's oaths, and smoke each other's pipes, and respect each other's lights o' love, and keep each other's secrets, and tell each other's jokes, and pawn each other's watches and merrymake together on the proceeds, and sit all night be each other's bedsides in sickness, and comfort each other in sorrow and disappointment with silent, manly sympathy – 'wait till you get to forty year!' (*Trilby*, 100)

A further restraining mechanism is the diffusion of passionate affection between three friends rather than two – even here, the expressions of love are indirect, mediated through the narrator's comments to the reader rather than being openly spoken between the three protagonists. In the opening pages, Little Billee 'looked at his two friends, and wondered if any one, living or dead, had ever had such a glorious pair of chums as these.' (*Trilby*, 8) and the narrator comments that they in turn 'loved him very much indeed' (9).

But the beautiful Trilby is introduced almost immediately after this comment, and attracts two of the three friends, later becoming the innocent cause of their temporary estrangement – ultimately, the Laird will explain that he too was in love with her. Little Billee, who nearly marries Trilby and tragically does not, is able to tell his friends that he loves them after he has confessed his love for a woman – but for much of the novel, this feeling is expressed in the negative form of longing retrospect, as he loses his powers of affection with the disappearance of Trilby and his own subsequent breakdown, and observes his own (scientifically analysed) indifference to his closest friends. Little Billee will suffer breakdown at two points in the novel, and both are explicitly associated with Trilby – on both occasions Taffy and the Laird share the nursing with his mother and sister, and at the end of the novel the Laird will marry this sister, after the death of Little Billee and despite the narrator's earlier refusal to provide such a resolution to the love triangle. *Fin de siècle* fiction could, then, promulgate the ideal of male romantic friendship, but the terms in which it could be presented were increasingly restrictive.

In 1896, the Bishop of Winchester was still able to claim that:

> Many … of those whom we, most deeply revere, thoroughly trust, and secretly love, we have never had a chance of seeing but twice or thrice in our lives. A quick glimpse at a golden opportunity has proved magically potent in attracting and uniting kindred natures; ;and there is a sort of tropical suddenness with which some characters bud, blossom and fruit into a close and undying regard. (Thorold, 6)

But the unexplained reference to 'secretly' loving immediately qualifies this comment, as does the ensuing passage on such friendships, that are maintained by correspondence alone. Critics have long noted the proliferation of interest in the 'double', most famously represented in Robert Louis Stevenson's *The Strange Case of Dr Jekyll and Mr Hyde* and in Wilde's own *The Picture of Dorian Gray*, first published in volume form in 1886 and 1892 respectively. Maintaining a respectable place in society, these characters' transgressions are the more disturbing for being so well concealed.

Wilde's transgressions, likewise concealed for a time, brought about a state of panic in the aftermath of his trials for gross indecency. As early as *The Portrait of Mr W. H.*, he was conflating the traditions of male romantic friendship with those ancient Greek traditions from which the nineteenth century was increasingly anxious to differentiate itself as the implications of pederasty became more pressing. The implications were so uncomfortable precisely because codes of friendship in all-male institutions were understood to lead to just such erotic exchanges. As I have argued, male bonding did not depend for its fervour on such erotic undertones, but the delicate balance of romantic friendship could hardly withstand such a deliberate identification with the sexual aspect of Hellenic ideals. As Jerusha McCormack explains, the idealisation of a working-class actor in this context undermines the class status by which the intensity of romantic friendship is justified:

> … the language that was being devised during the closing decades for 'the love that dare not speak its name' was largely a gentlemanly and encoded discourse, confined to allusions about crushes between boys at prestigious public schools: a kind of initiation into sexual activity common to the elite – who could justify it by citing their Plato in the original. Willie Hughes is an insult to such discourse. (McCormack, in Raby, ed., *The Cambridge Companion to Oscar Wilde*, 109–10)

In 1894, even before the notorious trials, Edward Carpenter was complaining: 'We find in some quarters that even the most naïve attachments between youths are stigmatized as "unnatural" (though, inconsistently enough, not those between girls) …' (Carpenter, *Homogenic Love and its Place in a Free Society*, in Guy, ed., *The Victorian Age: An Anthology of Sources and Documents*, 540). In the final years of the century, anxieties about male friendship could always be contained in the pursuit of imperialist adventure (conducted safely out of sight in the colonies). But English literature's most famous male friendship, that of Sherlock Holmes and Dr

Watson, may or may not owe something of its continued success to the professed passionlessness of the former.

But notwithstanding Carpenter's astute observation, the 1890s of course also saw a re-evaluation of female friendship, as sexologists disputed the grounds on which young girls formed such strong and exclusive attachments. Matt Cook argues that while an intellectual elite were aware of the theories of sexology as early as the 1870s, few people had access to their 'findings' even in the final years of the century. But women's friendships may not initially have appeared vulnerable precisely because they already had built-in defences against just such interpretations. Certainly, female romantic friendship was at first able to maintain its ground – and had indeed been doing so for much of the century in the face of close and sometimes severe scrutiny. While sexology may have got off to a slow start, Alexander Walker's *Intermarriage* offers some (admittedly cloudy) allusions to lesbianism, and its popularity is clear from the number of reprints between its first appearance in 1838 and its posthumous reappearance in 1897 (Walker died in 1852), two years after the Wilde trials and the same year as *Sexual Inversion*. In 1902, Frances Power Cobbe remarked on what she saw as a new fashion for emotional exchanges between women, again suggesting that confidence in female emotionalism as a legitimate means of expression had not abated by the turn of the century.

In *Feminist Lives in Victorian England*, Philippa Levine views intense female friendship, as Faderman also does, as inseparable from the feminist movement of the latter years of the century:

> The singular and distinctive characteristics of this common theme of friendship within the feminist movement of this period is ... the extraordinary closeness which ensued. Even women living at opposite ends of the country made attempts to get to know one another, to sustain contact even if only through correspondence, and to maintain links with other feminist women. (Levine, 68)

It is perhaps tendentious to claim intense bonds between women as the sole province of late Victorian feminists – close friendships between women had always been amenable to a conservative social order, after all; however, Levine goes on to make an important distinction between male and female friendship at this time, in the course of which she implicitly differentiates feminist understandings of friendship from the conservative ideals of mid-century. Specifically, she claims that:

> Women, in choosing female friendship as the primary source of emotional sustenance in lives that were often caught in contradiction, were meshing their political understandings with their social and emotional being; it was an explicit rejection of the division between public and private with which they had been so thoroughly inculcated. ... Whereas in choosing male friendship as a prerogative, men were rejecting the private sphere and embracing notions of masculine consonance and identification, women's friendships – certainly in a feminist context – involved a specific meshing of public and private, and thus a firm rejection of the dualism that divided the sexes. (Levine, 68–9)

The implications of this appropriation of the public sphere did not escape the attention of social and medical commentators. Faderman notes the setbacks caused to the feminist movement by sexologists in particular:

> Whether or not the process was a conscious one, those opposed to women's independence now could hurl, with credible support behind them, accusations of degeneracy at females who sought equality, and thereby scare them back to the hearth with fears of abnormality. (Faderman, 239–40)

Martha Vicinus likewise observes that:

> Women educators, etiquette-book writers, and other advice givers for over a century spoke the same language when discussing romantic friendships. This single discourse held as long as appropriate female roles were clearly defined both within the world of women and in the large middle- and upper-class society. ... As women gained a voice in the public sphere, their single-sex institutions came under attack. ('Distance and Desire: English Boarding School Friendships, 1870–1920', in Duberman, Vicinus and Chauncey Jr, eds, *Hidden from History*, 212)

But the logic of the above arguments, and novels of the period, similarly suggest that such invective was aimed primarily at *groups* of like-minded women, not at the individual friendships that women had been taught to regard as valuable for so much of the century. Faderman points out: 'Of course love between women had been encouraged or tolerated for centuries – but now that women had the possibility of economic independence, such love became potentially threatening to the social order' (Faderman, 240). In the final years of the century, New Woman fiction both represented and evoked anxiety about women's place in society, but works such as Gissing's *The Odd Women* (1893), Meredith's *Diana of the Crossways* (1885) and Sarah Grand's *The Beth Book* (1897) suggest that political solidarity and an organised drive towards economic independence cause more concern than individual relationships. In Grand's account it is Beth's conscious identification with a group of liberal women, centred round the aptly named 'Ideala', that particularly enrages her unprincipled but conventional husband.

First published in 1885, George Meredith's *Diana of the Crossways* is notably radical in its sympathy for married women's disadvantaged status – when her husband fails to divorce her for her supposed adultery, Diana is condemned to an ambiguous existence, having lost the protection enjoyed by married women, but denied the chance of finding a more suitable partner without further loss of reputation. But in marked contrast to a writer like Trollope, who made marital breakdown the pivot of *He Knew He Was Right*, Meredith barely outlines the causes of Diana's marital unhappiness or the resulting misunderstanding. The major relationship treated in the novel is that between Diana and her married friend Emma.

Written some years after the anxieties suggested by 'Carmilla' and the tensions revealed by *Armadale*'s exploration of male friendship and its effect on marriage, *Diana of the Crossways* still insists on a marked level of intensity between the central female characters. The inspiration is overtly Hellenic, 'They had often talked of a classic friendship between women, the alliance of a mutual devotedness men choose to doubt of' (*Diana of the Crossways*, 87), and Redworth compares them to Pythias and Damon. Emma's habit of addressing Diana with the masculine 'Tony', for Antonia, suggests a gender balance between the two that is reminiscent of Tennyson's presentation of a self-contained friendship in *In Memoriam*, but also recalls Diana Mulock Craik's monitions about the gender reversals enacted within female romantic friendship. At various points their shared language is highly charged to the point of superfluity. In explaining her failure to keep up a correspondence during her friend's absence, Diana blames the incursion of marriage:

> But your voice or mine, madre, it's one soul. Be sure I am giving up the ghost when I cease to be one soul with you, dear and dearest! … I was shy. I knew I should be writing to Emmy and *another*, and only when I came to the flow could I forget him. (*Diana of the Crossways*, 32)

Contained elsewhere within this passionate confession, however, is an indication of the conservative framework that validates it. Emma is both a privileged invalid and a recluse. Her marriage has temporarily all but severed her friendship with Diana, as the above conversation suggests. When the characters are first brought together in the novel, it is after a separation of four years, as Emma has accompanied her husband abroad. The close bond between the two women is developed only as Emma's marriage is shown to be circumscribed by her own ill health and her husband's desire for the pleasures of London. The absence of Lord Dunstane for prolonged periods obviates any conflict between him and his wife's friend, but even his occasional presence ultimately has disastrous results. The narrator comments wryly that, 'Women with otiose husbands have a task to preserve friendship' (66), and Dunstane's ill-advised attempt to flirt with Diana leads directly to her catastrophic marriage to a man she does not love.

The continuation of Diana's close friendship with Emma after both are married is unusual in Victorian fiction, but in narrative terms the circumstances are shown to warrant it. Diana is seen not as a threat, but more as a useful resource, by her friend's husband, who is often away from home, and Emma's illness allows her to function as a nurse, which in itself creates a privileged space for intense expression. Indeed, this unity in the sickroom suggests the wider context in which each friend inspires and elevates the other. In particular, Emma's physical frailty repeatedly saves Diana from moral corruption, influencing her directly after the divorce trial:

> There was in her bosom a revolt at the legal consequences of the verdict … and the burden of keeping it under, set her wildest humour alight … This ironic fury, coming of the contrast of the outer and the inner, would have been indulged to the extent of permanent injury to her disposition had not her beloved Emma, immediately after the tension of the struggle ceased, required her tenderest aid. (160)

Some time later, Diana is about to elope with Percy Dacier when she receives an urgent summons to her friend's bedside. On a subsequent visit, Percy himself is affected by the atmosphere surrounding them: 'The two women, striving against death, devoted in friendship, were the sole living images he brought away; they were a new vision of the world and our life' (302).

The narrator approvingly registers the complementary qualities each friend brings to the other:

> Diana and Emma enjoyed happy quiet sailings under May breezes on the many-coloured South-western waters, heart in heart again; the physical weakness of the one, the moral weakness of the other, creating that mutual dependency which makes friendship a pulsating tie. (307)

When the threat of Percy is finally removed by a somewhat unconvincing strategy (Diana is short of money and ingenuously repeats his parliamentary confidences to a newspaper editor, with predictable results), it is Emma who literally saves her life by sharing food and bodily warmth with her. In this climactic scene, the exclusivity of the women's feeling is unmistakeable, but by this stage the narrative has carefully prepared for such fullness of expression and it can be imbibed without suspicion, if not (by a modern reader) wholly without embarrassment:

> '... I have been unhappy. It is not hard to go.'
> Emma strained to her. 'Tony will wait for her soul's own soul to go, the two together.'
> There was a faint convulsion in the body. 'If I cry, I shall go in pain.'
> 'You are in Emmy's arms, my beloved.'
> Tony's eyes closed for forgetfulness under that sensation. A tear ran down from her, but the pain was lax and neighboured sleep, like the pleasure.
> So passed the short winter day, little spoken. (411)

Notwithstanding this seeming privilege of friendship over unsatisfactory marriage, the ending of the novel is wholly conservative in its treatment of female friendship. Despite Diana's clearly stated reluctance, she is married off to the loyal Redworth, Emma's friend. This outcome is comparable to the closing scenes of *Shirley*, in which the eponymous heroine likewise finds her freedom curtailed partly by the contrivance of her friend Caroline, who is in league with the determined suitor. In both cases the potential conflict is dispelled, as marriage to a relation or brother figure suggests the recreation of an ideal family group. Diana's transfer of loyalty is hinted at when the dying Emma expresses a hope that she will live to be godmother to the expected child.

Meredith is certainly unusual in beginning a novel with a friendship between women that is resumed at such an intense level after the marriage of one party. But if the central marriage plot, namely Diana's, is taken as being pivotal in its relation to romantic friendship, the treatment of female relations in *Diana of the Crossways* becomes far more conservative – even at this date – than it first appears. While the expressions of attachment between the two friends are certainly unrestrained, the full apparatus of a controlling mechanism emerges in the course of the novel. Emma's illness and her inadequate marital relations facilitate her close friendship with another woman, but Diana's heterosexual urges are stressed throughout, and her ultimate marriage is actually brought about by her much loved friend. It only requires Emma's final illness to glorify romantic friendship even as it is inevitably superseded by a suitable marriage of the heroine to an honourable and devoted admirer. This ending has been perceived as a failure of the narrator to sustain the radical status of strong feeling between women, as portrayed in their affectionate language and physical desire for each other's presence. But again, placing this relationship in the context of nineteenth-century romantic friendship actually diminishes rather than bolstering its claims to radicalism – the final marriage between Diana and Redworth has been anticipated from an early point in the novel, and Diana's effusions to her friend are contained within this fairly traditional marriage plot. The reader is never allowed to lose sight of this likely outcome, against which the licensed passion of the heroine is reassuringly set.

In illustration of the shift in attitudes taking place in the 1880s, Faderman cites George Moore's depiction of the amorous Cecilia in *A Drama in Muslin* (first published in 1886, a year after *Diana of the Crossways* had offered a largely uncomplicated endorsement of female friendship). From the outset, the friendship between Cecilia and the heroine Alice is compromised by the former's lack of control, and the suggestion of sexual attraction is present from the start: 'In one thing only was she constant – she loved Alice. There was love in those wilful brown eyes – love that was wild and visionary, and perhaps scarcely sane. And the intensity of this affection had given rise to conjecturing' (*A Drama in Muslin*, 3). But notwithstanding this authorial monition, Alice initially reciprocates her friend's passionate expression, and does so without herself incurring suspicion. Indeed, the friendship is life-sustaining in face of the vicissitudes each is to undergo:

> … the girls had found the world cold and heartrending, and, in the severance of ties, nought but their friendship had remained. Alice had accepted it at first from pity, and then had abandoned herself, overcome by the power of an all-giving love. But they who can always accept, think little of the worth; and until now, she had not even dreamed the meaning of it. A moment of effusion had revealed it. Words were unnecessary, and intent on their happiness, absorbed in the dolorous felicities of their sensations, the girls walked onwards in silence. (61–2)

Alice partially withdraws from this friendship when she meets an eligible man, to her friend's undisguised fury; it is at this point that Alice decides Cecilia's compliments are inappropriate and asks her to keep her distance. Cecilia later admits, in language reminiscent of 'Carmilla', that 'I had desired more than God had willed to give me, for I desired you. I desired to possess you wholly and entirely' (*A Drama in Muslin*, 298). However, she also claims the prerogatives of romantic friendship, declaring reproachfully: 'Ah, if you knew the lofty hopes that were once mine, of the high ideal life I once dreamed to live with you; a pure ecstatic life untouched by any degrading passion, unassailed by any base desires!' (300). By 'degrading passion', Cecilia means for the opposite sex, which by implication allows her to reject the stigma of abnormality while reserving the right to fulfil her own passion for Alice.

According to Faderman's interpretation:

> In earlier novels of romantic friendship her sentiments would have been seen as unquestionably noble and would have been very familiar to the women readers. By 1886, in the hands of an 'informed' writer such as George Moore, they are the utterings of a deformed crazy. (Faderman, 290)

But the narrator of *A Drama in Muslin*, sophisticated enough to introduce the possibility of lesbianism, is also subtle enough to distinguish it from romantic friendship proper. A number of exchanges between the two friends show Alice as welcoming and returning intense expressions of love far more extreme than the really quite tame 'There never was anyone so nice as you, Alice' that provokes the seemingly unwarranted retort, 'Cecilia, dear, you shouldn't talk to me like that.; it is absurd. Indeed, I don't think it is quite right' (*A Drama in Muslin*, 227). It is not romantic friendship itself that is being construed as sexually aberrant – at a seemingly arbitrary moment (although, tellingly, after her induction into heterosexual passion), Alice realises that her friend's interest is more than she quite likes, and only at that point does she reject the discourse of romantic friendship in defining their relationship. This rejection of the sexually aggressive figure at the end of the novel is quite in keeping with earlier treatments of the same theme: the similarity to 'Carmilla', for instance, has been noted in another context. Cecilia's retreat into convent life both confirms and sublimates her disappointment – as Frederick Roden has convincingly shown, the religious life could elevate same-sex desire, vindicating its purity at the cost of precluding its implied manifestation.

Ethel Arnold's *Platonics*, published in 1894, and Mary Cholmondeley's *Red Pottage* (1899) both present female friendships as intense and yet seemingly as transparent as any to be found in mid-century writing. Indeed, as I will suggest, *Red Pottage* is the most radical text of all those under consideration here in its treatment of female friendship – although admittedly in the years after Wilde's disgrace, the omission of Hellenism as a frame of reference is likely to be deliberate.

So why was female friendship seemingly immune to the initial retrenchment of passionate expression in the 1890s? One reason may have been the nature of the suspicion surrounding same-sex relations at this time. Matt Cook argues that same-sex sexual relations were associated largely with the city, crucially the locus of male friendship as mediated through gentlemen's clubs and bachelor chambers. For sexologists specifically:

> The environment and external factors became significant in awakening a latent predisposition or inciting an entirely new configuration of desire. Most suggested the importance of schools, universities, prisons and military institutions in this process, but also indicated how life in the city might prompt sexual experimentation and excess ... (Cook, 75)

Notably, female romantic friendship in a range of texts from *Shirley* to *Platonics* envisages a rural idyll as the setting for a life of the soul. More importantly in this context, Cook demonstrates that despite the work of sexologists, the authorities and the newspapers persisted in defining homosexuality in terms of an act rather than an identity:

> Importantly, men were not labeled as homosexuals or inverts by the newspapers or courts during the period and the emphasis continued to be on what they had done. ... (Cook, 59)

It is at least plausible to suggest that what was compromised in the aftermath of the Wilde trials was not the ideal status of romantic friendship *per se*, but its ability to distinguish itself from the manifestations of criminal desire. As stereotypes of the homosexual and his putative behaviour were popularised in the press, so writers such as Symonds and Edward Carpenter doggedly insisted on the 'purity' of same-sex love as derived from the ancients. As this was the very foundation on which male romantic friendship had modelled itself, the fear of one's behaviour being misunderstood – or even leading to arrest – must have been inhibiting to many. What becomes questionable, then, is not the straightforwardness of romantic friendship, but simply the difficulty of safely projecting or recognising it in a context where gesture, language or even personal appearance could all connote deviance. An otherwise perplexing scene in E.M. Forster's *Maurice* makes perfect sense in this context. While at Cambridge, Maurice and Clive form a close friendship, incorporating a level of physical intimacy – Maurice repeatedly strokes Clive's hair, and they habitually sit with their heads against each other's knees. When Maurice initially rejects Clive's declaration of love, however, the latter does not reproach him with his earlier responsiveness or accuse him of encouraging his attachment. Instead, he apologises for having, as he supposes, 'mistook your ordinary friendliness' (*Maurice*, 56) and feels relief that Maurice would at least not report him to the police. What is interesting here is the assumption that even in 1913, when the book was written, 'ordinary friendliness' between male undergraduates at least could involve hair-stroking and a high degree of physical contact. This episode strongly suggests that romantic friendship was compromised from the end of the nineteenth century, not because it implied sexual feeling in itself, but because its mannerisms were difficult to distinguish from a perceived code of homosexual behaviour. Writing in the 1930s, E.F. Benson enthuses about a bachelor don who had 'a romantic and devoted affection' for his father in the late 1840s or early 1850s (Benson, 59). The lack of embarrassment in this account (admittedly, he states that no response was expected from his father) again suggests an assumed audience that can accept the possibility of such a romantic friendship without automatically locating it on a spectrum of same-sex desire.

As lesbianism was notoriously not held to account either in the existing or in the new legislation, female friendship was under less pressure to clarify its intentions. This freedom – noted bitterly by Edward Carpenter and with insidious suspicion by Havelock Ellis, meant that the espousal of romantic friendship could not lead to threats or imprisonment if it failed to regulate its behaviour or distinguish itself sufficiently from sexual deviance. That sexologists such as Ellis did effortlessly conflate female romantic friendship with lesbianism is well known – but the suggestion that women were 'unknowingly' attracted to one another largely excluded sexual acts by definition. While this perception of an unacknowledged but insistent sexual responsiveness is a familiar enough concept at the beginning of the twenty-first century, it none the less allows scope for overt denial and counter-argument. Crucially, a failure to convince others of the limits of a female friendship at the end of the nineteenth century could not land its proponents in a police cell.

A brief consideration of *Red Pottage* and *Platonics* will show how, paradoxically, women's friendships could provide a certain freedom even in the closing years of the century, and how such friendships could be read in safely conservative terms even as they took on radical implications.

Platonics and *Red Pottage*

Ethel Arnold's *Platonics* was published in 1894, and as Ann Ardis points out, it 'offers a fascinating portrait of New Women's responses to the New Hellenism *before* Wilde's trials polarised modern gender distinctions and crystallised the New Hellenism's association with homosexual "deviancy"' (Ardis, in Richardson and Willis, eds, *The New Woman in Fiction and Fact: Fin-de Siècle Feminisms*, 115). The relationship between the central female characters reveals a tension between the desire for loving expression and the false philosophy that has led to Susan's attempt to 'shut her heart' against further inroads.

None the less, in common with earlier writers, Arnold situates the friendship between Susan and Kit within the wider context of heterosexual expectation.

Indeed, the story begins not with female relations, but with Susan's unorthodox friendship with her neighbour, Ronald Gordon. Unconventional but restrained, this friendship appears to be threatened by Kit's return from a four-year absence abroad. This opening crisis suggests a pattern whereby a proposed marriage will be disrupted by friendship, rather than the other way round. While Kit's love for and subsequent marriage to Gordon appears to privilege heterosexual attachment, this conventional outcome is subverted by her continuing love for her friend, whose importance is reasserted at the end of the novel.

Susan's unrequited love for the man whose proposal of marriage she has just rejected initially heightens the intense feeling between her and her friend, as Kit attempts to console her:

> Holding the frail, slight figure in her strong, young arms, bending over the small head and whispering loving, soothing words into her ear, there came a look into Kit Drummond's face which few people would have believed it capable of – a look of such tenderness, such benign loving-kindness, as almost raised friendship into a sacrament. (*Platonics*, 25–6)

Inevitably, it is the friendship between the women themselves that is damaged when Gordon transfers his attentions from Susan to Kit, but this very disruption allows for a more complete expression of the women's love for each other as it is thrown into crisis. Momentarily at least, Gordon is threatened with exclusion, as he indirectly affirms the strength and quasi-religious nature of the women's feeling for each other: 'Must my life be offered up too on the altar of friendship?' (78).

Characteristic of romantic friendship is both Susan's determination to sacrifice all for her friend, and Kit's warning to Gordon that he must not be jealous of their feeling for each other. Reworking the accepted terms of female friendship that ends with marriage, Kit insists that Susan, and not she, will withdraw from their intimate relations, and it is this that she regrets in accepting her suitor. She correctly predicts that: 'I shall be more and more shut out from her heart. And though I love you truly and deeply, I loved Susan first, and for ten years she has been my very life' (97). The narrator confirms that 'there are some women whom no man's love can altogether compensate for the loss of a woman's, and Kit was one of them' (109). As in *David Copperfield*, the friend who stands in the way of marital happiness is abruptly killed off in the final pages (this despite Susan's initial suggestion that all three could be friends). However, Susan's parting letter allows Kit to feel a sense of post-mortem union with her, reminiscent of Tennyson's depiction of his feeling for Hallam in *In Memoriam*. While Kit allows Gordon to read the maid's letter advising her of Susan's illness, it is wholly appropriate that the final words in Susan's own hand should be read by her alone.

Platonics is reminiscent of much nineteenth-century writing on romantic friendship, in so far as its extreme expressions of feeling between friends are enabled by a carefully constructed dynamic. The women's love – which the narrator specifically differentiates from passion – is mediated through their mutual feeling for a male figure who is otherwise largely irrelevant. It is interesting, of course, that this late-century novel should be wary of construing female friendship in terms of 'passion'. But this framework of a marriage plot overtaking the initial female friendship is complicated by the seemingly conventional death of the 'redundant' friend. In permitting Susan and Kit to share an intense union after the former's death, Arnold revitalises their friendship without rendering it threatening to the reader who saw Kit's natural fulfilment in her marriage to Gordon. In creating a relationship based almost entirely on absence (Kit reappears at the beginning only to marry and promptly disappear again), Arnold suggests ambivalence about the acceptable limits of the friendship she presents, and how it might be contained. But ironically, this very absence allows a fuller expression of love between women than might otherwise have been sustainable.

In her introduction to the 1995 edition, Phyllis Wachter acknowledges the ambivalence of Arnold's representation and the contention that her portrayal may have been limited by her anxiety about revealing a sexual aspect to her own relations with other women. She contends that:

> When all conjecture is done, what is known is that Ethel Arnold devoted one of her best creative efforts to the exploration of how female friendships are capable of fortifying a woman in ways which are both exclusive of and different from a woman's attachments to and with men. (introduction to *Platonics*, xxi)

What *Platonics* does not address is the nature of intense feeling between a Gordon and a Susan – it can only represent such a friendship as cordial liking on one side, and passion on the other. This is a problem that Hardy would address with limited success in *Jude the Obscure*, published the following year.

But if *Platonics* contrives to reconcile the collision between female romantic friendship and marriage through the traditional expedient of killing off the spare protagonist, it was left to a later novel – *after* the Wilde trials – to reverse the terms of this resolution in perhaps the most radical denouement since Wilkie Collins's *Armadale*. Mary Cholmondeley's *Red Pottage* comes close to killing one of the pair of female friends, and marries the other in the final pages of the novel. But it is the friendship that remains quite literally central throughout the course of the novel.

As the reception accorded to female friendship in a series of New Woman novels suggests, it was still possible to endorse romantic friendship between women even at the turn of the century without incurring hostility from reviewers. The very anxiety provoked by female political groupings might help to account for the toleration of intensely individual relationships, but it is none the less surprising that the advent of sexology seems to have had little initial impact, given the increasing levels of awareness discernible in much earlier texts. Questions remain about the availability of sexology to a popular audience at this time, but novels such as *Platonics* suggest an authorial awareness of a potentially critical audience. None the less, Frances Power Cobbe was able to comment in 1902 on the emotional content of women's language to each other as a supposedly new fashion, and early misreadings of Mary Cholmondeley's *Red Pottage* are similarly ironic, focusing on her satire of the clergy and her treatment of the marriage plot.

Red Pottage succeeds in portraying a female romantic friendship partly because it adheres at one level – as the reviewers might perhaps have noticed – to a conventional framework in which the heroine's love plot looks set to displace her early friendship. But even before this ending is abruptly sabotaged and unconvincingly patched up with a replacement husband (whose final appearance is mentioned seemingly as an afterthought), the novel has shown itself to be deeply concerned with the nature of female relationships. At the end of the century, Cholmondeley is still responding to the questions raised by earlier novelists about the durability and rôle of female friendship. The superficial Lady Newhaven,

> 'I loved you from the first moment I saw you' she said. 'I don't take fancies to people, you know. I am not that kind of person.' (*Red Pottage*, 44)

is wonderfully reminiscent of Thackeray's Blanche Amory. Indeed, the narrator acknowledges this tradition of male satire, conceding:

> Many sarcastic but true words have been said by man, and in no jealous spirit, concerning woman's friendship for woman. The passing judgement of the majority of men on such devotion might be summed up in the words, 'Occupy till I come.' It does occupy till they do come. (29)

Ann Ardis contends that:

> By contrast with Arnold's characterization of Susan and Kit's relationship, Cholmondeley is very careful *not* to assert the ultimate primacy of a woman's relationship with another woman. Writing in the wake of the scandal of Wilde's trials, perhaps she had no other rhetorical options … ('New Women and the New Hellenism', in Richardson and willis, eds, *The New Woman in Fiction and Fact*, 120)

But its deceptive concession having once been made, the narrator goes on to present a committed and important female friendship that will ultimately emerge as the most important relationship in the novel.

The relationship between Hester and Rachel bears all the hallmarks of an intensely felt romantic friendship. It is characterised by the familiar motifs of inspiration and willingness to die for the beloved. At crucial moments in the novel, each character expresses a desire to die for the other if it would do any good, and it is at one of these key moments that Hester adopts Rachel (to whom her doomed novel will later be dedicated) as her muse:

> And as Hester leaned against Rachel the yearning of her soul towards her suddenly lit up something which had long lain colossal but inapprehended in the depths of her mind. Her paroxysm of despair at her own powerlessness was followed by a lightning flash of self-revelation. She saw, as in a dream, terrible, beautiful, inaccessible, but distinct, where her power lay, of which bewildering hints had so often mocked her. (*Red Pottage*, 37)

This beneficent and transparent influence of one character on another contrasts favourably with anxieties about male influence an identity in texts of the *fin de siècle* (I have noted Robert Louis Stephenson's *Jekyll and Hyde* in addition to Wilde's *Dorian Gray*). But the radical claims of this friendship are made possible only by the careful limitations with which it is endowed. The narrator is particularly careful in delineating these limits and in modifying the very claims that this friendship will ultimately surpass:

> here and there among its numberless counterfeits a friendship rises up between two women which sustains the life of both, which is still young when life is waning, which man's love and motherhood cannot displace nor death annihilate; a friendship which is not the solitary affection of an empty heart nor the deepest affection of a full one, but which nevertheless lightens the burdens of this world and lays its pure hand upon the next. (*Red Pottage*, 29)

Negotiating Craik's prescriptions for spinster friends, this encomium acknowledges the topical suspicion of erotic interest in order to allay it (friendship is *not* the last resort of the lonely and unmarried, but nor is it 'the deepest affection'). The mutual love of Hester and Rachel then is not a temporary expedient, but nor is it overtly set to oust the supremacy of heterosexual union (Rachel's vigorous heterosexuality is stressed in her response to Hugh). It is further justified by the difference in their personalities (Rachel is more reserved and stoical than the mercurial Hester) and by their youth – this is the most obvious reason for the digression in which the narrator recalls their having met as children, allowing a high level of attraction to be depicted with impunity.

Moreover, the convention whereby an inconvenient friend is summarily killed off is threatened in Hester's illness (notably, this follows Rachel's engagement and the symbolic burning of the novel she had dedicated to her). Lord Newhaven had previously reassured his friend, himself in love with Rachel:

> 'It generally needs a magnifying glass to see a woman's friendship, and then they are only expedients till we arrive, Dick. You need not be jealous of Miss Gresley. Miss West will forget all about her when she is Mrs. Vernon.' (*Red Pottage*, 129)

Such dismissive cynicism appears justified when Rachel confronts her own feelings about Hester's illness:

she prayed the more fervently for her friend because she knew that even if Hester died, life would still remain beautiful; the future without her would still be flooded with happiness. … '… Are other women as narrow as I am? Can they care only for one person at a time like me? Ah, Hester! forgive me, I can't help it.' (344)

But in a dramatic volte-face, Hester recovers and it is Hugh who kills himself after his dismissal by Rachel when she learns of his part in Lord Newhaven's suicide. Again, she attempts to recall him, but it is too late to save his life, and he is reconciled to her only as he dies, significantly failing to recognise her actual presence and assuming that he has met her again in a post-mortem state. Redeploying the radical ending of *Armadale*, *Platonics* suggests the sacrificial death of a male figure who has had the temerity to come between two women. In a similar scene of compromise, the ending of the novel details the travels abroad of the two female friends, with a sketchily appended Dick Vernon as presumable husband to Rachel. As in Armadale's marriage to Neeley, heterosexual union is possible when it is so clearly inferior to the relationship between friends; meanwhile, intense friendship is protected by the indisputable precedence given to heterosexual love (it is not the fault of the protagonists that the objects of their love end by killing themselves). In this context, James Gresley's ironic assumption that the women are in pursuit of Dick in their travels together only serves to heighten the reader's sense of their all-importance to each other.

The concerns of *Red Pottage* in 1899 are strikingly similar to those of mid-century portrayals of romantic friendship. But what is astonishing, given the moral climate of the time, is its relegation of heterosexual attachment, even as the narrator ostentatiously defers – in theory – to the supremacy of marriage over friendship.

Both *Platonics* and *Red Pottage* subtly negotiate late-century concerns about the nature of romantic friendship, ostensibly allowing for the ultimate status and importance of marriage. This careful passage through potential objections is characteristic of literary portrayals throughout the century, but within these confines both writers convey a more subversive subtext. It is in this shift that the radical potential of romantic friendship becomes apparent. Where female friendship has been paramount in earlier treatments, it has provoked anxiety in the narrator (notably in 'Carmilla') – in these female-authored texts of the *fin de siècle*, it has become a source of power.

The Picture of Dorian Gray

But if the limits on female friendship could be successfully – if briefly – subverted at this point in the century, the similar constraints on masculine expression were contested only at considerable risk. In the case of Oscar Wilde, an open defiance of changing social codes would lead famously to disaster.

Wilde is remembered not least for his defiance of social and literary convention, but he was by no means the first to deprecate the constraints implied by the notorious cheek of the young person. Writers had been railing for decades against the demands of the three-volume novel and the circulating libraries with which it was associated – George Moore, who anticipated Wilde's dictum 'art for art's sake' in a vigorous argument in his *Confessions of a Young Man*, published in 1886, memorably complained of Mudie's that 'The villa made known its want, and art fell on its knees' (*Confessions of a Young Man*, 146). Again serving as a precursor to Wilde's more famous work, Moore's deliberately titillating autobiography takes self-centred indulgence as a central theme, admitting that its aim is to gain notoriety for the author, and claiming that in any case, morality has no place in art, to which it can only be incidental. Interestingly, the preface includes a letter from Pater (who has been persistently associated with the genesis of *Dorian Gray*), admiring the writing itself while pointedly deprecating its cynicism.

Rejecting the three-volume form, as writers at the end of the century were increasingly ready to do, Wilde, like Moore, offers in his novel a study of the limits of self-indulgence, and he too claims indebtedness to Pater, in exploring the relationship between the senses and the soul. But unlike the *Confessions*, the focus of *Dorian Gray* is on the dynamic of friendship, through which both sensory impressions and psychological analysis are minutely deployed. Opening in a London garden, where the headiness of the flowers create an artistic illusion that both suggests and parodies the pastoral idyll more usually associated with female friendship, the novel immediately sets up a triangular relationship between three male characters, and the only contender for 'female lead', Sybil Vane, dies because her failure to impress Lord Henry Wotton humiliates Dorian as her lover.

Given his aesthetic concerns as expressed in the preface, it would be reasonable to expect a work disclaiming the tradition of romantic friendship as deployed by earlier, 'mainstream' writers. In its much discussed inclusion of homosexual undertones, Wilde's exploration of romantic friendship necessarily diverges from the carefully defined parameters with which writers earlier in the century were so concerned. But *The Picture of Dorian Gray* none the less claims a relationship to the earlier tradition, noticeable in its – very deliberate – disruption of the approved models of behaviour and feeling I have identified as central to more orthodox portrayals.

While there are no specific references to homosexuality, in its intelligibly erotic designs the novel could be seen as taking romantic friendship to what some have seen as its logical conclusion. But such an ahistorical approach would involve automatically conflating eroticism and passion in a way that is resisted by most nineteenth-century formulations of friendship. Where the narrator of *Dorian Gray* diverges from such formulations is not in disguising sexual relations as more acceptable romantic friendships, nor in any discernible claim that intense friendship is necessarily sexual in its bearings. The divergence lies rather in the text's refusal to set out recognisable parameters – in his defence of his work during the Queensbury libel trial, Wilde deliberately refused engagement with the question of Dorian's crimes as either homosexual or not, and more importantly (given the context of his answers in response to legal cross examination), the text itself upholds the potential purity of passion irrespective of its source and without reference to its physical expression.

Linda Dowling's assessment of Oxford Hellenism is of crucial significance to Wilde's treatment of romantic friendship, in so far as it 'provides the means of sweeping away the entire accumulation of negative associations with male love which had remained strong through the beginning of the nineteenth century'

(Dowling, *Hellenism and Homosexuality in Victorian Oxford*, 79). The location of purity within passion is characteristic of romantic friendship, but in its refusal to exile the erotic from this ideal, as exemplified in the references to platonic thought, the narrator threatens to undermine the boundaries that determine the legitimacy of same-sex friendship.

What Wilde is doing in *The Picture of Dorian Gray* is more subtle then than simply disguising or encoding a proscribed erotic element within the male relationships he explores. Indeed, the roughly contemporaneous fictional account of Shakespeare's sonnets, in which an anonymous narrator becomes preoccupied with the detection of a putative Willie Hughes as dedicatee, clarifies the ways in which Wilde attempts to locate sexuality *within* an ideal of spiritual friendship. In discussing Renaissance Hellenism, this first-person narrator recognises a fascination:

> In its subtle suggestions of sex in soul, in the curious analogies it draws between intellectual enthusiasm and the physical passion of love, in its dream of the incarnation of the Idea in a beautiful and living form ... (*The Portrait of Mr W. H.*, 42)

In a striking parallel with the more famous novel, this anonymous narrator becomes obsessed with a portrait as representing a spiritual relation between Shakespeare and the young man who supposedly inspired his poetry, stressing that the physical dimensions of this relationship are unknowable and largely irrelevant. The point, as the narrator sees it, is that a beautiful form can inspire great works of art, and in so doing, reveal the soul of the artist:

> Art, even the art of fullest scope and widest vision, can never really show us the external world. All that it shows us is our own soul ... (*The Portrait of Mr W. H.*, 75)

This sentiment is famously echoed by the artist of *Dorian Gray*, whose secret is that he has revealed his own soul in the portrait of a beautiful youth. Indeed, the narrator and the various spokesmen of the novel picture Dorian as the inspiration for what the artist Basil Hallward terms:

> the lines of a fresh school, a school that is to have in it all the passion of the romantic spirit, all the perfection of the school that is Greek. The harmony of soul and body – how much that is! We in our madness have separated the two, and have invented a realism that is vulgar, an ideality that is void. (*Dorian Gray*, 8–9)

In this account, Basil can be seen to pinpoint and attack the very basis of traditional romantic friendship, whereby passion is expressible *because* it is ultimately distinguishable from sexual responsiveness. In a novel preoccupied with erotic suggestion, this traditional appeal to ancient Greece becomes highly charged. But as Linda Dowling notes with reference to Uranian poetry:

> [its] most radical claim ... would always be that it sang the praises of a mode of spiritual and emotional attachment that was, at some ultimate level, innocent or asexual. Uranian poetry as able to give voice to a counterdiscourse of spiritual procreancy underwritten by the authority of Oxford Hellenism to precisely the degree that it was able to represent itself as superior to the blind urgencies of a merely animal sexuality, either the imperatives

of heterosexual reproductivity or, in the language of ancient social and religious taboo, the bestial degradation of sodomy as anal copulation. This pure and intellectual dimension of Uranian love would allow Wilde to defend it so fearlessly from the Old Bailey witness box … (Dowling, *Hellenism*, 115)

Where earlier writers make careful appeals to Greek worship of the male form as a largely aesthetic embodiment of feeling, Wilde's artist (in line with progressive homosexual apologists of the time) offers the possibility that sexuality may be potentially cerebral and aesthetic in itself. In order to appreciate the subversive force of this conflation, it is important to remember the precision with which more traditional writers separate the purely aesthetic from the erotic, often splitting the two ideas between an approved hero and a more threatening figure whose teaching must be rejected. The narrator of *Dorian Gray* alludes to a tradition that he assumes his readers will still be able to endorse, but in so doing he conflates romantic friendship with the very elements from which it constantly sought to disentangle itself. In giving the language of romantic friendship to such an ambiguous set of relationships, Wilde effectively forces this ideal into alliance with his own position, namely the irrelevance of sexuality to questions of purity.

In responding closely to a tradition of romantic friendship, and indeed adopting many of its concerns, *Dorian Gray* is then all the better able to challenge the assumptions on which it is based. But as I will argue, the real focus of the novel ultimately rests on familiar questions of influence and control, irrespective of the sexual element it seeks to accommodate. Despite the repeated appeals to a new tradition, the motivating force of the novel really rests on its concern with older ideas. The possible inclusion of homosexual love *within* a recognisable formulation of romantic friendship has the potential to be radically subversive. But paradoxically, this very suggestion serves to displace the centrality of the homo-erotic. Sexuality in such an account is made highly visible – even ineluctable – even while it is rendered secondary to the wider (and recognisably traditional) moral concerns of romantic friendship.

The moral focus of the novel is represented by the idealistic Basil, who makes a strong claim for the dependency of art itself on passion. As his friendship with Dorian draws to an end he declares that his work as an artist is also over, recalling:

> Dorian, from the moment I met you, your personality had the most extraordinary influence over me. I was dominated, soul, brain, and power by you. You became to me the visible incarnation of that unseen ideal whose memory haunts us artists like an exquisite dream. I worshipped you. I grew jealous of every one to whom you spoke. I wanted to have you all to myself. I was only happy when I was with you. When you were away from me you were still present in my art. (*Dorian Gray*, 93)

There is no attempt here to distinguish the ideal passion of the artist from the intense emotion of the friend, still less to establish the parameters of that emotion. Basil's interest in Dorian may or may not contain an erotic element, but in a sense this is almost irrelevant. As Michael Gillespie notes:

In every instance, Basil frankly admires Dorian's beauty, and certainly an aura of homoeroticism seems to inform all their exchanges. On closer scrutiny, however, his admiration seems always to be a preliminary sensation. Events clearly show that Basil draws on Dorian for a far more complex set of responses, extending well beyond the gratification of physical desire ... (Gillespie, 82–3)

Where *David Copperfield*, for instance, carefully delineates the context and nature of David's passion for Steerforth, *Dorian Gray*'s focus on the relationship between passion, hedonism and morality seems able to bypass the question of whether or not such attraction is sexual or simply, to use David's term, enthusiastic. It is arguably one of the most modern features of the novel that sexuality becomes irrelevant in determining moral worth.

Dorian's rejection of the moral anchorage offered by Basil signals his acceptance of New Hedonism, as represented (or perverted) by the more fascinating Lord Henry Wotton. The influence of Pater's *The Renaissance: Studies in Art and Poetry* on this aspect of the novel has been well documented, his *Marius the Epicurean* rather less so. In the earlier novel, Marius's philosophy of sensation is determined by his moral outlook, as the narrator is quick to point out: 'Not pleasure, but a general completeness of life, was the practical ideal to which this anti-metaphysical metaphysic really pointed' (*Marius the Epicurean*, 142). Marius reacts with horror to the tortures of the Roman amphitheatre, and ends his life as a convert to Christianity. But stripped of its moral impetus, epicureanism for Dorian becomes simply the search for new sensations in the face of a growing ennui. The text that influences him most is not the religious and philosophical journey of the Roman Marius, but the 'poisonous' story of a modern Parisian, often identified with Jean des Esseintes, the nihilistic protagonist of Huysman's *A rebours* (Wilde himself denied that this was the book responsible for Dorian's fall, making the fine distinction that *A rebours* suggested to him the type of book that Dorian might have read). Either way, this positioning of alternatives is reminiscent of earlier Victorian texts, and with its suggestion of 'good and bad angels' in the placing of Basil versus Lord Henry, we would appear to be in the familiar territory of Dickensian moral triangles (although this is not a comparison that Wilde would necessarily have relished).

Indeed, the visible vitiation of Dorian's soul suggests an earlier tradition yet, that of the Faustian pact. Lord Henry violates the apparently Edenic calm of Basil's garden, subtly playing on Dorian's hitherto unacknowledged desires in order to gain influence over him. In his suggestion of an intuitive rapport, 'you have had passions that have made you afraid' (*Dorian Gray*, 15), Lord Henry already lays claim to a greater understanding of the younger man's character than he knows himself to possess. His desire to captivate Dorian is partly related to intellectual curiosity: 'he had begun by vivisecting himself, as he had ended by vivisecting others' (46). It also reveals the desire for influence and control over others embodied by that similarly world-weary gentleman, James Steerforth. Lord Henry is ten years older than Dorian, and uses his greater experience as a means of controlling him. Where Basil admits to being fascinated by Dorian's personality, such as it is, the more perceptive Lord Henry aims to impose his own personality on what he perceives to be simply a beautiful form:

There was something terribly enthralling in the exercise of influence. No other activity was like it. To project one's soul into some gracious form, and let it tarry there for a moment; to hear one's own intellectual views echoed back to one with all the added music of passion and youth; to convey one's temperament into another as though it were a subtle fluid or a strange perfume: there was a real joy in that … (29)

John Herdman is surely right in seeing the rapport between Dorian and Lord Henry as narcissistic (Herdman, 140) – where Dorian sees his own attractiveness reflected back to him, somewhat vampiristically, Lord Henry celebrates the absorption of his own personality into another form. It is under the influence of Lord Henry's encomium on youth that Dorian first wishes to rupture the interdependence of body and soul, thus undermining the accepted Victorian register for identifying the state of one's soul by appeals to physiognomy. By repeatedly encouraging Dorian to court new impressions, Lord Henry dangerously remains – as Wilde himself remarked – a 'spectator' of life, disregarding the moral consequences of the influence he exercises. Nothing could be more distant from the democratic spirit enshrined in the Socratic ethos that sought to strengthen emotional and physical bonds between men. Little wonder the picture of Dorian Gray undergoes the most appalling kinds of disfiguration, as he becomes tyrannised by passions that need to be disciplined – not exploited – by the care and affection constituting paiderastia (Bristow, in Raby, ed., *The Cambridge Companion to Oscar Wilde*, 213).

But as Michael Gillespie points out, the question of responsibility is a complex one – Lord Henry acts as a deliberate tempter, but Dorian later complains that Basil first taught him to be vain of his good looks. And Dorian himself must bear the ultimate responsibility for his actions (a conclusion he rashly tries to evade in his final stabbing of the portrait).

The precise stance of the narrator is not made clear, indeed there are moments of seeming complicity in Dorian's fall:

Self-love is the sin by which Dorian falls, but the tone of the writing repeatedly attests Wilde's complicity in Dorian's self-love. A subtle transposition of values is repeatedly at work. Sin and vice are not essentially reprehensible because they are evil, but because they are *ugly*; or rather, evil is seen almost solely in terms of ugliness. And after all, is there not a kind of beauty in ugliness, and therefore a kind of beauty in sin? It is impossible to escape the impression that at times Wilde finds Dorian's sin attractive. (Herdman, 139)

This impression is borne out by a disturbing comment in the text whereby Dorian's consciousness and the narrator's become momentarily indistinguishable:

Is insincerity such a terrible thing? I think not.
It is merely a method by which we can multiply our personalities.
Such, at any rate, was Dorian Gray's opinion. (*Dorian Gray*, 117)

If the question of responsibility is never fully resolved, the novel does maintain a strong focus on the theme of control and influence so characteristic of literary romantic friendships. Basil occasionally doubts the appropriateness of his own intense feeling, although it is he who is dominated by Dorian, seeing in him on their first meeting:

some one whose mere personality was so fascinating that, if I allowed it to do so, it would absorb my whole nature, my whole soul, my very art itself. (5)

This exchange of influence makes for a complex rendering of the traditional themes of romantic friendship, particularly as Dorian's fascination for Basil is entirely unintentional. That Dorian himself is so vapid a character in the first chapter simply confirms the power of the abstract ideal encapsulated in this declaration. Intense feeling for the beauty of form, here represented by a flawless male figure, inextricably links art, romantic idealism, and arguably, erotic responsiveness. Basil, the most trustworthy proponent of romantic idealism, represents the most sincere moral voice in the novel, but he is marginalised almost from the beginning.

The dominant voice throughout is that of Lord Henry, either directly or in his recommendation of 'poisonous' reading matter – references to the insidious effects of poison recur with considerable frequency in the narrative description of Dorian's fall. Where Basil is helplessly mesmerised by Dorian, Lord Henry initially sees himself as controlling the younger man and guiding his responses. Only gradually does he come to realise: 'It often happened that when we thought we were experimenting on others we were really experimenting on ourselves' (48). Towards the end of the novel, he reveals his own passion, although by this stage Dorian is too preoccupied to listen, confessing obliquely that the smell of lilacs has a profound effect on him, and mentioning some minutes later that 'I don't think there have been such lilacs since the year I met you' (180). What becomes clear in the course of the novel is that influence operates in several directions simultaneously, whatever the ostensible dominance of one character over another. The danger of passion is that it is not ultimately controllable, as Lord Henry has tried to believe, or containable within art, as Basil would desire. In portraying Dorian's moribund degeneracy, the narrator implicates both aesthetic values and the pursuit of physical sensation in the loss of control experienced by all three of the central characters.

What *The Picture of Dorian Gray* does, as I have suggested, is to take the tradition of romantic friendship and systematically disrupt its precepts. Notably, the ideal of self-sacrifice becomes the self-love of a character who attempts to evade all moral responsibility. Dorian's obsession with his own portrait causes him both relief at the physical deterioration he has escaped, and anxiety lest his true self be revealed to others. Where Basil refuses to exhibit the picture for fear that it shows the secret of his own soul, namely his adoration of the sitter, Dorian employs it as the accurate reflection of his soul that various characters ironically claim to see in the purity of his ever-youthful face. If the picture represents Dorian's soul, Basil could be taken as the embodiment of his conscience, and it is this that he does succeed in destroying. Where the ideal of romantic friendship offers an elevating moral influence, Dorian is concerned to avoid the guilt that this would represent in his own case. This refusal of salvation is in keeping with the idea of the 'devil's bargain' satirically raised by a woman Dorian has ruined – it is no coincidence that he is moved to murderous rage just as Basil is trying to remember a prayer that might move him to repentance.

Dorian in a sense becomes the vampiristic successor to Lord Henry, rejoicing in his corruption of the most promising young men who come in his way and perpetuating the corruption of his own soul by deluding and corrupting a series of women (it should not be forgotten that the known victims of his predatory sexuality are all female). In the ultimate rejection of romantic friendship, Dorian actually murders the friend whose passionate devotion embodies this ideal, and the narrator is at pains to point out that he sleeps particularly well that night. This final act of defiance not only parodies the sanctity of romantic friendship, but reverses the norm according to which the central protagonist resists the influence of a dubious friend. Even in the subversive 'Carmilla', which I explored in Chapter Three, the vampire is ultimately vanquished by the victim she has claimed to love. In Wilde's rendering, the intended object of a benign influence literally extirpates the redemptive possibilities offered by the narrative, as the more moral character is expelled in the final pages.

The Picture of Dorian Gray is, then, firmly rooted in the tradition it seeks to disrupt. Fascination is linked both to ennui and the desire for new sensation, and the idealism associated with artistic inspiration. The exercise and loss of control are central to the development of Dorian's personality, and form the focus of the novel as a whole. The nature of Dorian's guilt is necessarily hard to pinpoint, not only because his homosexual crimes can only be implied, but because it involves the marginalisation and ultimately the expulsion of the only figure who remains committed to a moral (if not an orthodox religious) position. In distorting and disrupting the concerns of romantic friendship, *Dorian Gray* draws attention to its own place in that tradition, and is able to exploit the latent threat contained within such an intensely felt influence as the accepted model of romantic friendship seem to endorse. In this sense, it both works within the tradition and exposes the fractures endemic to it, hitherto suggested most clearly by the sensation writer Sheridan Le Fanu.

But where *Dorian Gray* is most radical, and therefore most disturbing, is in its refusal to conflate youthful purity and innocence. Dorian is largely responsible for his own downfall even at the moment where he is shown at his most naïve, wishing decay on the portrait in order to preserve his own youth. He subsequently resists all attempts to reform him, a narrative device that draws attention to his complicity in his own decay. The location of corruption in Dorian himself rather than in the picture is confirmed in the final scene, where his face takes on the visible signs of corruption. This transference confirms the inevitability of an ultimate retribution, as in his final desperate attempt to destroy the visible emblem of his soul, he simply destroys the soul itself.

Working within a recognisable framework of male romantic friendship, *Dorian Gray* reworks several of the themes to be found in an earlier model such as *David Copperfield*. Like Steerforth, or the even earlier Henry Fortescue of 'Early Friendship', Lord Henry Wotton is a jaded member of the upper class who finds transient interest in fascinating others. In Wilde's version, however, the moral certitudes represented by Basil are relegated to the sidelines before being unceremoniously murdered with him; the corrupt Lord Henry himself becomes fascinated by Dorian, who is himself held accountable for his crimes even as sympathy for Lord Henry's unhappiness increases. This increasing uncertainty in texts detailing male friendship is echoed in novels centring on female relationships, an issue that becomes increasingly fraught towards the latter years of the century.

Conclusion

I never used it lightly; unto me
A sacredness hung round it; for a sign
I held it of our common words that be
Initial letters of a speech divine:
Oh, take this coin, too oft to worthless ends
Profaned, and see upon its circlet shine
One Image fair, one Legend never dim;
And whose but Caesar's? for this word by Him
Was used at parting, 'I have called you "*Friends*".'
(Dora Greenwell, 'To A Friend')

The excesses of romantic friendship may now make it appear remote – perhaps even alien – as an ideal, and its history is notoriously difficult of recovery. But whatever ambiguities later scholars have identified, in the nineteenth century demonstrations of love between friends could escape condemnation from, or even be deployed by, otherwise conservative commentators, who applauded same-sex friendship as a union of souls even as they relegated self-styled 'romantic friendship' in theory to the realm of the adolescent imagination.

The standard prescriptions for conduct and even feeling in friendship extended through a series of life stages with diminishing returns at each stage: different expression was appropriate to the phases of school, early adulthood and after marriage respectively, with a sometimes grudging and sometimes relieved concession for close friendship being made to women in particular who did not marry. But various writers suggest that these prescriptions may not always have been adhered to – the heroes of Collins's *Armadale* defiantly place their friendship above marriage itself, for instance, while *David Copperfield* pre-empts any possible tension by strategically placing the breakdown of the friendship with Steerforth before the introduction of Dora. Proscriptive moralists such as Ouida, and in this context, Thackeray, continually praise reticence as a more 'English' and 'aristocratic' virtue, in an effort to recommend it to a middle-class readership; but their technique of throwing the excesses of romantic friendship into relief by contrasting passionate expression with ostensible reserve, attempts to suggest a greater divide than really exists between romantic friendship and the expression permitted to their own characters (indeed, the inconsistencies of Thackeray's narrators itself undermines his ostensible disdain for emotionalism).

None the less, novels that depict friendship as a central concern do tend to focus on specifically youthful feeling (Gaskell's *Cranford* being a famous exception as the ultimate example of a community of single, mainly middle-aged women). Even in that most expansive form, the three-volume novel, there is admittedly rarely space for the adventures of a hero's entire lifetime. But in the wide range of characters such a format encourages, it is surprising to find so few middle-aged friends.

Gissing offers a moving and ultimately tragic portrayal of male friendship after 40 in the Reardon–Biffen pairing, in *New Grub Street*, and a more optimistic account of supportive female community in *The Odd Women* (in which he redeploys the stereotype of unmarried women living together for mutual comfort). But the appeals to the power of friendship made by other writers are more often addressed implicitly or explicitly to the young.

Thackeray for one regrets the tendency to worldliness that he sees as impeding the course of friendship after a certain age, when the exigencies of a career necessarily cramp youthful sensibilities, and nostalgic appeals to youthful friendship are common (Disraeli's invocation of Eton is defined in terms of a lost and necessarily transient idyll that he sees as irrecoverable; its essential power is to influence conduct in later life and to moderate the ruthlessness demanded of men in the world).

Despite these reservations, writers continued to analyse what they saw as the inevitably changing nature and rôle of friendship as adult responsibilities superseded youthful ties – William Alger went so far as to prescribe friendship as a cure for the ills of modern life:

> Thoughtful observers agree, that the most ominous characteristic of the present age is, its complication of interests, its doubts, its weariness, its frittering multiplicity of indulgences, cares, and obligations, the best individual remedy for this evil is friendship. (Alger, 416)

In the course of the twentieth century and at the beginning of the twenty-first, such a distinctive form of expression has variously been taken to denote the irretrievable innocence of an age less socially and sexually aware than our own, and an accepted outlet of sorts for culturally proscribed same-sex sexual passion. The notion of a 'homosexual panic' overtaking a long-unregulated form of same-sex desire somewhere in the 1890s is a highly persuasive one, but it works uncritically in this sense within the terms of late nineteenth-century thought. While the 'panic' is not in dispute, such an analysis presupposes the accuracy of the sexologists' observation in locating an erotic element in romantic friendship.

While this abrupt clampdown on homosexual expression at the end of the century did inevitably involve a corresponding diminution in expressions of passionate regard between friends, the traditionally accepted account leaves several questions unanswered. Why, as the most obvious one, would an age so preoccupied with self-control and sexual regulation as the Victorian simply fail to notice the excesses of romantic friendship, and even give it a licence not accorded to other areas of social and cultural life? Again, given the medical interest in the supposed evils of masturbation, that most clandestine and well-hidden form of sexual deviance, is it likely that female friends could openly share a bed without arousing suspicion, purely on the grounds that unmarried women lacked sexual awareness?[1] Finally, and most

---

1   Martha Vicinus raises this very issue, arguing that 'Women together, especially in bed together … were not above suspicion. The legal profession struggled to define, or to leave carefully undefined, passion between women. Recognition and denial went hand in hand' (Vicinus, 61). But this remark serves to contextualise a particular scenario (Vicinus is talking about the accusations of female sexual deviance raised by the Dame Cumming Gordon libel case of 1811) – throughout the century, women openly shared beds without necessarily

importantly, there is the seemingly insuperable difficulty of negotiating the Platonic account of male friendship and repackaging it for the consumption of a Victorian middle class with circumscribed notions of morality. The widespread endorsement of this ideal necessarily bypasses the issue of pederasty, but with its eyes very much open, as the accounts of various writers testify. The cultural investment in romantic friendship as derived from Platonic love suggests a deliberate consensus to extract certain elements and not others – again, this conscious adaptation of Greek ideals can hardly be consistent with a lack of sexual awareness.

Once these questions about conscious intent begin to be asked, a more complex pattern is discernible in Victorian accounts of romantic friendship long before the retrenchments of the *fin de siècle*. Despite its apparent boundlessness, the template for such friendships is actually quite proscriptive, and largely dependent on both external scrutiny and the internalisation of certain mores. The best-known 'rule', observed by a succession of critics and historians, is that they should not survive the marriage of the proponents involved. The ideal itself is associated almost entirely with the young, and impingement of the designated boundaries may lead to ridicule or reprimand, either from one of the parties or from a fictional narrator. The course of literary romantic friendships itself points to the largely unspoken rules that are assumed to govern them. There may be no suggestion of erotic exchange or even acceptance of such a possibility – *Bleak House*'s Esther and Ada show no sexual interest in each other, neither do Caroline and Shirley in Brontë's novel; the male friendship in *Armadale* is highly charged, but its most damning commentator, the sexually transgressive Lydia, does not seem to contemplate any homo-erotic element. That this refusal to accept an erotic element is not based on ignorance is implied in the lengths nineteenth-century texts go to in order to expel any such threat or to withstand this interpretation in the first place. Tennyson's repeated positioning of himself as Hallam's widow in *In Memoriam* is made possible – and would have been rendered acceptable to his first readers – precisely by his awareness of where the lines needed to be drawn. An alternative framework posits one party as remaining wholly unconscious of the erotic possibilities of intense same-sex friendship, an innocence that their dangerously knowing friend attempts to exploit (Steerforth's manipulation of David *circa* 1850 is a notorious case in point). In these narratives of 'split' characteristics, the subversive figure is ultimately expelled from the text, either with or without the final realisation by the innocent friend of what has been at stake.

The imposition of these rules allowed the Victorians to invest in an ideal of friendship that emphasised elements of self-sacrifice (Tennyson's regret that he cannot 'thro' his lips impart / The life that almost dies in me' may often be read as sexual, but the real issue here, as the poet narrator sees it, is that he has failed to give his life for that of his friend) and inspiration (Robert Audley and the fair-haired

---

inviting conjecture, and such practices are described under ordinary circumstances with a casual matter-of-factness. It is for precisely this reason that the more suspicious among medical writers felt they must warn parents to be vigilant about the sleeping arrangements made for their children – that such advice was largely ignored suggests the stronghold same-sex friendship inhabited in the Victorian imagination.

Armadale both develop resolution and earnestness as a direct result of their respective friendships, while Rachel becomes Hester's muse in *Red Pottage*). In most accounts of romantic friendship, the ideal is only viable as long as the relationship remains within the realms of the non-erotic, and this status must be constantly reinforced and displayed for the reader's reassurance – the difficulty for a narrator is to do this without suggesting any obvious consciousness on the part of the protagonists themselves.

But to articulate the ideal of romantic friendship in the terms I have employed is not to deny its tensions, aberrations and failures. This much is implied in the necessity for outlawing or even killing such predatory figures as Steerforth and Carmilla and in the very necessity writers perceived for enforcing prescribed limits. Anxieties about the loss of control associated with intense emotion are suggested by the frequent susceptibility of romantic friends to nervous illness – most frighteningly, Robert Audley fears that he will literally succumb to insanity. Various writers were similarly concerned with the conflict between friendship and marriage lurking beneath the rhetoric of a rehearsal for life's 'great drama'. In *David Copperfield*, *Diana of the Crossways* and *Platonics*, a friend conveniently dies to make way for the marriage of the hero or to allow the heroine to focus her attention (at least ostensibly) on her new husband. But as early as *Bleak House*, and likewise in *Lady Audley's Secret*, *Armadale* and *Red Pottage*, something goes very wrong with the mechanism, and it is the lover or spouse who dies, allowing to the bereaved party a full restoration of rights in an earlier romantic friendship – in the final tableau of *Red Pottage*, the successful suitor for Rachel's hand is seen slightly off-centre while she and Hester appear together harmoniously centre-stage.

If later treatments of same-sex romantic friendship suggest a greater level of anxiety or subversive potential, still the conventions governing female friendship need only the most minor adjustments in the last years of the century in order to be celebrated safely. Indeed, as *Red Pottage* demonstrates, novels of the 1890s can depict a subtle displacement of heterosexual union by female friendship and still attract notice mainly for a love plot or for satirising the Church. What no writer could do with impunity, as Hardy would discover in 1895, was to apply the rules of romantic friendship to an ambiguous study of youthful male–female relations.

The realignment of loyalty along gender lines, changes in the relations between men and women, and the ubiquitous spectre of 'the breakdown of the family' – all these issues inform literary portrayals of romantic friendship in the course of the century. But more threatening even than such incursions was, of course, the identification of such a highly valued form of friendship with homosexual feeling, most publicly by the highly articulate Oscar Wilde at the end of the century. The resulting furore did nothing to reverse the tendency of male-centred texts in the last years of the century either to contain their friendships within strict limits or at least to take them abroad in the name of empire and adventure. I have argued none the less that this disruption did not wholly destroy the ideal itself for even its most orthodox adherents. Romantic friendship was not necessarily conflated with homosexuality – it may often have been damned by association, but that is not the same thing.

As an ideal in literature, romantic friendship is deeply flawed by contradictions: it is implicitly feminised even while impugning the female capacity for sincere friendship; almost by definition unconscious of erotic potential, it none the less depends for its status on a constant rejection of the sexual; upholding the sickroom as the site of intimacy and self-sacrifice between friends, it uses illness as a signifier of unhealthy emotion; taking Greek pederasty as a model, it recoils from the arguments of Uranian intellectuals at the end of the century. Dangerously unrestrained but simultaneously proscriptive, sacrosanct but transient and frequently satirised, its energy and complexity exemplify the preoccupations of the age that was finally to disavow it.

Bibliography

Primary Sources

Alger, William, *The Friendships of Women* (Boston, MA: Roberts Brothers, 1868).
Anon., *Famous Friendships of Men and Women eminent in politics and literature etc.* (London: Ward, Lock, 1883).
Anon., *Sayings about Friendship; with some reflections thereon. An unphilosophical essay* (London: Jarrold and Sons, 1864).
Anon., *Thoughts on Friendship* (London: Geo. Burns & Co., 1858).
Armstrong, Isobel, *Victorian Scrutinies: Reviews of Poetry 1830–1870* (London: Athlone Press, 1972).
Arnold, Ethel, *Platonics* (Bristol: Thoemmes Press, 1995).
Barker, Juliet (ed.), *The Brontës: A Life in Letters* (London: Viking, 1997).
Benson, E.F., *As We Were: A Victorian Peepshow* (London: Penguin, 2001).
Bentley's Miscellany (1840).
Black, Hugh, *Friendship* (London: Hodder and Stoughton, 1897).
Braddon, Mary, *Lady Audley's Secret* (Oxford: Oxford University Press, 1987).
Brontë, Charlotte, *Shirley* (Oxford: World's Classics, 1998).
Brookes, John, *Manliness: Hints to Young Men* (London: James Blackwood, date unknown).
Broomfield, Andrea and Sally Mitchell (eds), *Prose by Victorian Women: An Anthology* (New York: Garland, 1996).
Browning, Elizabeth Barrett, *Aurora Leigh* (Oxford: World's Classics, 1993).
Burstall, Sara, *Retrospect and Prospect* (London: Longman, Green, 1933).
Cambridge Review, vol. 4 (1882/1883).
Cholmondeley, Mary, *Red Pottage* (London: Virago, 1985).
——, *Sir Charles Danvers* (New York: Harper Brothers, n.d).
Collins, Wilkie, *Armadale* (Oxford: World's Classics, 1989).
Dickens, Charles, *David Copperfield* (Oxford: World's Classics, 1999).
——, *Our Mutual Friend* (Oxford: World's Classics, 1998).
Disraeli, Benjamin, *Coningsby, or The New Generation* (London: Longmans, Green, 1879).
du Maurier, George, *Trilby* (Oxford: World's Classics, 1998).
Edgeworth, Maria, *Helen* (New York: Macmillan, 1896).
Edwards, B.B. and E.A. Park, *Selections from German Literature* (New York: Gould, Newman and Seaton, 1839).
Eliot, George, *The Mill on the Floss* (Oxford: World's Classics, 1998).
Ellis, Havelock and John Addington Symonds, *Sexual Inversion* (London: Wilson and Macmillan, 1897).
Ellis, [Sarah], *The Daughters of England: Their Position in Society, Character and Responsibilities* (London: Fisher, Son & Co., [1845]).

——, *The Women of England: Their Social Duties and Domestic Habits* (London: Fisher, Son & Co., 1839).

Erith, Francis Norton, *The Pleasures of Friendship, and other poems* (London: Whittaker, 1849).

Falconer, Lanoe, *Shoulder to Shoulder: A Tale of Love and Friendship* (London: Griffith Farran Oheden and Welsh, 1891).

Feminist Studies, 18 (1992).

Forster, E.M., *Maurice* (London: Edward Arnold, 1971).

Gaskell, Elizabeth, *Wives and Daughters* (Harmondsworth: Penguin, 1969).

Gissing, George, *The Odd Women* (Oxford: World's Classics, 1992).

Grand, Sarah, *The Beth Book* (London: Virago, 1980).

Greenwell, Dora, *Selected Poems* (London: Walter Scott).

Guy, Josephine M., ed., *The Victorian Age: An Anthology of Sources and Documents* (London and New York: Routledge, 1998).

Hamilton, Lucilla, 'Love or Friendship?' (ProQuest Information and Learning Company, PCI Full Text: taken from *Temple Bar*, 104, January/April 1895).

Herbert, Sir Maxwell, 'The Conduct of Friendship', *Nineteenth Century*, 34 (1893), 399–415.

Hughes, Thomas, *Tom Brown at Oxford* (Reading: Puffin Classics, 1983).

——, *Tom Brown's Schooldays* (Reading: Puffin Classics, 1983).

——, *True Manliness: From the Writings of Thomas Hughes* (Boston, MA: D. Lothrop, 1880).

Huysmans, J.K., *A rebours/Le drageoir aux épices* (Union Générale d'Éditions, 1975).

Jackson, Henry, *A First Friendship* (London: Parker Son and Bourn, 1863).

Jump, John D. (ed.), *Tennyson: The Critical Heritage* (London: Routledge and Kegan Paul, 1967).

Lang, Cecil Y. and Edgar F. Shannon Jr (eds), *The Letters of Alfred Lord Tennyson*, vol. 1 (Oxford: Clarendon Press, 1982).

Le Fanu, Sheridan, *In A Glass Darkly* (Oxford: World's Classics, 1993).

Meredith, George, *Diana of the Crossways* (London: Constable, 1910).

Moore, George, *A Drama in Muslin* (Buckinghamshire: Colin Smythe, 1993).

——, *Confessions of a Young Man* (London: Penguin, 1939).

Miller, Walter J., *Offerings to Friendship and Truth* (London: Hamilton, Adams & Co., 1877).

Nadel, Ira Bruce (ed.), *Victorian Fiction: A Collection of Essays From the Period* (New York: Garland Publishing, 1986).

Nineteenth Century, 34 (July–December 1893).

North American Review, 139:6 (December 1884).

Ouida, *Under Two Flags* (Oxford: Oxford University Press, 1995).

——, *Views and Opinions* (London: Methuen, 1896).

Pater, Walter, *Marius the Epicurean* (London: Jonathan Cape, 1927).

——, *The Renaissance: Studies in Art and Poetry* (London: Collins, 1961).

Patmore, Coventry, *The Angel in the House/The Victories of Love* (London: Routledge).

Pickering, Percival Andree, *An Essay on Friendship* (London: H. Sotheran, 1875).

Ray, Gordon N. (ed.), *The Letters and Private Papers of William Makepeace Thackeray*, vols I and II (London: Oxford University Press, 1945).

Reade, Charles, *Hard Cash* (London: Chatto and Windus, 1922).

Showalter, Elaine (ed.), Christina Rossetti, *Maude*, Dinah Mulock Craik, *On Sisterhoods/A Woman's Thoughts About Women* (London: William Pickering, 1993).

Storey, Graham, Kathleen Tillotson and K.J. Fielding (eds), *The Letters of Charles Dickens*, vol. V (Oxford: Clarendon Press, 1981) .

—— (eds), *The Letters of Charles Dickens*, vol. viii (Oxford: Clarendon Press, 1995).

Symonds, John Addington, *In the Key of Blue and Other Prose Essays* (London: Elkin Mathews and John Lane, 1892).

Tennyson, Alfred, *A Critical Edition of the Major Works* (Oxford: Oxford University Press, 2000).

Thackeray, Anne, *Toilers and Spinsters and Other Essays* (London: Smith, Elder & Co., 1874).

Thackeray, William Makepeace, *The History of Pendennis* (London: Penguin, 1986).

——, *Vanity Fair* (Oxford: World's Classics, 1998).

Thorold, Anthony W., *On Friendship* (London: Ibister, 1896).

Trollope, Anthony, *An Autobiography* (Oxford: Oxford University Press, 1999).

Trumbull, Henry Clay, *Friendship the Master-passion; or, the nature and history of friendship, etc.* (Philadelphia, PA: J.D. Wattles, 1892).

Tytler, Sarah [Henrietta Keddie], *Papers for Thoughtful Girls, with illustrative sketches of some girls' lives* (London: Hamilton, Adams & Co., 1862).

Walker, Alexander, *Intermarriage; or the mode in which, and the causes why, beauty, health, and intellect result from certain unions, and deformity, disease and insanity from others* (Birmingham: Edward Baker, 1897).

Wilde, Oscar, *The Picture of Dorian Gray* (Oxford: World's Classics, 1998).

——, *The Portrait of Mr W. H.* (London: Hesperus Press, 2003).

Wilton, J.H., *The First Crime: or, True Friendship* (London: Piper, Stephenson and Spence, 1854).

Yonge, Charlotte, *Womankind* (1876).

Secondary Sources

Abelow, Rachel, 'Labors of Love: The Sympathetic Subjects of *David Copperfield*', *Dickens Studies Annual*, 31 (2002), 23–46.

Adams, James Eli, *Dandies and Desert Saints: Styles of Victorian Manhood* (Ithaca, NY: Cornell University Press, 1995).

Auerbach, Nina, *Our Vampires, Ourselves* (Chicago, IL: University of Chicago Press, 1995).

Bachman, Maria K. and Don Richard Cox, 'Wilkie Collins's Villainous Miss Gwilt, Criminality, and the Unspeakable Truth', *Dickens Studies Annual*, 32, pp. 319–38.

Bailin, Miriam, *The Sickroom in Victorian Fiction: The Art of Being Ill* (Cambridge: Cambridge University Press, 1994).

Barickman, Richard, Susan MacDonald and Myra Stark, *Corrupt Relations: Dickens, Thackeray, Trollope, Collins and the Victorian Sexual System* (New York: Columbia University Press, 1982).

Barker, Juliet, *The Brontës* (London: Phoenix Press, 1994).

Barreca, Regina (ed.), *Sex and Death in Victorian Literature* (Basingstoke: Macmillan, 1990).

Bashford, Alison, *Purity and Pollution: Gender, Embodiment and Victorian Medicine* (Basingstoke: Macmillan, 2000).

Blair, Emily, '"The Wrong Side of the Tapestry": Elizabeth Gaskell's *Wives and Daughters*', *Victorian Literature and Culture* (2005), 33, 585–97.

Bristow, Joseph, *Effeminate England: Homoerotic Writing After 1885* (Buckingham: Open University Press, 1995).

Carey, John, *The Violent Effigy* (London: Faber, 1991).

Chandos, John, *Boys Together: English Public Schools 1800–1864* (New Haven, CT: Yale University Press, 1984).

Cook, Matt, *London and the Culture of Homosexuality, 1885–1914* (Cambridge: Cambridge University Press, 2003).

Cooper, Helen, *Elizabeth Barrett Browning, Woman and Artist* (Chapel Hill, NC: University of North Carolina Press, 1988).

Cosslett, Tess, *Woman to Woman: Female Friendship in Victorian Fiction* (Atlantic Highlands, NJ: Humanities Press International, 1988).

Cvetkovich, Ann, *Mixed Feelings: Feminism, Mass Culture, and Victorian Sensationalism* (New Brunswick, NJ: Rutgers University Press, 1992).

Dellamora, Richard, *Masculine Desire: The Sexual Politics of Victorian Aestheticism* (Chapel Hill, NC: University of North Carolina Press, 1990).

Dolin, Tim, *Mistress of the House: Women of Property in the Victorian Novel* (Aldershot: Ashgate, 1997).

Donoghue, Emma, *Passions Between Women: British Lesbian Culture 1668-1801* (London: Scarlet Press, 1993).

Dowling, Andrew, *Manliness and the Male Novelist in Victorian Literature* (Aldershot: Ashgate 2001).

Dowling, Linda, *Hellenism and Homosexuality in Victorian Oxford* (Ithaca, NY and London: Cornell University Press, 1994).

Duberman, Martin Bauml, Martha Vicinus and George Chauncey Jr (eds), *Hidden from History: Reclaiming the Gay and Lesbian Past* (Harmondsworth: Penguin, 1991).

Faderman, Lillian, *Surpassing the Love of Men: Romantic Friendship and Love Between Women from the Renaissance to the Present* (London: Junction Books, 1980).

——, *Odd Girls and Twilight Lovers: A History of Lesbian Life in Twentieth-century America* (New York: Penguin, 1992).

Feminist Studies, vol. 18.

Gaskell, Elizabeth, *The Life of Charlotte Brontë* (Oxford: World's Classics, 1996).

Gelder, Ken, *Reading the Vampire* (London: Routledge, 1996).

Gillespie, Michael Patrick, *The Picture of Dorian Gray: 'What the World Thinks of Me'* (New York: Twayne Publishers Masterwork Studies, 1995).

Green, Laura Morgan, *Educating Women: Cultural Conflict and Victorian Literature* (Athens, OH: Ohio University Press, 2001).

Guy, Josephine M., *The Victorian Age: An Anthology of Sources and Documents* (London and New York: Routledge, 1998).

Hall, Donald, *Muscular Christianity: Embodying the Victorian Age* (Cambridge: Cambridge University Press, 1994).

Hall Caine, Thomas Henry, 'The New Watchwords of Fiction', *Contemporary Review*, 57 (1890), 479–88.

Hardy, Barbara, *Forms of Feeling in Victorian Fiction* (London: Peter Owen, 1985).

Harman, Barbara Leah, *The Feminine Political Novel in Victorian England* (Charlottesville, VA: University Press of Virginia, 1998).

Herdman, John, *The Double in Nineteenth-century Fiction* (Basingstoke: Palgrave, 1990).

Hood, James W., *Divining Desire: Tennyson and the Poetics of Transcendence* (Aldershot: Ashgate, 2000).

Houghton, Walter, *The Victorian Frame of Mind, 1830–1870* (New Haven, CT: Yale University Press, 1985).

Jackson, Margaret, *The Real Facts of Life: Feminism and the Politics of Sexuality c1850–1940* (London: Taylor and Francis, 1994).

Jeffreys, Sheila, *The Spinster and Her Enemies: Feminism and Sexuality 1880–1930* (London: Routledge and Kegan Paul).

Jenkyns, Richard, *The Victorians and Ancient Greece* (Oxford: Basil Blackwell, 1980).

John, Juliet, *Dickens's Villains: Melodrama, Character, Popular Culture* (Oxford: Oxford University Press, 2001).

Kucich, John, *The Power of Lies: Transgression in Victorian Fiction* (New York: Cornell University Press, 1994).

Leighton, Angela, *Elizabeth Barrett Browning* (Brighton: Harvester Press, 1986).

Lettis, Richard, 'The Names of David Copperfield', *Dickens Studies Annual*, 31 (2002), 67–86.

Levine, Philippa, *Feminist Lives in Victorian England* (Oxford: Blackwell, 1990).

Logan, Deborah Anne, *Fallenness in Victorian Women's Writing* (Columbia, MO: University of Missouri Press, 1998).

Luftig, Victor, *Seeing Together: Friendship Between the Sexes in English Writing, from Mill to Woolf* (Stanford, CA: Stanford University Press, 1993).

Manning, Sylvia, ;'Death and Sex from Tennyson's Early Poetry to *In Memoriam*', in Regina Barreca (ed.), *Sex and Death in Victorian Literature* (Basingstoke: Macmillan, 1990), pp. 194–210.

Marshall, William, *Wilkie Collins* (New York: Twayne Publishers, 1970).

Mavor, Elizabeth, *The Ladies of Llangollen: A Study in Romantic Friendship* (London: Penguin, 1971).

Michie, Helena, *Sororophobia: Differences Among Women in Literature and Culture* (Oxford: Oxford University Press, 1992).

Moore, Lisa L., *Dangerous Intimacies: Toward a Sapphic History of the British Novel* (Durham, NC and London: Duke University Press, 1997).

Myers, Margaret, 'The Lost Self: Gender in David Copperfield', in John Peck (ed.), *New Casebooks: David Copperfield and Hard Times* (London: Macmillan, 1995).

Nestor, Pauline, *Female Friendships and Communities: Charlotte Brontë, George Eliot, Elizabeth Gaskell* (Oxford: Clarendon Press, 1985).

Newey, Vincent, *The Scriptures of Charles Dickens: Novels of Ideology, Novels of the Self* (Aldershot: Ashgate, 2004).

Ormond, Leonée, *Alfred Tennyson: A Literary Life* (Basingstoke: Macmillan, 1993).

Peck, John, ed, *New Casebooks: David Copperfield and Hard Times* (Basingstoke: Macmillan, 1995).

Peters, Catherine, *Thackeray's Universe: Shifting Worlds of Imagination and Reality* (Oxford: Oxford University Press, 1987).

Pykett, Lyn, *Critical Issues: Charles Dickens* (Basingstoke: Palgrave Macmillan 2002).

Raby, Peter (ed.), *The Cambridge Companion to Oscar Wilde* (Cambridge: Cambridge University Press, 2000).

Reed, John R., *Dickens and Thackeray: Punishment and Forgiveness*, (Athens, OH: Ohio University Press, 1995).

Reynolds, Kimberley and Nicola Humble (eds), *Victorian Heroines: Representations of Femininity in Nineteenth-century Literature and Art* (New York: New York University Press, 1993).

Richardson, Angelique and Chris Willis (eds), *The New Woman in Fiction and in Fact: Fin de Siècle Feminisms* (Basingstoke: Palgrave, 2001) .

Robson, John M., *Marriage or Celibacy? The Daily Telegraph on a Victorian Dilemma* (Toronto: University of Toronto Press, 1995).

Roden, Frederick S., *Same-sex Desire in Victorian Religious Culture* (Basingstoke: Palgrave Macmillan, 2002).

Rosenberg, John, 'Stopping for Death: Tennyson's *In Memoriam*', *Victorian Poetry*, 30:3–4, 291–330.

Sage, Victor, *Le Fanu's Gothic: The Rhetoric of Darkness* (Basingstoke: Palgrave Macmillan, 2004).

Schroeder, Natalie, '*Armadale*: A Book That Is Daring Enough to Speak the Truth', *Wilkie Collins Society Journal*, 3 (1983), pp. 5–16.

Sedgwick, Eve Kosofsky, *Epistemology of the Closet* (New York: Harvester Wheatsheaf, 1990).

——, *Between Men: English Literature and Male Homosocial Desire* (New York: Columbia University Press, 1985).

Shairp, J.C., 'Friendship in English Poetry', *North American Review*, 139:6 (December 1884), 580–98.

Showalter, Elaine, *A Literature of Their Own: British Women Novelists from Brontë to Lessing* (London: Virago, 1982).

Shuttleworth, Sally, *Charlotte Brontë and Victorian Psychology* (Cambridge: Cambridge University Press, 1996).

Sinfield, Alan, *The Wilde Century: Effeminacy, Oscar Wilde and the Queer Movement* (New York: Cassell, 1994).

Smith-Rosenberg, Carroll, *Disorderly Conduct: Visions of Gender in Victorian America* (Oxford: Oxford University Press, 1985).

Stedman, Gesa, *Stemming the Torrent: Expression and Control in the Victorian Discourses on Emotions, 1830–1872* (Aldershot: Ashgate, 2002).

Stokes, John, *Oscar Wilde: Myths, Miracles, and Imitations* (Cambridge: Cambridge University Press, 1998).

Stone, Marjorie, *Elizabeth Barrett Browning* (Basingstoke: Macmillan, 1995).

Sussman, Herbert, *Victorian Masculinities: Manhood and Masculine Poetics in Early Victorian Literature and Art* (Cambridge: Cambridge University Press, 1995).

Tromp, Marlene, Pamela K. Gilbert and Aeron Hanyie (eds), *Beyond Sensation: Mary Elizabeth Braddon in Context* (New York: State University of New York Press, 2002).

Turner, Frank M., *The Greek Heritage in Victorian Britain* (New Haven, CT: Yale University Press, 1981).

Tuss, Alex J., *The Inward Revolution: Troubled Young Men in Victorian Fiction, 1850–1880* (New York: Peter Lang, 1992).

Vicinus, Martha, *Intimate Friends: Women Who Loved Women 1778–1928* (Chicago, IL: University of Chicago Press, 2004).

Victorian Literature and Culture (2005).

Victorian Poetry, vol. 30 (Morgantown, WV: West Virginia University Press, 1992).

Welsh, Alexander, *Dickens Redressed: The Art of Bleak House and Hard Times* (New Haven, CT: Yale University Press, 2000).

Wilkie Collins Society Journal, vol. 3 (1983).

Wood, Jane, *Passion and Pathology in Victorian Fiction* (Oxford: Oxford University Press, 2001).

Woodham-Smith, Cecil, *Florence Nightingale 1820–1910* (London: The Reprint Society, 1952).

Wright, Terence, *Elizabeth Gaskell: 'We Are Not Angels'. Realism, Gender, Values* (Basingstoke: Macmillan, 1995).

Index